Chihuahuas For Dummies®

D0479787

Selecting a Chihuahua puppy

Follow these suggestions to help choose a Chihuahua with your head as well as your heart (and check Chapter 4):

- Trust your instincts. Does one puppy catch your eye immediately? First impressions are important, and love at first sight can last a lifetime. But take time to assure that your furry favorite is healthy and has a pleasing personality.

- Be observant. Watch the puppies play together for several minutes without human interference. Your best bet is a puppy in the middle of the pecking order — neither the bully nor the scaredy-cat.

- Eye the eyes. They should be bright, alert, and clear of mucous. (Don't mistake clear tears for mucous.)

- Check the coat. A healthy coat is smooth to the touch and glossy, with no bald patches. No puppy should have skin showing through on its back or sides.

- Know the nose. Breathing should be quiet and rhythmic and the nostrils should be free of mucous.

- Note how puppies move when they play. Despite a bit of baby clumsiness, they should appear quick, bouncy, and agile, standing straight on legs that look strong enough to carry their bodies.

Shopping for puppy gear

If you are introducing a Chihuahua to the household, here's your shopping list (see Chapter 5 for more details):

- Two dishes, one for water and one for food
- Puppy (or dog) food
- Collar
- Leash
- Grooming equipment, including a natural bristle brush, nail clipper, toothbrush, doggie tooth-paste, and shampoo. Long coated Chihuahuas also need coat conditioner, a hard rubber comb, and a mat splitter.
- Three or four toys
- Dog crate
- Dog bed (optional)
- Warm sweater (if it's chilly outdoors)
- Poop scooper
- Identification
- An excellent veterinarian

Finding a good veterinarian

Sharpen your search for a good vet with one or more of these tactics:

- Ask your Chihuahua's breeder. Even if the breeder lives far away, he or she may have sold pups to people in your area who can recommend a vet.

- When you see people walking toy dogs in your neighborhood, ask them what vet they use and if they are satisfied with the quality of care.

  Call the nearest major veterinary referral hospital for recommendations.

See Chapter 13 for more details on veterinarians and canine health.

For Dummies: Bestselling Book Series for Beginners

Chihuahuas For Dummies®

Cheat Sheet

Visiting the vet

Use this checklist to prepare for your Chihuahua's first check-up:

- ✔ To reduce the probability of carsickness, feed your dog a couple of biscuits an hour or more before driving to the clinic.
- ✔ Take along a roll of paper towels and a container of the wet wipes in case a quick clean-up is necessary.
- ✔ Take a copy of your dog's health record.
- ✔ Transport your dog in a crate. Secure the crate so it won't tumble if you have to swerve or make a quick stop.
- ✔ Make a list of your dog care questions and bring it along. Vets are glad to answer appropriate questions about feeding, grooming, toenail trimming, and anything else related to your Chihuahua's health.
- ✔ Take notes when the veterinarian gives instructions.
- ✔ Follow instructions exactly. Medications must be given at the right time and in the correct dosage or they won't work.

Housebreaking a young pup

The secret: Stay on schedule. You may have to get up 15 minutes earlier; come home for lunch (or hire a dog walker); and come straight home from work; until Pepe is a little older. Here's a schedule for a young puppy:

Morning

- ✔ First thing, take Pepe outside for several minutes. Praise him for a job well done.
- ✔ Feed and water him.
- ✔ Take him out again after he eats breakfast. If you are leaving, confine him to his crate.
- ✔ Take Pepe outdoors mid-morning if you are home.

Afternoon

- ✔ Take Pepe outside as soon as you get home at lunch time.
- ✔ Give Pepe lunch and fresh water.
- ✔ Take him outdoors after he finishes eating. Then confine him if you can't keep an eye on him or won't be home.

Evening

- ✔ When you arrive home in the evening, take Pepe outdoors right away and enjoy a nice walk (weather permitting).
- ✔ Feed and water Pepe for the last time each day between 6 and 7 p.m. Then remove the water bowl until morning.
- ✔ Take Pepe outside when he finishes eating.
- ✔ Take Pepe outside just before you go to bed. Confine him for the night.

For more on housebreaking and other good manners, see Chapter 10.

For Dummies: Bestselling Book Series for Beginners

TM

References for the Rest of Us!®

BESTSELLING BOOK SERIES

Do you find that traditional reference books are overloaded with technical details and advice you'll never use? Do you postpone important life decisions because you just don't want to deal with them? Then our *For Dummies*® business and general reference book series is for you.

For Dummies business and general reference books are written for those frustrated and hard-working souls who know they aren't dumb, but find that the myriad of personal and business issues and the accompanying horror stories make them feel helpless. *For Dummies* books use a lighthearted approach, a down-to-earth style, and even cartoons and humorous icons to dispel fears and build confidence. Lighthearted but not lightweight, these books are perfect survival guides to solve your everyday personal and business problems.

> *"More than a publishing phenomenon, 'Dummies' is a sign of the times."*
>
> — The New York Times

> *"A world of detailed and authoritative information is packed into them…"*
>
> — U.S. News and World Report

> *"…you won't go wrong buying them."*
>
> — Walter Mossberg, Wall Street Journal, on For Dummies books

Already, millions of satisfied readers agree. They have made For Dummies the #1 introductory level computer book series and a best-selling business book series. They have written asking for more. So, if you're looking for the best and easiest way to learn about business and other general reference topics, look to For Dummies to give you a helping hand.

Wiley Publishing, Inc.

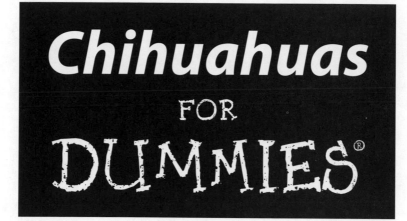

Chihuahuas

FOR

DUMMIES®

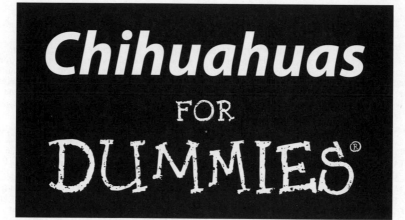

Chihuahuas FOR DUMMIES®

by Jacqueline O'Neil

WILEY

Wiley Publishing, Inc.

Chihuahuas For Dummies®

Published by
Wiley Publishing, Inc.
111 River Street
Hoboken, NJ 07030
www.wiley.com

Copyright © 2001 by Wiley Publishing, Inc., Indianapolis, Indiana

Published by Wiley Publishing, Inc., Indianapolis, Indiana

Published simultaneously in Canada

For general information on our other products and services or to obtain technical support, please contact our Customer Care Department within the U.S. at 800-762-2974, outside the U.S. at 317-572-3993, or fax 317-572-4002.

Wiley also publishes its books in a variety of electronic formats. Some content that appears in print may not be available in electronic books.

Library of Congress Cataloging-in-Publication Data:

Library of Congress Control Number: 00-107690

ISBN: 0-7645-5284-8

Manufactured in the United States of America

15 14 13 12 11 10 9 8 7

3B/QR/QW/QU/IN

About the Author

Jacqueline O'Neil is an award-winning author of more than a dozen books and a couple hundred magazine articles on animal care and training. She and her husband, Tom, a wildlife photographer, follow the sun around North America in a motor home. Favorite stops include the Florida Keys, Montana, Alaska, and the Yukon.

Before morphing into a Gypsy, Jackie was a successful dog breeder and trainer, handling her own dogs to top awards in the show and obedience rings.

A graduate of the University of Florida, Jackie is a member of the Outdoor Writers Association of America, the National League of American Pen Women, and the Dog Writers Association of America, where she also served two terms as a director. In addition to dogs, she's into horses, birds, fishing, scuba diving, and fiddling.

Jackie has two grown daughters, Peggy and Sunny Fraser, who have recently started their own menageries. The whole family is proud to be owned by a three-pound Chihuahua named Manchita.

About Howell Book House
Committed to the Human/Companion Animal Bond

Thank you for choosing a book brought to you by the pet experts at Howell Book House, a division of Wiley. And welcome to the family of pet owners who've put their trust in Howell books for nearly 40 years!

Pet ownership is about relationships — the bonds people form with their dogs, cats, horses, birds, fish, small mammals, reptiles, and other animals. Howell Book House/Wiley understands that these are some of the most important relationships in life, and that it's vital to nurture them through enjoyment and education. The happiest pet owners are those who know they're taking the best care of their pets — and with Howell books owners have this satisfaction. They're happy, educated owners, and as a result, they have happy pets, and that enriches the bond they share.

Howell Book House was established in 1961 by Mr. Elsworth S. Howell, an active and proactive dog fancier who showed English Setters and judged at the prestigious Westminster Kennel Club show in New York. Mr. Howell based his publishing program on strength of content, and his passion for books written by experienced and knowledgeable owners defined Howell Book House and has remained true over the years. Howell's reputation as the premier pet book publisher is supported by the distinction of having won more awards from the Dog Writers Association of America than any other publisher. Howell Book House/Wiley has over 400 titles in publication, including such classics as The American Kennel Club's *Complete Dog Book,* the *Dog Owner's Home Veterinary Handbook, Blessed Are the Brood Mares,* and *Mother Knows Best: The Natural Way to Train Your Dog.*

When you need answers to questions you have about any aspect of raising or training your companion animals, trust that Howell Book House/Wiley has the answers. We welcome your comments and suggestions, and we look forward to helping you maximize your relationships with your pets throughout the years.

Howell Book House Staff

Dedication

To my daughters, Peggy and Sunny Fraser, who have been mommies to a munchkin named Manchita for the last decade, including their college and early career years.

Author's Acknowledgments

My husband, Tom O'Neil, took some of the photos for this book and proof-read the manuscript before I sent it to my editor.

My mother, Dori Freedman, taught me that anything worth doing is worth doing right, and that once started, projects must be finished. Perhaps that's why I've been able to make writing my career.

My stepdad, Needham Parrish, contributed to the research in a big way by sending me books, articles, and videos on Chihuahuas. He also took the photos of the Chihuahua named Chiquita.

My daughter, Peggy Fraser, who hates posing for pictures, did it anyway. Thanks, honey.

Taco Bell Corp. provided information about Gidget, the world's most recognizable Chihuahua, and included photos of their superstar.

Publisher's Acknowledgments

We're proud of this book; please send us your comments through our online registration form located at www.dummies.com/register.

Some of the people who helped bring this book to market include the following:

Acquisitions, Editorial, and Media Development

Project Editor: Norm Crampton

Acquisitions Editor: Scott Prentzas

Copy Editor: Neil Johnson

Technical Editor: Deborah Wood

Editorial Manager: Pam Mourouzis

Media Development Manager: Heather Heath Dismore

Editorial Assistant: Carol Strickland

Cover Photo: American Kennel © Alice Su

Production

Project Coordinator: Nancee Reeves

Layout and Graphics: Amy Adrian, Kristin Pickett, Jill Piscitelli, Brent Savage, Jacque Schneider, Rashell Smith, Kendra Span, Brian Torwelle

Proofreaders: Valery Bourke, Angel Perez, Carl Pierce, York Production Services, Inc.

Indexer: York Production Services, Inc.

Publishing and Editorial for Consumer Dummies

Diane Graves Steele, Vice President and Publisher, Consumer Dummies
Joyce Pepple, Acquisitions Director, Consumer Dummies
Kristin A. Cocks, Product Development Director, Consumer Dummies
Michael Spring, Vice President and Publisher, Travel
Brice Gosnell, Associate Publisher, Travel
Suzanne Jannetta, Editorial Director, Travel

Publishing for Technology Dummies

Richard Swadley, Vice President and Executive Group Publisher
Andy Cummings, Vice President and Publisher

Composition Services

Gerry Fahey, Vice President of Production Services
Debbie Stailey, Director of Composition Services

Contents at a Glance

Cartoons at a Glance

By Rich Tennant

page 5

page 39

page 105

page 151

page 209

page 191

Fax: 978-546-7747
E-mail: richtennant@the5thwave.com
World Wide Web: www.the5thwave.com

Table of Contents

Introduction

Years ago, the then editor of the *AKC Gazette* asked me to cover the Chihuahua National Specialty, the breed's most prestigious annual dog show. The article I wrote was entitled, "Chihuahuas Charm Chicago," but the truth is, those Chihuahuas charmed me. Although I bred and exhibited American Staffordshire Terriers, and was a veteran writer — used to studying a breed, attending a national specialty show, and submitting an article — I was smitten as surely as a young girl who's first date brings her flowers. From that day on, I had to have a Chihuahua.

Who else has been captivated by these audacious little dogs?

A couple months ago, when I visited an old college friend, a half dozen Chihuahuas frolicked in her elegant Miami home. They kept her company while she studied the theories that helped her become a world class bridge player.

At an RV camp in Oklahoma, my husband Tom and I met a retired couple who travel with three Chihuahuas. Because the dogs love to wear costumes and show off their repertoire of tricks, that couple finds friends wherever they go.

At a resort in central Florida, we met a recent widower who thanked God he had "let his wife get a Chihuahua," because now the dog gives him a reason to keep going.

My daughters took their Chihuahua to college. Besides graduating with them from the University of Florida, three-pound Manchita has lived in three major cities — Miami, New York, and Atlanta — plus several smaller ones, and never minds traveling or moving. To her, home is where one of her humans is.

Two weeks ago, our fishing buddies from Key Largo, Florida, brought their motor home to Montana and visited us on their way to Alaska. Their Chihuahua Cricket sees her world change from swaying palms to snow-dusted ponderosa pines and back again, and always takes it in stride.

And just last evening, at an RV camp in Idaho, we were greeted at the office by the owner's Chihuahuas . . . three oldsters competing for our attention with puppyish enthusiasm.

From singles on the fast track to seniors out seeing the world, many of my friends and acquaintances share their lives with a Chihuahua or two. And do you know what? Every single one of us had our first Chihuahua years before television commercials boosted the breed's popularity.

Today you can't turn on the TV or browse in a gift shop without seeing Chihuahuas. From fashion centers to flea markets, they have become one of our nation's most popular pets. But just because these critters attract attention with their incredible cuteness isn't enough reason to run out and get one. That would be kind of like asking the prettiest cheerleader to marry you when you don't even know her name. Instead, let me introduce you.

The first part of this book reveals the Chihuahua's personality and helps you think about how *your* personality can blend with the unique disposition of this diminutive breed of canine. But the book isn't just for new owners. I wrote *Chihuahuas For Dummies* to make living with a Chihuahua easy and fun. Whether you have one Chi or half a dozen, the book simplifies daily care, tells you how to train your dog, and even helps you organize a nonviolent coup to take leadership away from a tiny tyrant.

When I brought home my first Chihuahua, I discovered that no matter how successful I had been with a bigger breed, Toy dogs are different. And as the tiniest of the Toys, Chis are the most different of all. They are more fragile as pups, but they outlive bigger breeds by several years. They take a little longer to housebreak, but they love performing tricks and never forgot what they learn. Some of them have a tendency toward shyness, but well-socialized Chis are every bit as bold as a feisty terrier. Some bark too much, but that's their owner's fault, because all it takes is a little guidance to raise a Chihuahua that sounds off only when it has a good reason.

A little guidance — that's what I'm here for. So turn to Chapter 1, or anywhere in the book for that matter, and let me do my job. Whether you're a new owner or have enjoyed the companionship of Chihuahuas for years, this book helps you and your dog make the most of your relationship.

How This Book Is Organized

Chihuahuas For Dummies is divided into six sections. If you are looking for a Chihuahua, you may want to begin in the early chapters. If you already have a Chi, you can skip around, going quickly in and out at chapters that address your curiosity or urgent need to know. Here's what you'll find.

Part I: Getting to Know Chihuahuas

Adopting a dog has a lot in common with adopting a soul mate of the human species: You know you're in for a lot of give and take! But don't let that scare you — bringing a Chihuahua into your life is both a serious commitment and one of life's huge pleasures. This section shows you what's in store.

Part II: Fitting a Compact Canine into Your Life

What do you look for in a healthy Chihuahua? How do you prepare your home for your little amigo. What do Chihuahuas eat? How much exercise do they need? Part II provides the information you need to welcome a Chi into the household and make a good beginning on a special new relationship.

Part III: Training Your Chihuahua

Part III is your ready reference and everyday problem-solver, from training for basic good habits to having fun. Housebreaking? Barking? Shyness? Dominance? All the typical Chihuahua needs are covered here.

Part IV: Keeping Your Chihuahua Healthy

Finding the right veterinarian for your dog — at a convenient location — is job one on the health plan. Part IV shows you how to find a good vet and make the most of your visits to the clinic. Use this section as a reference to identifying and dealing with common health needs of Chihuahuas.

Part V: Taking Your Chihuahua on Stage

Have some fun — teach Pepe or Manchita a trick or two and entertain family and friends with your talented little canine. Part V also answers your questions about showing your Chihuahua.

Part VI: The Part of Tens

So much to tell you about Chihuahuas, so little time! Part VI is packed with more useful data, like a handy list of questions when you are buying or adopting a dog, and Web sites where you can find a huge variety of additional information. Finally, I raise the curtain on a stageful of celebrity Chihuahuas, including Gidget, of course.

Appendixes

The two appendixes in this book direct you to interesting a enlightening information about Chihuahuas. Appendix A, "More Good Reading," lists and describes Web sites that offer their own unique pathways along the Chihuahua information superhighway. Appendix B, "Clubs and Connections," gives you pertinent information about Chihuahua-related clubs, organizations, and connections that help you discover the particulars about training, showing, caring for, and even putting your Chi to work for you and others.

Icons Used in This Book

The pages of this book are peppered with icons in the margins. Besides adding a little salsa, they also give you a quick bite of Chihuahua information. Here's what's on the menu:

True stories, exceptions to the rules, trivia, and fun facts that make colorful conversation.

You'll see this icon most often. It contains advice on Chihuahua care, training techniques, and shortcuts to simplify life with a dog.

Whoa! This Chihuahua is on full alert. That's a caution signal for you to keep you from skidding into common but potentially serious mistakes.

Every species has its own language. These icons define the terms dog owners in general, and Chihuahua owners in particular, will want to know.

Part I
Getting to Know Chihuahuas

The 5th Wave   By Rich Tennant

At one time, Chihuahuas were used to hunt hippopotamus, rhinos, and Cape buffalo. In packs of 5 to 6 hundred, these small dogs were able to subdue the largest of African mammals over the course of an attack which could last several hours

In this part . . .

This part reveals the Chihuahua's distinctive personality and body structure. I help you think about the ups and downs of dog ownership and what you can and can't expect from your pet. In short, Part I is the key to deciding whether the Chihuahua's unique disposition fits your lifestyle.

Chapter 1

Adopting a Dog: Big Decision

In This Chapter

▶ Examining your motives for acquiring a dog

▶ Focusing on the Toy breeds

▶ Making a match with a Chihuahua

C an money ever buy you love? Sure. Just use it to buy a dog. Your Chihuahua won't waffle about making a permanent commitment. In fact, expect Pepe to envelop you in affection, do his best to protect you, and maybe even improve your health. No kidding. Scientific studies show that a pet's companionship alleviates stress and helps people relax. In many cases, dogs (and other pets) get credit for lowering their owner's blood pressure. But while most Chihuahua owners are crazy about their pets, a few wish they had never brought a dog (or *that* dog) home. I don't want Chihuahua owner-ship to disappoint you, so in this chapter, I talk about the ups and downs of living with dogs in general and Chis in particular. Is the portable pet with the king-sized heart the right breed for you? In this chapter, you find the answer.

Deciding Why You Want a Dog

If you are *dog-deprived,* you know it. You greet all your friend's dogs by name, eye every dog that goes by on the street, and sometimes even ask strangers if you can pet their pup. Maybe you surf through your favorite breeds on the Internet or browse through the dog magazines at the bookstore. Do you have a list of possible puppy names in your head? You're already a *dog-goner.* It won't be long before other dog-deprived people are asking to pet your new puppy.

Ideally, you are drawn to dogs and playing with them makes you feel good. But your reason for buying a dog may be less than ideal yet work out well anyway. For example, maybe you're lonely or bored and hope a dog can fill the void. The truth is, a little fur wrapped around a pleasant personality (like Manchita, in Figure 1-1) spices up a bland life if you let it. Being loved by a dog is fulfilling in itself, while taking it a step further and becoming involved in dog activities (see Chapter 9) can bring you excitement, new friends, and a sense of purpose.

So what's the problem? The glitch is that puppies purchased to relieve monotony often are ignored when the novelty wears off. So before buying a Chihuahua, decide whether you will always appreciate your pet or you just crave some instant entertainment. Still not sure? Ask yourself this: Am I ready to love a dog for the duration (possibly 15 years for a Chihuahua) or can a cruise to the Caribbean be just as effective for banishing my boredom?

Getting a dog is a big decision. After all, dogs are dependent, make demands on your time, cost money, and inhibit your freedom. Are they worth it? Absolutely. That's why more than 52 million dog-owning households exist in the United States alone. But just because dogs and people have been best buddies since before recorded time doesn't necessarily mean you need to run out and get a puppy right away. Maybe dog ownership isn't right for you; maybe it is right for you, but not right now. Let's find out by taking a look at the upside and downside of having a dog.

Chihuahuas are either smooth or long coated. Smooths have short hair that is soft and shiny. Long coats have (you guessed it) long hair that may be straight or wavy.

Figure 1-1:
Manchita is a smooth coated Chihuahua.

Welcoming a Dependent That's Not Tax Deductible

Like a child, Pepe relies on you for food, housing, education, affection, toys, and medical care — and the IRS won't even let you declare him. Unlike a child, your puppy won't ever become independent. Pepe never fixes his own dinner, brushes his own hair, or pays his own medical bills. Instead, he depends on you for his health and happiness all his life.

On the upside, most dog owners enjoy the small chores that make up daily dog care. For some, interacting with their dogs is a restful transition from a too-busy day. Others say their dogs keep the nest from feeling empty, and add laughter to their lives. When you have a doggy dependent you always are the most important thing in his life. Pepe needs you from puppyhood through old age. He doesn't graduate, get a job, marry, or move halfway across the country.

Discuss division of labor with your family before getting a dog, but don't expect even the most logical schedule to be carved in stone. In the end, someone — one person — must take responsibility, making sure Pepe is fed, watered, groomed, trained, and exercised outdoors when he indicates a need to eliminate. Since you're the one reading this book, I bet that someone is you. Will you relish or resent the responsibility?

Even though Pepe's poops are small, they make a big mess on the bottom of someone's shoe. Don't forget to clean up after your dog every time you walk him. In many places, it's the law!

Figuring the long-term cost

Can you afford a dog? No, I'm not talking about just the price of the dog (which will probably be between $300 and $600 for a Chihuahua puppy), but also the price of upkeep.

Some breeds, Chihuahuas for example, don't eat much, but they still need quality food, puppy shots, an annual checkup complete with vaccinations, regular worming, minor surgery to spay or neuter, medication to prevent heartworm, a crate, grooming equipment, a collar and leash, dog dishes, and a variety of toys and treats. And although Chis tend to be healthy, Pepe may rack up a big bill if he ever is in an accident and requires emergency surgery.

Fitting Pepe into your schedule

Darn right you can afford a dog. As hard as you work, you can swing that cruise to the Caribbean, if only you had time to take a vacation. Truth is, you seldom even make time for a social life. At least you deserve the pleasure of an adoring dog when you finally get home from work at night.

So you're doing fine financially but working crazy hours to reach the next rung up the corporate ladder. In that case, Pepe's excited antics when you come through the door can be just the ticket to turn your mood from office mania to bemused tranquility. Forget fuming over a frustrating meeting. Your dog needs to be walked and fed, and both of you look forward to snuggling through a sitcom or two. Just keep in mind that no matter how frazzled you are, and no matter how late it is, Pepe still needs your attention and affection. If you and he live alone, then you are his entire world.

The downside of having a dog during the most demanding years of your career is that after an 11-hour workday, Pepe's joyful greeting at the door may feel more like pressure than privilege. Upward mobility in your company can also involve moving rather often, and finding a nice rental that permits pets isn't always easy.

Some offices allow employees to bring well-behaved pets to work. My Chihuahua spent many hours in the office when I worked for the American Kennel Club (AKC) in New York City. Sure, that's a special case, but while we walked to work, I saw plenty of other pooches accompanying people carrying briefcases.

Fitting Pepe into the family structure

Your spouse's feelings about having a dog, your children's ages, your activity level, and your travel plans are important considerations when deciding whether to make a dog part of your family. Bringing home a dog when your spouse doesn't want one is unfair to everyone. So is buying a breed your other half hates. Sure, the reluctant spouse, in some cases, learns to love the dog, but in just as many other cases, one partner never quite comes around. Having to defend your dog on a daily basis gets old real fast and you don't need that. Furthermore, no dog deserves to be dumped at the pound because everyone got tired of the hassles at home.

Are you hoping to settle down and start a family in the near (or distant) future? Some breeds (Chihuahuas are one of them) are long-lived, so with luck, plan on Pepe being with you for your wedding and the births of your babies. But as sweet as that sounds, it may not be a good thing. Will your spouse also love your dog or will he or she consider Pepe excess baggage? Another potential problem is that some breeds (yes, Chihuahuas are one of them) don't thrive around toddlers. It's a no-fault, lose-lose situation. Tiny dogs are too delicate for young children, and kids under the ages of 6 or 7 still are geared toward stuffed animals. Imagine how long poor Pepe would last if a toddler tripped over him, or swung him by one leg like a stuffed teddy.

Picking up after Pepe

What kind of housekeeper are you? Is your home casual and relaxed, the kind of place where friends gather to munch popcorn and watch videos. Or is your house so immaculate that family members remove their shoes before stepping on the cream-colored carpet?

Puppies aren't perfect. Chances are you'll have to clean up some accidents while housetraining Pepe. Not only that, he'll shed at intervals (or constantly) all his life. Long after Pepe is reliably housebroken — maybe years after you've moved into your dream home — he can get sick and upchuck on the new sofa. When that happens, will you view the mess as a minor annoyance or a major tragedy?

Making a Match with a Toy Breed

After reading the ups and downs of dog ownership, you still decide that you want a canine companion. Right on! You're going to love living with a dog. That is, if your dog lives up to your expectations. Humans breed dogs capable of doing an extraordinary number of things, but dogs are specialists in a sense, and no one breed does it all. A wrong match between dog and owner usually brings misery, like a bad marriage, while a good match means years of satisfaction and fun.

Some Toy dogs, such as the Toy Poodle, are downsized versions of their larger cousins. Others, like the Miniature Pinscher, have been around longer than the larger dogs that resemble them. The Chihuahua is not a scaled down version of anything. It's a true Toy.

What's terrific about Toys

What do all the Toy breeds have in common? They are living proof that great things really do come in small packages. Here's the upside:

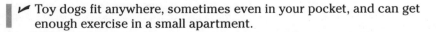 Toy dogs fit anywhere, sometimes even in your pocket, and can get enough exercise in a small apartment.

- Toy dogs are cuddly and love human attention. They form extremely strong bonds with their people and many of them are content to warm a lap for hours.

- Toy dogs are portable. They are ideal for people who travel a lot and like to take their dog along with them.

- Toy dogs love to show off. Most of them enjoy learning new things from an upbeat trainer.

- Toy dogs are often welcome where larger breeds are not. For example, some condo associations limit the size of pets.

- Toys are real dogs. They are intelligent and affectionate, with bold, fun-loving temperaments. Many of them make alert watchdogs.

In the lingo of the dog fancier, the Chihuahua is considered a *natural* dog. That means his coat isn't trimmed, shaved, stripped or plucked, and his ears and tail are left the way nature made them — not trimmed or docked in the style of the Miniature Pinscher (among others). In dog-fancier slang, that makes the Chihuahua a wash-and-wear breed.

Toy breeds on parade

The American Kennel Club (AKC) recognizes more than 150 different dog breeds and divides them into seven groups, depending upon the function each breed originally performed. The Chihuahua is a member of the Toy Group — a collection of breeds created for the sole purpose of being companions to people. The AKC recognizes the following Toy breeds:

- Affenpinscher

- Brussels Griffon

- Chihuahua (Smooth or Long Coat)

- Chinese Crested (Hairless or Powderpuff)

- English Toy Spaniel (Blenheim, Prince Charles, King Charles, and Ruby)

- Havanese

- Italian Greyhound

- Japanese Chin

- Maltese

- Manchester Terrier (Toy)

- Miniature Pinscher

- Papillon

- Pekingese

- Pomeranian

- Poodle (Toy)

- Pug

- Shih Tzu

- Silky Terrier

- Yorkshire Terrier

According to AKC statistics, the top three most popular Toy breeds in 1998 were the Chihuahua, the Yorkshire Terrier, and the Pomeranian. Toy Poodles are also popular, but knowing where they rank is impossible because all three varieties of Poodle (Standard, Miniature, and Toy) are counted as one.

Digging up the Mexican connection

Chihuahuas are lap warmers and their purpose is companionship. But in tougher times, before people owned pets for pure pleasure, every creature had to have a function and "just for fun" didn't cut it. Historians are still uncertain about the precise origins and uses of the earliest Chihuahuas, but legends about their beginnings abound — a combination of fact and fantasy that makes the dog world's littlest breed one of its biggest mysteries.

Relics from ancient Mexico include sculptures of small dogs that archeologists discovered while studying the remains of the Mayan, Toltec, and Aztec cultures. While some of the statues (you can see them at the National Museum in Mexico City) don't look much like our modern Chihuahuas, and little is known about the Mayans, some information is available about the Toltecs.

The Toltec Indians lived in Mexico during the ninth century, and possibly even earlier. They had a dog called the *Techichi,* which some historians believe is the ancestor of today's Chihuahua. Stone carvings of these dogs are found at the Monastery of Huejotzingo (on the highway between Mexico City and Puebla), and they look much more like our modern Chihuahua than do the statues that are believed to be Mayan.

Potential problems with portable pets

Toy dogs need careful owners. Depending on your nature, that's one potential downside risk of owning a Chihuahua. Although most Chis think they're tough, they're more vulnerable to injury (especially being stepped on or tripped over) than larger dogs. Here are some other concerns:

- When Toy dog owners overdo carrying and cuddling and skimp on training, their pets often become spoiled. And that turns them into tiny tyrants or nervous wimps.

- Toy breeds view the world from a different perspective — just above ground level, which can be scary. Developing that typical Toy spirit means they need plenty of social interactions with a variety of people from puppyhood on.

- Toy dogs that are neglected during puppyhood, or that come from inferior stock, may suffer myriad physical and/or mental problems at maturity.

- Some people dislike Toy dogs and may make rude remarks about Pepe when you walk him. If you answer at all, smile and say something like, "Shhh. He thinks he's a tiger."

- Toys are real dogs. Like every other breed, they need training and guidance. In other words, if you don't train Pepe, Pepe will train you.

Finding the Things You Have in Common

All the Toy breeds make exceptional companions, but they aren't inter-changeable. The 18 breeds come in a variety of shapes, coat types, and colors, and their temperaments and activity levels vary from lazy and laid-back to extremely active. Is the Chihuahua the right choice for you? Here's a synopsis of what Pepe can and can't bring to a relationship. (And for more on the Chihuahua disposition, see Chapter 3.)

- ✔ Pepe thrives on togetherness. A Chihuahua is the ideal dog for someone who is home a lot and spends some time sitting. That's because Chis love to sit beside you, or better yet, on your lap. If you work from a home office, or if some of your favorite things are watching television, reading, or surfing the net, Pepe will be in puppy paradise. But if you are on the go all the time, and can't make space in your schedule to accom-modate an accomplished lap warmer, then this is not the breed for you.

- ✔ Pepe enjoys a brisk walk around the block when the weather's nice, but if you want a jogging or hiking companion, check out some of the larger breeds. No, a Chihuahua isn't wimpy when it comes to walking. He gets tired because he takes several strides to keep up with just one of yours.

- ✔ Pepe is an alert watchdog with a bark much bigger than he is. But he isn't a guard dog or an attack dog, no matter what he thinks.

- ✔ Pepe is loyal and loving. He believes in family first and is vigilant and discriminating when you have visitors. Your friends may become his friends after he gets to know them.

- ✔ Pepe is easy to groom whether he is a smooth or a long coat. If you are looking forward to fussing with hair, many other Toys have thicker, longer coats.

- ✔ Pepe is a housedog. He can't tolerate cold or rainy weather, garages or drafty basements.

- ✔ Pepe is the perfect pet for singles in small living quarters and for seniors who may have trouble handling a stronger dog. He's also an excellent family dog, provided the children are gentle and older than 7.

- ✔ Pepe is super-short. That means you, your family, and your guests must watch where you walk. Don't worry. It becomes second nature in a day or two. But when you or your children have friends over, they must be reminded.

- ✔ Pepe plays games with you (you can find some in Chapter 16). He may even learn to fetch a ball or chase a small Frisbee, but he won't be able to handle any rough stuff. If you want a tough dog that plays hard, get a larger pet.

✔ Pepe probably is a good traveler. Most Chihuahuas adapt well to the open road and love to watch the world go by from the passenger's seat of a vehicle (especially when there's a passenger in the seat). Of course, a crate (see Chapter 5) is safer.

✔ Pepe must be taught manners, the same as any other dog. Little and cute loses its charm real fast when it's accompanied by bad habits.

✔ Pepe is a natural born show-off with a good memory. After he learns a trick or two, he's proud to perform for your friends (once he's familiar with them).

✔ Pepe is sensitive. He tries to comfort you when you are sad and dances for joy when you are happy. He won't feel secure in a house full of friction.

✔ Pepe is delicate. He needs your protection from bigger dogs even if he doesn't think so. And not just when he's on the ground, either. Big dogs have been known to snatch tiny ones right out of their owner's arms (yes, that's rare, but I thought I should warn you). Do you tend to get physical when you are angry? Then it's best not to have any pet, especially not a Chihuahua. The first hot-tempered blow a Chihuahua receives will probably be its last.

✔ Pepe is intelligent and highly trainable. In fact, he's capable of becoming competitive in active events like agility and obedience. But don't expect miracles. He'll prefer indoor activities to performing on damp grass.

Loyal, intelligent, trainable, portable, and incredibly cute to boot, if all those endearing Chihuahua charms have you captivated, you have lots of company. In 1998, 43,468 new Chihuahuas were registered with the American Kennel Club. That ranked the breed eighth among the 146 AKC breeds. Only a year before, Chihuahuas ranked 12th. The little guys are on the move!

Chapter 2

Building the Unique Chihuahua Look

In This Chapter

▶ Picturing the perfect Chihuahua

▶ Examining heads, tails, and other body parts

▶ Keeping perspective — nobody's perfect!

*L*ots of little dogs have compact bodies, big eyes and erect ears, so what makes a Chihuahua unmistakably a Chihuahua? Details. A whole bunch of details combine to create a dog that looks and acts like a Chihuahua and nothing but a Chihuahua. This chapter focuses on appearances and gives you the official (honest!) word picture of Chihuahua perfection.

You may already have a mental picture of a Chihuahua from watching the old TV ads showing Gidget, the Taco Bell dog (see Figure 2-1), mouth his polite request for a little grub. Of course, I should have said *her* request because Gidget is, after all, a gal dog playing a guy, but that's neither here nor there.

Next to its diminutive size, the Chihuahua's most recognizable feature is its apple-domed head, which you can plainly see in Manchita in Figure 2-2. Attached to Manchita's signature head are big eyes, brimming with intelligence and an inquiring gaze (Gidget's gaze is intense). Erect ears, a bit bigger than you might expect, add to her aspect of alertness. On top of many Chihuahua heads, practically invisible but easily discernable through touch, is the *molera* — a soft spot similar to the one found on newborn babies. The molera is also called the *fontanel*.

A Chihuahua's body is surprisingly sturdy, and although Manchita's feet are dainty, her legs are muscular and swift. Her back is level, she's a little longer than she is tall, and she carries her tail confidently — either in a semicircle or in a loop over her back.

Figure 2-1:
Head study
of the best-
known
Chihuahua
on
television.

Photo courtesy of Taco Bell Corp.

The apple-shaped head and a few other features pretty much describe a Chihuahua's distinctive appearance, but building a complete little superdog takes lots more anatomy. Although knowing the details is important to successfully showing your Chihuahua (see Chapter 17), you don't need to know the finer points to love and enjoy your pet. So if you want details, stick with me. But if anatomy isn't your thing, skip this section.

Figure 2-2:
Manchita
presents the
classic
Chihuahua
look: apple-
shaped
head,
prominent
leg muscles,
level back,
and
confident
tail.

Looking for the Picture-Perfect Chihuahua

Believe it or not, a blueprint exists for building a Chihuahua (and every other AKC registered breed). The blueprint is called *the "Official Standard for the Chihuahua,"* and it describes the ideal or picture-perfect Chihuahua. Of course no dog is perfect (just as no person — not even a Miss America — is perfect), so no matter how charming a Chihuahua appears, the knowledge-able eyes of a good breeder or dog show judge always find room for improvement. That's why even the best breeders always have something to strive for.

Breed standards are serious stuff. Selecting breeding partners with the standard in mind is how breeders produce generation after generation of dogs that look and act like Chihuahuas — or Doberman Pinschers or Labrador Retrievers or . . . name your favorite. The best breeders try to produce dogs that come as close to matching the standard as possible, and dog show judges select winners by comparing how closely each competitor matches its breed standard.

In Figure 2-3, you see dog lingo describing the external features of the Chihuahua. That's a handy diagram to refer to as you cruise through the details ahead. Pretty soon you'll be able to speak the language of *dog people* — breeders, show exhibitors, and judges.

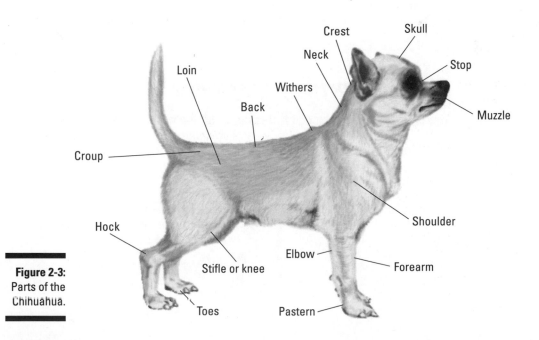

Figure 2-3:
Parts of the Chihuahua.

Just like school, Chihuahuas have a parent group

Every breed of dog that the American Kennel Club recognizes is backed by a national organization known as a parent club. Parent clubs educate owners and breeders and create the standards of excellence for their breeds. Respected breeders within the parent club write standards that the club membership must first approve. The standards are created for the long term, and seldom change. The parent club for the Chihuahua is the Chihuahua Club of America (CCA).

What can reading the Chihuahua standard do for you? It helps you develop an eye for an excellent specimen and understand what makes the breed unique. The problem: The standard is hard to follow because it was written as a guide for judges and breeders who understand dog lingo. Not to worry: Throughout the rest of this chapter, I translate the official talk into plain English.

General appearance

The Chihuahua is a graceful, alert, swift-moving, compact little dog with a saucy expression and terrier-like qualities of temperament.

Manchita — as I'm going to refer to that perfect Chihuahua throughout this little tour — is compact, feels solid in your hands, and appears well-proportioned — not long of body or lanky or too tall. She has terrier-like qualities; she's confident, animated, spirited, curious, and interested in everything happening around her.

Size, proportion, substance

Manchita is a well balanced little dog, weighing not more than 6 pounds (to qualify for the show ring). Her body is *off-square,* to quote the official standard. So, she's slightly longer when measured from point of shoulder to point of buttocks than she is tall at the *withers, or* the top of her shoulders. Somewhat shorter bodies (length) are preferred in males. Manchita's height is the distance from the highest point of her withers to the floor, while her length is the distance from the point of her shoulder to the point of her buttock. (Remember to check Figure 2-3 to see all the technical terms applied to the dog.)

In general, many breeds are considered *square,* meaning that their height is the same as their length. But the Chihuahua is supposed to be just a little longer than it is tall. The reason a little more length is desired in females than it is in males is because females need the extra space to carry puppies.

A Chihuahua needs a balanced appearance. That means every part of its body must be in proportion with its other parts. If its legs appear too long for its body or its head appears too small for its neck, the Chihuahua looks like it's made from spare parts.

Head

To meet the standard, the shape of Manchita's head looks sort of like an apple — rounded but not completely round. If she has a molera, you'll feel a slight indentation, like the soft spot on a baby's skull, when you gently stroke the top of her head. Her eyes are better if they're large, set well apart, radiant and shiny — not close together, protruding, smallish, or dull. For perfect proportions, the middle of the eyes lines up with the lowest part of the ears.

Ears

If Manchita has ideal ears, they'll be at a 45-degree angle to her head when she's resting, but come to attention, held high, when she's alert. Manchita may also flatten them against her skull when she's moving fast or when something makes her uneasy.

Chihuahua ears must be left as nature made them. *Cropped ears* (surgically shaped or shortened ears) are not permitted on Chihuahuas in the show ring. A Chihuahua with broken ear cartilage, resulting in a droopy or lopsided ear, is grounds for disqualification from showing.

How a dog holds its ears (for example, alertly erect or relaxed), is called its *ear carriage.*

Muzzle (snout)

The standard calls for a muzzle, or snout, that is moderately short, but that doesn't mean shorter is better. A super-short muzzle is incorrect in the Chihuahua. That's because extremely short muzzles can cause breathing problems and crowd the teeth. Ideally, the muzzle should emerge from the skull at a right angle.

Soft spot on head suggests Malta homeland

While many historians contend that the Chihuahua is a native Mexican breed, others argue that the breed originated in the Mediterranean, particularly on the island of Malta. According to proponents of the Malta theory, a tiny dog with a *molera* (a soft spot on its head and a trait unique to Chihuahuas) became established there and traveled on trading ships to European ports. To back up their theory, these historians point out that many paintings produced by European masters include a small dog resembling the Chihuahua. The most famous of these paintings is a fresco in the Sistine Chapel created by Sondro Botticelli around 1482. Part of a series illustrating the life of Moses, *Sons of Moses* includes a little dog with a round head, big eyes, large erect ears, and other Chihuahua characteristics. The painting was completed ten years before Columbus dropped anchor in the New World, so it's a sure bet that Botticelli never saw or heard of a Mexican dog. Yet he painted something incredibly close to a Chihuahua.

Still another theory contends that Chihuahuas originated in China and were brought to Mexico about 200 years ago. Supporters of this theory say that the Chinese were known for dwarfing plants and animals, and when wealthy Chinese merchants established homes in Mexico, they brought their little canine companions with them.

Although no actual proof can be offered, the most widely accepted hypothesis on Chihuahua origins concludes that the breed evolved when the ancient Mexican Techichi crossbred with small European dogs that traders brought to the New World during the 14th and 15th centuries.

Teeth

If Manchita's upper front teeth meet tightly outside her lower front teeth, she has a scissors bite, while if her upper and lower incisors (front teeth) meet flush with each other when her mouth is closed, her bite is level. The scissors bite is the strongest bite and is considered ideal. Also, the teeth wear down faster when the bite is level.

Neck, topline, body

An attractive neck from a side view flows smoothly and gracefully into your Chihuahua's withers (top of her shoulders) without wrinkles or folds. Ideally, her neck is of medium length. Too short of a neck may be the result of improperly placed shoulder blades, which prevent Manchita from moving well (see "Gait" later in this section). Besides, if her head appears to be attached directly to her shoulders, she'll look unbalanced and front-heavy. On the other hand, an extremely long neck may be a sign that a dog lacks substance (appears weak). It may be accompanied by too-long legs and a lanky body. Look for graceful lines. All the dog's parts should be well balanced in relation to one another.

Manchita's topline flows along the top of her back from the withers to the root of her tail (where the tail meets the body). Ideally, it should be level or straight, without a dip in the middle or a downward or upward slope. Manchita's body appears rounded rather than flat along the sides, and she needs a roomy rib cage to house her heart and lungs.

Tail

Figure 2-4 illustrates the Chihuahua's three correct tail positions and the sorry-looking tail-tuck. When a Chihuahua puts its tail between its legs, something is wrong. The dog may be timid, frightened, cold, or sick. A cropped tail or bobtail disqualifies a dog from the show ring.

A dog's *conformation* is the shape of her body from the top of her head to the tips of her toes and tail. It encompasses balanced body proportions and size, both of which need to be correct for the breed.

Forequarters

Sloping shoulders can also be described as *well laid back*. That means Manchita's shoulder blade, or *scapula*, connects her upper arm bone with her vertebrae with an obvious backward slope from its bottom end (at the arm) to its top (just in front of the withers). Why are well-laid-back shoulder blades important? Because sloping shoulder blades allow Manchita's front legs to have a good range of motion. Shoulders that lack this slope are called *straight shoulders*. They are faulty because the upper end of the shoulder blade is too far forward — crammed right into the dog's neck. Besides making the neck look too short, straight shoulder blades shorten a dog's gait by limiting the forward reach of the front legs.

Ideally, Manchita's front legs are straight while her toes point forward. Being *bowlegged* is a fault and so is an *east-west front* (toes pointing to either side) or *toeing in* (toes pointing toward each other).

Feet that are elongated like a rabbit's foot or rounded like a cat's paw are not desirable. Instead, Manchita's feet need to reach a happy medium between the two, with the toes separated but not *splayed* (flat and spread apart).

The *pasterns* are the lowest points on Manchita's front legs, just above her feet. They need to be slender and straight.

Figure 2-4:
Three
correct tail
positions —
and one
sorry tail
tuck.

Hindquarters

To give you a little taste of dog talk, the perfect Chihuahua's rear end is officially described as "Muscular, with hocks well apart, neither out nor in, well lct down, firm and sturdy. The feet are as in front." Have you got that? Well the first word, muscular, is obvious, and what the rest of it means is a dog's hind leg has an upper and lower thigh, separated by the *stifle,* or knee joint, which is located on the frontal part of the dog's hind leg (don't forget Figure 2-3). The upper and lower thighs need to have sufficient muscle. Between the stifle joint and the foot is the *hock joint.* Hock joints that are not in the middle of the hind leg, but much lower, are better. So *well let down* means the hock joint is rather close to the ground.

Rear legs that are absolutely parallel when viewed from behind are ideal. On the other hand, hocks turning toward each other, known as *cowhocks,* and hocks turned outward (bowed or spread) are faulty.

Coat

Chihuahuas come in two varieties — *smooth coat* and *long coat.* If Manchita has a smooth coat, her hair is short and close to her body, and she may or may not have an *undercoat, or* a protective layer of shorter fur underneath the outer or top coat. A smooth Chihuahua that has an undercoat appears more thickly coated than one that doesn't, and usually has a furrier tail and a *ruff* of thicker hair around its neck. If Manchita has no undercoat, her hair is sparser. In fact, it may be so thin that she appears nearly bald on parts of her head, ears, chest, and belly. Don't worry. It's not a problem. The thin coat simply means she's a smooth Chihuahua without undercoat.

If Manchita, on the other hand, is long coated, she has an undercoat and her outer coat is between an inch and an inch-and-a-half long. Her ears are decorated with longish hair called *fringe* or *feathering,* and she has an abundant ruff around her neck, long hair called a *plume* on her tail, and wispy hair on the back of her legs. She also sports *natural pants* — long hair on her buttocks. Aside from that, she should look exactly like a smooth Chihuahua, because the two varieties have exactly the same conformation (body structure) underneath their coats.

A sparse coat disqualifies only long-coated Chihuahuas from the show ring. Short-coated dogs with thin hair are considered normal, although a thicker coat usually is more attractive.

Color

Any color — solid, marked, or splashed, take your pick — and all colors or combinations of colors and markings are acceptable in Chihuahuas, and none are considered better or worse than others.

Gait

If you walk at a normal pace, Manchita is easily able to keep up with you by moving along at a smart trot. When she gaits properly, no motion is wasted — no high-stepping hackney or goose steps. Her feet don't turn in toward each other or wing out to the side. In fact, her movement is lively but effortless, and only her legs are involved. Her back (topline in dog lingo) remains level, not rolling from side to side, bobbing up and down, or appearing concave *(dip in the topline)* or convex *(roached back)*.

One way to check Manchita's movement is to watch while someone else trots her squarely toward you and away from you on a leash. If her movements are ideal, you see only her front legs as she approaches you and only her rear legs when she moves away. While watching her from the side, if her front legs reach out but stay close to the ground and her rear legs (which actually power the dog) have good drive, and none of her legs interfere with each other, chances are she's a good mover. If you're not sure about rear drive, watch her trot away from you again. Can you see the pads of her back feet? If so, she probably has plenty of drive.

When a Chihuahua stands relaxed, her front feet may turn ever so slightly away from each other toward either side and still be correct. In fact, if they point perfectly front when the dog is in a casual stance, chances are they'll point toward each other (toe in) instead of straight ahead when she moves.

Temperament

Manchita appears bright, bold, and saucy, but that's just the gist of it. Chihuahua temperament deserves a full chapter, not a paragraph. Read all about it in Chapter 3.

Oh No! Manchita Doesn't Match the Standard

It's true. The real Manchita misses out on matching the standard in several places. Yet she's happy, healthy, and pushing 12 years old, with the attitude and energy of a puppy. Her bite is wrong, but she chews just fine. She's *fiddle-fronted* (bow-legged with toes turned out), but she's agile and likes going for brisk walks. So if you've just read about the Chihuahua standard and discovered that your precious pet isn't perfect, don't worry. As long as her faults don't affect her health and mobility, only a top breeder or judge knows or cares.

The truth is, no dog, not even an AKC Champion, matches every word of the standard, but show dogs have to come pretty close or their careers end early. Naturally, it's most important that dogs used for breeding comply with the standard, since their quality is reflected in the next generation. Remember that breeding to its own standard is what makes each breed of dog unique. Ignore the details and soon Chihuahuas, Papillons, Miniature Pinschers, and other Toy dogs begin to resemble each other, and the individual breeds gradually are lost.

Chapter 3

Getting to Know You: Chihuahua Charm

*W*hat makes the world's smallest dog one of our nation's most popular pets? That perky personality, of course. Yes, this unique breed has more going for it than a serious case of the cutes. Chihuahuas are protective despite their size and react appropriately to their owner's moods. They love lovin', travel well, and adore creature comforts. In this chapter, I talk about the traits of a typical Chihuahua — complete with all its characteristics and quirks.

Packing a Lot of Character into a Tiny Dog

The breed standard for the Chihuahua describes its temperament as terrier-like, so let's start by talking about typical terrier personality. Most small terriers (think Fox Terriers and Scottish Terriers) originally were bred to *go to ground* after prey. They helped keep wily foxes out of henhouses and rats from fouling the feed in barns, and they didn't hesitate to take on badgers, snakes, or anything else that intruded near their people or property. Although few terriers do their traditional work today, most retain their feistiness and are brave to a fault. Alert to their surroundings, quick to defend home and family, and positive that they are tougher than the biggest dog on the block, terriers make alert watchdogs and energetic, playful companions.

Petite protectors

While few Chihuahuas care to go rat hunting (aren't you glad), they do have several terrier traits. Bravado is one example. When Pepe trots down the street with you, he appears animated and confident — a bantam rooster with a proud posture.

Most Chihuahuas don't realize that they're small. Given the opportunity, some approach big dogs in play, and occasionally — especially if the large dog is invading their territory — aggressively. While a tiny terror, barking and running full force, sends some gigantic dogs packing, this situation isn't safe. Toy breed owners need to exercise caution around strange dogs, because even the friendliest medium-sized dog can seriously injure a small one during rough play.

The Chihuahuas' bravado also makes them good watchdogs. Like terriers, they're alert and have amazingly keen hearing and a bark that's loud for their size and shrill. To top it off, they can tell the difference between a family member's footsteps or a stranger's stride nearing the door, and they know when a vehicle other than the family car pulls up to the house. Chihuahuas have an unjust reputation for excessive barking. Most bark an alarm when a stranger approaches, but when properly trained (see Chapters 10 and 12), they're not any noisier than most other breeds.

Most Chihuahuas are good eaters. In fact, some Chihuahua owners have to watch their pet's weight to prevent obesity.

Close companions

Pepe's an affectionate animal who dogs your footsteps from room to room, because awake or asleep, he wants to be near you. While some breeds always seem in search of mischief, the typical adult Chihuahua is content with its owner's company (see Figure 3-1). After Pepe grows out of his busy puppy stages, he's happiest when you and he are close — preferably touching. An accomplished cuddler, he lies on your lap for as long as you let him, helping you relax as you read the paper or watch television. Pepe adores being stroked when you have a free hand, and a gentle massage transports him to puppy paradise. Don't be surprised if he rolls over to beg for a belly rub.

After all that togetherness, Pepe may not want you to leave him even at bedtime. Many Chihuahuas sleep in their owner's bedrooms, but not necessarily in their beds. Train Pepe to snooze in his own soft bed or crate, and that's where he curls up when the lights go out. It's safer than sharing space with him in your own bed. Sure he'd rather snuggle up with you, but he can easily get hurt if you happened to roll over onto him during the right.

Figure 3-1:
Chihuahuas
need
affection
and thrive
on together-
ness.

Comfort-loving creatures

Chihuahuas are heat-seekers and masters of the art of relaxation. Indoors, Pepe plays bathing beauty, stretching out on the carpet right where a sunbeam shines through the window. On gray days, he seeks out another source of warmth, napping near a heating vent or in his own bed — that is, if your lap isn't available.

You'll know your Chihuahua is a little chilly when he curls up into a ball with his nose under one leg. Dogs do that because it allows them to breathe air that was preheated by the warmth of their bodies. Inhaling the warm air helps keep them cozy.

The ultimate house dog

Pick up a leash and say, "Wanna go for a walk?" and most breeds beat you to the door while dancing in ecstatic circles. Nevertheless, don't be surprised if Pepe plants his feet and gives you a longsuffering look that translates into, "Do I have to?"

Most Chihuahuas (some exceptions live in semi-tropical climates) prefer their homes to the great outdoors. Lovers of warmth and softness, they consider cold concrete and dewy grass hardships to be endured, not enjoyed. If Pepe is a smooth coat, he chills easily, sometimes shivering from ear tips to toes. He also hates rain, and it's no wonder. Imagine being so low to the ground that every step you take splashes cold water onto your bare belly! Of course, you must take your pet outside no matter what the weather so he can eliminate on schedule (see Chapter 5 for accessories that help keep him comfortable). On cold days, it's amusing to see how fast some Chihuahuas get it over with so they can rush back to their warm homes. When I lived in Manhattan, I carried Manchita to the curb during winter; otherwise, she squatted the second her toes touched the sidewalk.

Cautious compadres

Typical adult Chihuahuas are sassy with strangers but discriminating about making new friends. Few Chihuahuas, no matter how well-socialized, run pell-mell up to a houseguest and vie for his or her attention. Instead, Pepe makes sure you know a stranger's in the house by barking at the intruder until you tell him "Enough!" (see Chapter 10). After that, he probably takes a position with a view of your visitor from across the room for several minutes before deciding that person deserves canine company. Then his likely approach is a slow and gradual offering of his furry friendship — provided your guest lets him make the first move and resists the temptation to grab at him.

To speed up the buddy-making process between your friends and your dog, tell guests to ignore Pepe until he approaches them. Then they can reciprocate by tickling him on the chest or under the chin. That's less threatening than reaching over him to pet his head. Chihuahuas don't like it when strangers swoop down on them from above like hungry hawks. But if your friends squat down and let Pepe check them out, they'll soon become best buddies.

Pepe probably makes friends much faster on neutral ground (such as a park) than he does in his own home. That's because he doesn't feel the need to defend neutral territory.

Spirited, but not hyper

Although they are playful pets, Chihuahuas are not hyper little dogs. In fact, most of them don't have an especially high activity level.

Rather than racing around the living room, Pepe prefers spending part of his day on your lap or burrowed beneath a blanket. His attitude about exercise is easy going — ready to play when you are but content to relax when you aren't in an active mood.

CHIHUAHUA TALES

Environment trumps heredity

Although caution in choosing friends is a Chihuahua trait, not every adult Chihuahua is persnickety about meeting new people. Three-pound Manchita, for example, makes a merry dash into the arms of anyone who shows interest in her. When she was a puppy, my daughters were teenagers with friends coming and going daily. All the kids fussed over her during her formative months, so she grew up believing every human is a potential petting machine. Manchita is almost 12 years old now, and still falls for friendly people at first sight.

As Chihuahuas mature, they tend to take on the same activity level as their people. The same dog that is frisky when part of an active family turns into a contented cuddler when grandma and grandpa dog-sit.

TIP

Even though Chihuahuas prefer human company, properly trained adult dogs are able to occupy themselves for hours without looking for trouble or demanding attention.

Unusually adaptable

Chihuahuas thrive in living quarters ranging from country estates to studio apartments. Don't worry about stairs or elevators. Once Pepe is introduced to them (see Chapter 9), he handles them just fine.

Because Chihuahuas are so small, they don't need a fenced yard or kennel run to get their exercise. Give Pepe a few toys (see Chapter 5) and he plays active games right in the living room. Or better yet, join in the fun, and both of you get some exercise. I suggest some games to play together in Chapter 8.

Chihuahuas are good travelers and adjust to moving better than many breeds — feeling at home wherever their owners are. That attitude, plus their small size, makes the Chihuahua an ideal dog for people who have to move frequently and for retired couples crisscrossing the country in RVs. If you move often, your Chihuahua won't mind — but think twice before buying one anyway. Finding rental housing that allows dogs is often difficult. My daughters faced that problem when they took Manchita to college, but finally solved it by taking her along to meet potential landlords. When one landlord saw how petite and polite Manchita is, he made an exception. And the girls did their part by keeping their pet in a well-equipped playpen (the type meant for an infant) when they weren't home to supervise.

Male and female Chihuahuas are equally affectionate and appealing and initially take about the same amount of time to housebreak. But many males (if they haven't been neutered) disregard their training when they get old enough to lift their leg and mark their property (a sign of sexual maturity). Correct the problem by catching it early and returning them to their crate-training puppy schedule (see Chapter 10) for a few weeks. If that doesn't do it, help for hard cases can be found in Chapter 15.

Sensitive supporters

Chihuahuas sense their owner's moods and react accordingly. When you arrive home after receiving a promotion, Pepe recognizes right away that something wonderful happened and dances around you with glee. But he also senses when you're sick or sad, and tries to be consoling. Stories abound about Chihuahuas that stopped playing, and had to be reminded to eat and even eliminate, when a family member was bedridden with a serious illness. Instead, they tried to spend all their time with the sick person.

Easily trained

While housetraining any dog (see Chapter 10) is a chore, most of the other training you give Pepe should be pure pleasure for both of you. That's because Chihuahuas love being center stage and are eager to learn — provided the training is gentle, upbeat, and complete with plenty of positive reinforcement (read: praise and treats). Because they are so people oriented, Chihuahuas have longer attention spans (once they are past the puppy stage) than many other breeds. Make training fun and Pepe focuses his big eyes on you and pirouettes happily every time you praise him. Once he learns a new trick, he never forgets it. He may, however, try to improvise. Some Chis are so clever that as soon as they perfect a trick, they invent a new way to ham it up. Many Chihuahuas are successful in competitive sports such as obedience and agility. Read all about those activities in Chapter 11.

Contrary to false advertisements, Chihuahuas are not classified by size. Typical Chihuahuas weigh between three and six pounds. Dogs a little larger than six pounds make excellent pets, especially when children are in the family, but think twice before buying an especially tiny Chihuahua. Pups wrongly advertised as *miniature* or *teacup* are often too delicate for the average home and may have health problems.

Long-term friend

If Pepe is a healthy, well-bred Chihuahua and you take good care of him, chances are he can live well into his teens. Chihuahuas are one of the longest-lived breeds. And that's great news for humans who love them.

Socializing with Other Critters

While Chihuahuas may sass strange dogs when out for a walk (basic obedience training cures that), they usually get along with the other pets in your home. After introductions are made (see Chapter 5) and they all get used to each other, Pepe's likely to curl up with your cat, ignore your caged birds, and become buddies with your bigger dog. Don't be surprised if he shows a jealous streak over who gets the most attention. Dogs usually work these things out for themselves (with the Chihuahua often becoming the dominant dog). Just be sure to supervise the animals closely until they get used to each other and obviously get along.

Remember those terrier traits we talked about earlier in this chapter? Keep little critters like hamsters, gerbils, iguanas, and small birds out of Pepe's reach, or pouncing on them may be just too tempting.

One unique Chihuahuaism is that the breed recognizes, and almost always welcomes, its own. Even though Pepe seems sassy or even scared around strange dogs, in most cases he becomes ecstatic at the sight of another Chihuahua, and the two quickly make friends.

Deciding between Long-Coated and Smooth

When deciding whether you want a long-coated or a smooth Chihuahua, considering more than just the length of coat you want to cuddle is important. That's because the differences are more than skin deep. In general (there are exceptions), slight personality differences exist between the two coat types. The following sections discuss the more obvious.

Long coats and smooth coats are often *littermates*. That means they are brothers and sisters born in the same litter.

Long coats can handle cold better

While no Chihuahua can stand cold for long, many long coats enjoy a short walk in brisk weather and may even play in the snow (provided it's only a couple inches deep). Not so with smooth coats. Chihuahuas with short hair are miserable in cold weather (see Pepe shiver) and should wear a sweater outdoors on chilly days even when going for a short walk.

Smooth coats cuddle closer

Short-coated Pepe enjoys feeling the warmth of your body on his nearly bald belly and lies on your lap while you read or watch TV. His long-coated counterpart wants your company too, but he's more likely to sit beside you instead of on you. Differences also are noticeable if you decide to bed down with Pepe. A smooth coat curls up under the covers while a long coat usually lies on top of the blankets.

Long coats shed less

No, that's not a misprint. Long-coated Chihuahuas shed seasonally, usually twice a year. During those periods, they lose a lot of hair quite quickly. But a few good brushings, plus vacuuming the carpets and furniture, puts an end to the problem for several months. Smooth coats, on the other hand, shed old hair and replace it with new all the time. Consequently, a few tiny hairs always work their way into your clothes, furniture, and carpets.

Long coats are a bit more reserved

Smooth coats are often more outgoing and accept new friends faster than long coats. While long coats like attention too, they tend to be a little more reserved and need more time to warm up to friendly strangers.

According to an old wives' tale, at least one long-coated Chihuahua appears in every litter of smooth coats — a gift from Mother Nature to keep its short-coated littermates warm. Although it's a sweet story, it doesn't always happen that way. Besides, smooth-coated pups don't need the help. They do just fine by cuddling up to their dam and to each other.

Checking a Pup's Resume

Several things must go right before a Chihuahua puppy grows up to be typical of the breed. A puppy matures with the characteristics that people admire if it:

- Is well bred (comes from good stock)
- Receives adequate daily care (a clean habitat and quality food)
- Was socialized by a caring breeder
- Was further socialized by its owner (see Chapter 9)
- Was raised with attention and affection
- Was taught basic house manners (see Chapter 10)
- Was never abused or neglected

If any of the necessities in the list above were missing during the dog's upbringing, or if it was neglected or abused, chances are it won't behave like a typical Chihuahua. Unfortunately, Chihuahuas often get a bad rap from people who meet a sorry excuse for a dog and decide that the entire breed behaves badly. The following undesirable traits are the ones that frequently plague poorly bred, undernourished, unsocialized, untrained or unloved members of this breed. They are, in a sense, typical of the atypical:

- Timid, shy or extremely nervous
- Frail and sickly
- Temperamental
- Refuses to accept friendly strangers
- Yappy
- Vicious — snaps at people without warning, and for no reason
- Possessive — defends his food dish, toys, or favorite chair, even from his owners

Oh my! That's a scary list, isn't it? I bet it doesn't sound like anything you want in a dog. Don't panic. In Chapter 4, I tell you how to avoid the unhappy traits and find a Chihuahua puppy with the potential to grow up with all the breed's best characteristics.

Part II
Fitting a Compact Canine into Your Life

The 5th Wave   By Rich Tennant

"Okay, before I let the new puppy out, let's remember to be real still so we don't startle him."

In this part . . .

In this part, I help you choose a healthy Chihuahua with a great disposition and tell you how to keep it glowing with good health from puppyhood to old age. You discover what your Chi needs and doesn't need in the way of food, toys, grooming, housing, exercise, and preventative medical care.

Chapter 4

Selecting a Healthy Dog

*W*hew! You've made the really big decisions. You're sure you want a dog and think a Chihuahua is the breed for you. But you aren't finished yet. Now you have to make the most important decision of all — picking the one special Chihuahua to share your life.

Easy now. Don't rush. Picking your pet may be your only opportunity (outside of marriage) to actually choose a member of your family. All Chihuahuas aren't created equal, so let's go shopping together. I can help you find a healthy dog with that charming Chihuahua character.

Buying from a Breeder

The first step toward finding a fabulous four-legged family member is locating a respected breeder. The best breeders usually specialize in Chihuahua's, devoting years to preserving the breed's finest traits. Whether they have just a few adult dogs or a large kennel, their breeding stock is excellent, they give their puppies plenty of affection, and they probably exhibit at dog shows.

Several suggestions to help find a good kennel in your area include:

✔ Contacting the American Kennel Club (see Appendix B) and asking for the address of the Chihuahua Club of America. The address changes whenever a new club secretary is elected, but the AKC keeps up-to-date records.

- Asking the Chihuahua Club of America for literature on the breed and for the address of the regional Chihuahua club closest to you and then contacting that club for a list of member-breeders.

- Talking to local veterinarians. They know which breeders have healthy dogs with terrific temperaments.

- Finding the all-breed kennel club nearest you. Almost every city of any size has an all-breed kennel club. Ask at a veterinary clinic or call the library. Then contact the all-breed club to find out if any of their members are Chihuahua breeders.

- Looking at the breeder ads in dog magazines like *AKC Gazette*, *Dog World*, and *Dog Fancy*. Besides being available by subscription, the magazines are sold in many bookstores and at newsstands.

- Going to a dog show. Breeders travel many miles to show their dogs and are glad to talk to you after they finish competing. (Don't bother them during the heat of competition). Dog shows are fun and educational even if you have no interest in showing your own dog. With luck, you'll see several Chihuahas in the show ring. Watching them helps you decide what traits especially appeal to you. If several of your favorites come from the same breeder, you know where to look first. Ask your local all-breed kennel club or the American Kennel Club (AKC) when shows are scheduled in your area.

Make some decisions before you go Chihuahua shopping. Finding your ideal dog is easier if you've already decided whether you want a smooth or long coat, a male or a female, and a puppy or an adult.

Visiting breeders

Most reputable breeders cherish their Chihuahuas as a hobby, not a business. They're proud to show you their facilities and tell you about their dogs. Just be sure to contact them ahead of time and set up an appointment. Breeders don't keep regular business hours like pet shops do, and their facilities are almost always attached to their home or close to it. So meeting a breeder and seeing his stock is a lot like visiting someone socially.

Small size doesn't mean small price tag

Just because Chihuahuas are little, don't expect the purchase price to be less than for a larger dog. Chihuahuas have small litters. The cost of breeding them (including stud service, and possibly a Caesarean section) is high. And raising healthy, outgoing Toy dogs takes a lot of time and energy. Good breeders are happy to break even. They do it for love, not money.

A mature female dog is a bitch, no matter how sweet she is. And when used for breeding, she is a brood bitch.

Making a list of what you want in a Chihuahua and letting the breeders know your criteria before you visit simplifies things. For example, tell the breeder if you are set on a male or a female, a smooth or a long-coat, a certain color, and whether you plan to show your dog (see Chapter 18). That way, the breeders can save you a trip if they don't have what you want, and may be able to send you to another kennel where your dream dog awaits. Try visiting a few breeders and seeing several puppies before making a decision.

Oh gee, why the third degree?

All responsible breeders are going to grill you, so don't be surprised or insulted when you're asked about your lifestyle. Instead, be glad you found a breeder who truly cares about the puppies' welfare. It all evens out in the end. After all, you're going to evaluate the breeder while he or she assesses you.

Here are some of the questions many breeders are likely to ask you, and why they want to know:

- ✔ **What made you decide on a Chihuahua?** The breeder's making sure you choose the breed because you truly like Toy dogs and especially Chihuahuas — not that you just want one because its stylish, or think a little dog costs less to feed, or is easier for your 2-year-old to tote around.

- ✔ **Have you had dogs before and what happened to them?** Good breeders want their puppies to have loving permanent homes. If you never had a dog before, the breeder probably wants to fill you in on the facts of dog ownership just to make sure you know what you're getting into. If you had a beloved dog that eventually died of old age, the breeder's happy to sell you a puppy. But if your previous dog ran loose and got killed by a car, or died of a disease that could have been prevented, a responsible breeder won't sell you a dog. Truthfully, you don't deserve one — unless you learned something from the sorry saga and won't let that happen again.

- ✔ **What are your hours? How much time do you spend at home?** The breeder wants to be sure the puppy gets enough attention. Puppies must be fed and walked on a regular schedule to become housebroken.

- ✔ **How old are your children? Are they gentle with animals?** Tots and Chihuahuas aren't a good match. Toddlers are too young and uncoordinated to safely handle a small dog, and Chihuahuas are too tiny for rough handling. Teasing by youngsters also turns nice dogs into holy terrors.

✔ **Do you have a fenced yard?** The breeder wants to make sure your dog won't be turned loose to be flattened by a car, mauled by a bigger dog, or poisoned by eating something spoiled. Although fenced yards make dog ownership easier, many Chihuahua owners live in apartments or condos and exercise their dogs by walking them on the leash.

✔ **Is everyone in your family looking forward to getting a Chihuahua?** It isn't fair to the Chihuahua if someone in the family despises little dogs but was out-voted. The dog can sense the disdain immediately, and the person may go so far as to sabotage the socializing or training.

✔ **What do you expect from your Chihuahua?** Tell the breeder if you want a dog solely as a companion, or if you also want to show the dog. Will your Chihuahua live only with adults, or are there kids in the family? Will your dog live at home or travel in your RV? Will you have your pet spayed or neutered, or are you considering using the dog for breeding? Is obedience or agility competition a possibility?

The more the breeder knows about your plans for the pup, the better he or she is able to help you in making a selection. After all, the breeder observed the litter since birth and knows each puppy's personality.

When choosing your Chihuahua, avoiding orphan puppies or litters of only one is a good idea. That's because hand-raised orphans and solo pups get everything they want instantly. Consequently, they don't learn how to handle frustration or get along with other dogs. In general, puppies that are raised by their *dam* (the puppies' mother) along with at least one littermate make better companions.

Evaluating the breeder

Now it's your turn to be the judge. Here's how to make sure you found a good breeder:

✔ You already know that the best breeders specialize in one or two breeds, enjoying their dogs as a hobby rather than a business and adoring their puppies. They may exhibit their stock at dog shows. So if you see brood stock of several different breeds on the premises or notice that the puppies are treated like merchandise, don't purchase a puppy there.

✔ Healthy puppies come from clean kennels. Check out the floor or grass the puppies are playing on. Has it been washed or pooper-scooped recently, or is it covered with miniature messes? Sneak a peek at the food and water dishes. Is the food dish clean, or is ancient goop stuck to the sides? Is the water clear or has yellow slime invaded the bottom of the dish? Use your nose. Sure, you'll catch a whiff of fresh puppy poop, but if the stench is stale or overwhelming, try another kennel.

✔ Is the puppy play area bare, or do the puppies have a few toys? Toys serve a purpose. They stimulate puppies physically and mentally, motivating them to exercise, play together, and learn.

Even the healthiest pups become limp as dish rags when they are sleepy. If the pups you're visiting can't seem to stay awake, ask the breeder to schedule another visit at a different time of day.

✔ A good breeder knows the puppies' personalities inside out and gladly discusses them with you. In fact, he or she may talk nonstop and tell you even more than you want to know about the puppies, their parents, and extended family. Yes, breeders brag about their dogs, but that's a good sign. It proves they're proud of their breeding and spend enough time with their dogs to know them well.

✔ Did the breeder give you the grilling I told you to expect? Good. That means he or she wants to be sure that a Chi is the right breed for your family and that you'll give the puppy a good home. Steer clear of money-hungry puppy vendors who pretend Chihuahuas are ideal pets for everyone. It simply isn't so.

✔ Chihuahua puppies need to stay with their dam and littermates until they are at least 8 weeks old. Steer clear of any breeder lets a pup leave for its new home any sooner than that.

✔ Did the breeder tell you that if you ever have to give up your Chihuahua, he or she offers to take her back and find her a new home? That's a good sign that you're dealing with a responsible breeder.

✔ Did the breeder feed you endless data about how to raise and care for a Chihuahua? You may be annoyed by all the *you shoulds,* but cut this over-protective *mommy* some slack. You're talking to a caring person who willingly shares information and who someday, when you need advice, you'll be glad to know is willing to help.

✔ Did the breeder display the puppies' pedigree with pride? That's a good sign that the litter came from a well-planned breeding.

✔ Do you like the breeder? Okay, maybe not for a best friend but well enough to call on if you need advice about your Chihuahua's health or training? Or do you hope you never need to talk to the breeder again? If you have a bad feeling about the breeder, the facility, or any of the dogs, trust your intuition and look elsewhere for your puppy.

What about pet shops?

The darling "Doggie in the Window" can cost you a small fortune if you run into hereditary health problems.

The pet shop itself usually isn't the problem. The puppies in most pet shops are clean and well nourished, have toys to keep them occupied, and are often petted by the employees. The problem is where they came from before arriving at the pet shop. You see, good breeders plan matings carefully, breed to the standard, socialize their puppies, and after all that, want to check out every potential puppy owner. But the people who sell puppies to pet shops breed only to make money. They choose breeding partners for convenience instead of quality, and willingly sell the entire litters to middlemen without caring who ends up with the pups. Sometimes their facilities are crowded and dirty, and they usually have far too many dogs to give any of them individual attention. And that's a serious problem.

Lack of human attention early in life results in puppies that are nervous and shy, and a dirty habitat during their formative weeks can make them hard to housebreak. Sure, time and affection helps, but the bottom line is: No matter how hard you try, you can't cure bad breeding.

Dog lovers have a name for the over-crowded, filthy facilities that breed litter after litter and sell hundreds of poorly bred puppies every year. We call them *puppy mills*.

Classified canines

Should you check out the ads for Chihuahua puppies in your local newspaper? That depends on what's on your Chihuahua wish list. With the right knowledge, you may be able to find a nice pet through the classifieds. But if you dream of owning a show champion, buying from an established breeder is your best shot at success. Why? Because puppy sellers who advertise only in the paper, and not through the dog journals, probably bred their pets to their friends' pooches without studying the standard or comparing pedigrees. While both parents may be healthy Chihuahuas with excellent dispositions, it's better to have plenty of knowledge about picking puppies before trying to select a pet from the litter. Don't worry. Help is coming right up.

Pick of the litter

Gotta have it! But which one is it?

Everyone wants the *pick of the litter,* but it's a different puppy for different people. To a show exhibitor, the pick is the puppy that comes closest to the description of the ideal Chihuahua in the breed standard. To the woman who lives alone in the city, the pick is the puppy that alerts instantly to strange sounds. To the young couple with kids in elementary school, the pick is the largest and liveliest puppy. To the retired couple in the condo, the pick is the quiet puppy that loves to cuddle.

The truth is, the pick is the puppy that appeals to you — provided it is healthy and has the right temperament to share your lifestyle (see Figure 4-1). If you're dealing with a show breeder, but have no intention of showing, you don't need the puppy the breeder considers the pick of the litter. Chances are, the breeder won't sell it to you anyway. It's destined to become a show dog, and possibly, the *sire* (father) or dam of the breeder's next generation of show champions. But its litter brother or sister may make you the perfect pet.

At the best kennels, show puppies and pet puppies come from the same litters. In fact, the last choice in a top breeder's litter may be of higher quality than the first choice in a mediocre litter.

If you want to show your Chihuahua, let the breeder know that up front so he or she can steer you toward the puppy with the best conformation. Before buying, discuss guarantees. And expect to pay considerably more for your guaranteed show-potential puppy than you would for a pet.

Figure 4-1:
Pick a puppy that appeals to you on first sight, but check its health and disposition before making a purchase. This pup's name is Ginny.

Whether you decide to pick your own puppy or ask the breeder for input, the following four sections offer helpful suggestions to you on the big day.

Bring on the puppies

You better have a plan when meeting puppies, or canine Cupid will sting you with an arrow. The following suggestions help you choose a puppy with your head as well as your heart:

- **Trust your instincts.** Did one puppy catch your eye immediately? Do you keep going back to her even though you want to give them all equal time? Are you already naming her in your mind? First impressions are important when picking a puppy, and love at first sight can last a lifetime. But take the time to make sure your furry favorite is healthy and has a pleasing personality.

- **Be observant.** Watch the puppies play together for several minutes without human interference. (Chihuahua litters are small, so you'll probably observe two to four littermates interacting with each other). Your best bet is a puppy in the middle of the pecking order — neither the bully nor the scaredy-cat. One sign of superior character is a puppy that stands up to the bully, then goes on about her business peacefully.

- **Eye the eyes.** The eyes need to be bright, alert and clear of mucous. Don't mistake clear tears for mucous. Many Chihuahuas (and other Toy breeds) have too-small tear ducts, so tears occasionally fall from the eyes. A telltale sign is a small water stain at the inner corner of each eye. This is not a sign of sickness, but don't convince yourself that the stains fade away as the puppy matures. More than likely, the dog will always sport tear stains, but they won't affect her health or happiness.

- **Check the coat.** Bald may be beautiful on my husband, but it's a bad sign on a puppy. A healthy coat is smooth to the touch and glossy, with no bald patches. Smooth-coats without undercoat may have thin hair on their temples and practically bald bellies, but no puppy should have skin showing through on its back or sides.

- **Know the nose.** Breathing must be quiet and rhythmic and the nostrils should be free of mucous.

- **Watch the puppies move when they play.** Despite a bit of baby clumsiness, puppies appear quick, bouncy, and agile. Puppies standing straight on legs that look strong enough to carry their bodies is a good sign.

- **Take along someone who's knowledgeable about show dogs.** If you want a show puppy but don't have a clue how to select one, taking along someone knowledgeable about show dogs (and better yet, Chihuahuas) when you look at puppies is a wise move. Another option is making absolutely sure you're dealing with a successful show breeder and then letting him or her choose a puppy for you.

✔ **Check the teeth.** If a show career is in your puppy's future, don't forget to check her teeth for a *scissors bite* (the upper front teeth meet tightly outside the lower front teeth). Although it isn't easy to do with a tiny puppy, try to evaluate her *gait* (the way she moves at a trot) by watching her move both straight toward you and directly away from you. Front legs moving parallel with each other as she comes toward you and rear legs moving parallel with each other as she moves away are good signs. Study the breed standard (see Chapter 2) before selecting a potential show dog.

One on one

After watching the litter play together, it's time to meet your favorites up close and personal. But first you need to know how to hold a puppy. Novices often hold puppies high, with their back legs dangling, but dogs hate being held that way. Instead, when lifting a puppy (or an adult Chihuahua), use both hands. Place one hand under her chest and brace her bottom in your other hand. Then cradle the puppy close to your body. Little puppies are wiggly and a fall can be fatal, so keep your grip gentle but firm. And don't let your fingers push the pup's elbows outward or squeeze her front legs together, as either error could damage the dog.

Be smart and sit on the floor to play with puppies. You'll enjoy it more because you won't have to worry about dropping a pup, and the breeder's blood pressure will normalize.

Now you're ready to see how well each puppy relates to people — especially you — so here's the rest of your *check-it-out* list:

✔ Ask if you can take your favorite puppy or puppies out of sight (one puppy at a time) of the breeder, their dam, and their littermates, so you can test their temperaments. Then begin by giving each puppy at least a full two minutes to survey her surroundings (time it or you won't wait long enough). Watch her attitude while she explores. Is she curious or fearful? Lively or laid-back?

✔ Next, kneel down and try coaxing the pup into coming to you. When she does, praise her. Then get up, move away from her slowly, and try talking her into following you. If she does, that's a good sign that she enjoys human company and likes you just fine.

✔ Show the puppy a small ball or other dog toy just the right size for her, and roll it about three feet away from (never toward) her. Does she seem interested? If she doesn't respond right away, that's okay. It may take three or four tries before she understands the game. Does she eventually chase or follow the rolling toy and examine it when it stops moving? That's a good sign that she learns quickly, isn't afraid to try new things, and is willing to play on your team. If she picks up the toy in her mouth and carries it part of the way back to you, that's even better.

✔ Now pick up the puppy and cradle her securely against your body. She should feel strong (for her size) and solid in your hand. The puppy may struggle briefly, but she should soon relax and enjoy the attention. After she loosens up, does she sniff your hands, maybe even lick you? These are signs that she has a good temperament and was well socialized by the breeder.

✔ Try a little TLC. When you pick up the puppy and cradle her in your arms, does she stiffen with fear or struggle nonstop? Neither reaction is good, but don't give up too soon. The puppy may just need a little more time. Talk to her while stroking her soothingly. Does that tight little body relax? Good. If not, she may have missed out on early socialization. Pick another puppy.

✔ Never lift a puppy by its front legs. Not only is it painful, but it can cause permanent injury to the puppy's shoulders.

✔ No matter how super a puppy looks and tests, make sure some chemistry exists between you. During your first couple months together, both of you go through a period of adjustment. But a Chihuahua that charms a smile out of you makes all the adjustments seem minor.

Potential problem pups

Not every puppy aces your tests. Here are signs that may warn you away from a pup:

✔ Don't buy a skinny puppy, or one with pimples or raw patches on its skin, excessive dander, mucous seeping from the nostrils or the corner of the eyes, or diarrhea.

✔ Please don't purchase a puppy out of pity. When an active litter of puppies vies for your attention, but one hangs back or hides in a corner, she isn't an abused baby in need of comfort. If the breeder neglected or mistreated the pups, every one of them would shy away from people. The truth is, that puppy has a temperament problem. Yes, she might improve a little with time and a lot of socialization (see Chapter 9), but her apprehensive attitude is probably a permanent problem. Unfortunately, turning that poor puppy into the secure and cheerful companion you and your family deserve may take more love than exists in the world, let alone in your home.

✔ Go for impy, not wimpy. Don't pick a puppy that shies away from its littermates' games. I know it's tempting to take home a little underdog, but resist as hard as you can. Pups that allow themselves to be terrorized by their littermates seldom become confident pets.

✔ Avoid anxious Annie. Don't buy a puppy that runs away or crouches fearfully in one spot when you take her out of sight of her breeder and four-legged family. It's okay if it takes her a couple minutes to get her bearings, but after a few moments, expect her to show some interest in her surroundings and be curious about you.

✔ When tempted to buy a bargain puppy that doesn't turn you on, remember that the purchase price is only a small part of what you spend on your dog during her lifetime. It's smarter to pay more and get a dog that makes your heart sing.

✔ A puppy that tests well probably can make someone a wonderful pet, but that someone may not be you. How do you feel when you play with the pup? Is she the tiny soul mate you've been searching for? Or are you thinking of buying her only because she tested well and you're tired of Chihuahua shopping? When tempted to think that way, remember that you're choosing family. Then keep looking until you know you found your canine counterpart.

If you are buying a show potential puppy, don't be surprised if the breeder insists on keeping it until it is 6 months old. That's perfectly normal. Why? Because it takes that long to be positive (well almost, anyway) that a puppy has what it takes to become an AKC champion.

Seeing the extended family

When looking at a litter of puppies, ask to see their dam and any other close relatives that live with the breeder. With luck, you may get to meet the puppies' grand-dam, a couple of aunts or uncles or even an older brother or sister from a previous litter. You may also see the sire, but don't be disappointed if he lives far away from the breeder. Good breeders find the best possible match for their brood bitch. Then, no matter where he lives, they take (or ship) their bitch to him and pay a fee (or possibly a puppy) for his *service*. If the sire isn't on the premises, the breeder should be able to show you his pedigree and probably his picture.

The mother of a litter of puppies is their *dam* and the father is their *sire*.

The more of your potential puppy's close relatives you meet, the better. Why? Because their attitudes and appearances give you a good indication of how the puppies may turn out. For example, does the pup come from a friendly family? Or do its relatives aggressively attack your ankles or cringe behind the couch in terror? Do you find the family attractive, or do most of the dogs have a trait that you would rather avoid?

Choosing a Mature Chihuahua

After a brief period of adjustment, an adult Chihuahua bonds to a new owner just as strongly as a puppy does. But why would you want an adult dog? Maybe because even though puppies are precious, they're also babies. Like infants, they're sloppy eaters, go potty often, and sleep a lot — but not always on your schedule. They need constant supervision for several weeks or they may teethe on the table legs and leave puddles (or worse) on the carpet. So a mature dog may be easier on some people's schedules.

While not every mature Chihuahua is housebroken, and unsupervised young adults may still exercise their choppers on the chair legs, grown dogs have bigger bladders and longer attention spans than puppies, so they tend to learn the house rules rather quickly. But isn't acquiring an adult dog kind of like buying a used car? Isn't it merely someone else's problem just looking for a new place to happen? Maybe, but certainly not always.

Practically perfect adult dogs often find themselves homeless because of a divorce or death in their families, family members' allergic reactions to dog hair, or owners moving and being unable to find housing that allows pets. Many breeders also won't breed their bitches past a certain age and are happy to place them in loving homes. And lost or abandoned dogs are often available for adoption through a rescue or humane organization. See Appendix B for Chihuahua rescue organizations.

Every member of the family needs to meet an adult Chihuahua before a decision is made to buy or adopt it. That's because something in its past may have caused it to love men but hate women (or vice versa), or become defensive around children.

Selecting an adult Chihuahua is a lot like choosing a puppy but without some of the guesswork. Here's some tips to help you sift through the problem pets and single out your future best friend:

- ✓ When meeting a mature Chihuahua, remember that you are a stranger and adult dogs are more discriminating than puppies. Don't force your attention on the dog. Instead, sit down and talk to the owner for a few minutes until the dog warms up to you.

- ✓ Check for general good health by looking at the dog's eyes, nose, coat, skin, and movement. The eyes are clear and bright (not cloudy). The nose is free of mucus. The coat covers the body with a healthy shine. The skin is smooth and supple, without bumps, lumps, or pimples. And movement is easy and animated — not stiff or labored.

✔ You and the dog need to appeal to each other. Give her time to accept you and then pet her if she allows it. Does she relax and enjoy your company, or is she fearful or aggressive? Ask the owner to place her on your lap. Is she content to cuddle? Or is she scared stiff or frantic to escape?

✔ Ask if you may put a leash on the dog and take her for a walk. Encourage her to walk beside you with soft, happy talk. Does she trot down the street with you willingly, or does she freeze in place, cry, balk, or try to make a break for home?

✔ Now for the smile test. Does looking at this dog make you smile? That's good chemistry, but it works both ways. Once the dog knows you, does she wag her tail and dance a few happy steps when you talk to her? Liking each other is the most important criteria of all.

Many dogs are protective of their homes but warm up to friendly strangers easily on neutral ground. It's worth a try if you like everything about an adult Chihuahua but she doesn't seem to like you.

Understanding Pedigree

The word *pedigree* is often used incorrectly — especially in classified ads where the term *pedigreed puppies* almost always means purebred puppies. The truth is, every dog has a pedigree whether it's purebred or not. Honest. A pedigree is nothing more than a list of ancestors, just like a family tree. For example, one of your grandparents may be Hungarian, another Russian, another Irish, and the fourth may be British, but each one of them appears on your family tree. By the same token, a mutt's grandparents (grandsires and granddams) may be a Miniature Pinscher, a Chihuahua, a Yorkshire Terrier, and a Toy Poodle, and that is the dog's family tree. The dog has a pedigree, but is not a purebred.

What is a purebred? It's a dog that descended from dogs that were all the same breed. A purebred Chihuahua has two Chihuahuas for parents, four Chihuahuas for grandparents and eight Chihuahuas for great-grandparents, and so on, as far back as records can be traced.

Through studying pedigrees you learn a lot more than just the names of a dog's ancestors. For example, if any of the ancestors won a title, it shows up on the document. The titles found most frequently on Chihuahua pedigrees are show champion (*Ch* in front of the dog's name), an obedience title (CD or CDX after the name), or an agility title (NA or AD) after the name, but there may be others. Breeders are delighted to decipher the titles for you — and with good reason. They illustrate the beauty, trainability, and temperament of the dog's ancestors.

Registering your new dog

When you purchase a dog or puppy that is AKC registrable, you receive a registration application that has been filled out and signed by the seller. The form includes a section for the new owner (congratulations, that's you!) to complete. Do it ASAP and send it to the American Kennel Club (the address is on the form), along with the required fee. As soon as your dog's paperwork is processed and recorded, you receive a registration certificate. Finally, you own a registered dog.

Thousands of eligible dogs aren't registered even though their owners think they are. That's because the owners put the registration application in a safe place but never read it. That official-looking piece of paper is only an application. It means your dog is eligible to be AKC registered. For the dog to actually *be* registered, you must fill out the form and send it in.

One of the more important things you write on the registration application is your dog's name. Decide carefully, because once your dog is AKC registered, the name stays the same forever.

Don't be surprised if the kennel where you purchased your Chihuahua wants to either name her or include its kennel name as part of your dog's registered name. That isn't an unusual request. Breeding superior dogs is an art form, and putting a kennel name on a top quality dog is the same as an artist signing his or her work. Most of the time, you and the breeder can both get what you want. For example, if you bought your dog from Talko Chi Town Kennels and want to name her Susie, her registered name may be Talko Chi Town Susie. In dog show lingo, Susie is her *call name.*

Careful!

If the seller doesn't have a registration application for your puppy, but assures you that one is coming, proceed with caution. Maybe the seller didn't apply to AKC soon enough and expects the paperwork in a week or two. If you trust the seller enough to buy on that basis, ask for a bill of sale signed by the seller that includes your dog's breed, date of birth, sex and color, the registered names and AKC numbers of the pup's sire and dam, and the full name and address of the breeder. That way, if you don't receive official paperwork in a week or so, you can write to the AKC and fully identify your dog.

If you want a registered dog, and the seller can't give you either the registration application or every bit of the above information, pass up the puppy.

Crossbreed fables abound

One fable about Chihuahua origins contends that the Chihuahua came from a cross between a dog and a rodent and ran wild in the desert surrounding Chihuahua, Mexico. Another theory claims the Chihuahua evolved from a cross between the Techichi and a small wild dog called the *Perro Chihuahueno,* which lived in the area now known as the state of Chihuahua. And if that isn't enough, a few historians think the Techichi may have been crossed with a small hairless dog that was brought across the Bering Strait from China to Alaska.

Chihuahuas without credentials

If you adopted your Chihuahua from a rescue or humane organization, she probably came to you without papers. Does it matter? Only if you want to compete in AKC events such as obedience or agility. The American Kennel Club allows purebred dogs with no papers to compete in those events, if they have an *Indefinite Listing Privilege* (ILP) number. Write to the AKC (see Appendix B) and request the forms.

Chapter 5

Welcoming Home Your Little Amigo

● ●

In This Chapter

▶ Timing the arrival

▶ Puppy-proofing your place

▶ Going shopping for Pepe

▶ Sailing through the first 48 hours

▶ Blending dogs, kids, and other critters

▶ Resisting the freedom fantasy

● ●

*I*t's almost dog day! Excitement is in the air. I bet you can hardly wait to bring your puppy home, but first, let's do a little organizing. This chapter helps you decide when to bring Pepe home and tells you how to keep his curious tongue out of toxic things. It also helps you decide what your new dog needs and doesn't need, so you won't be tempted to buy every toy in the pet shop.

Are you wondering how to handle your Chihuahua when he's the new dog on the block? How to guide your children or grandkids into a good relationship with their little pal? How to introduce Pepe to your other pets? Don't worry. That's all here too.

Picking the Right Time

The best time to bring home a new puppy is when nothing new is happening at your place. Waiting until the repair people are finished, the relatives have gone home, and the holiday season is over gives Pepe quiet time to get to know you and adjust to his new home.

If Pepe is a holiday gift from your husband to you or vice versa, settle for a photo of him under the Christmas tree or beside the Hanukah candles. If you have kids at home, gift wrap a collar and leash, a food and water dish, and dog toys to go with the photo. Then bring Pepe home after the parties are over and the decorations have been boxed. A normal home has enough gizmos to tempt a puppy into trouble. Halls decked out for the holidays can be downright dangerous.

Don't ever give a dog as a present unless you are absolutely sure the recipients want one and that the breed you picked is their favorite too. Better yet, before you pay for the pup, invite the potential owners to meet him and check out the chemistry between them.

Dogs are social animals, so being alone in a strange place makes Pepe feel lonely and insecure. It's better if you can bring him home when you have a vacation or a long weekend and can be around to help him settle in. Is a regular weekend the best you can do? Then bring him home as early as possible on Saturday morning. Don't opt for Friday night, because bedtime without his dam and littermates is the hardest time for a puppy, and he'll feel better if he has a whole day to acclimate first.

Selecting the Right Room

Until he's housebroken, the right place for Pepe (when no one is able to supervise) is in one easily cleaned room of your home. Most people find the kitchen ideal, unless it's exceptionally large. In that case, a bathroom may be suitable. A wire mesh baby gate across the doorway works better than a solid door, which isolates the puppy, adding to his loneliness and frustration, and leads to incessant barking, temper tantrums, and tiny tooth prints in that darn door. Make sure the mesh is strong enough to withstand sharp teeth and that the mesh pattern is too small for Pepe to chew through or get caught in.

Pepe's room must be puppy-proofed for his safety. Puppies are curious, and because they don't have fingers to feel things, they try to taste everything (no matter how yucky it smells to us). Keep all cleaning agents, pesticides, antifreeze, and other household and garden chemicals out of your puppy's reach. The same is true with electrical wires. If it isn't possible to eliminate every electrical cord that Pepe can reach, coat them with Bitter Apple. It's a safe, evil-tasting liquid, formulated to prevent chewing and available in many pet stores.

Do you have houseplants? Then identify every one (not just the ones in the puppy-proofed room) and look them up to find out if they are poisonous (or take a leaf to the nursery and ask). Many popular houseplants are deadly, including poinsettia leaves and those merry mistletoe berries. Placing all plants, even the safe ones, out of Pepe's reach is a good idea, because no puppy can resist playing with a plant. But extra precautions are necessary with the poisonous ones. They shed leaves and berries even though they may be hanging high, and Pepe is bound to pick them up. Best bet? Get rid of them.

If you like your nonpoisonous houseplants right where they are, and want Pepe to know he needs to leave them alone, spray them with Bitter Apple leaf protector.

When young and unsupervised, Pepe tries to teethe on everything he can reach, from your bedroom slippers to your shower curtain . . . even a box of dishwasher detergent, if the cupboard door is left ajar. But keeping his curious mouth out of mischief isn't as hard as it sounds. Once you have your precious puppy, securing closet and cupboard doors, or flipping the shower curtain up over the rod becomes second nature in no time.

If you can't give Pepe the run of a whole puppy-proofed room, a baby's playpen with mesh sides is a good (and portable) alternative.

When Manchita was a puppy, she earned the nickname, Hoover, because she behaved like a vacuum cleaner, inhaling everything in her path. One day while we were out walking, she snatched up a small rock and swallowed it before I could get it out of her mouth. The next day, she strained to eliminate, couldn't pass the rock, and became sick. Luckily the veterinarian was able to dislodge it by medicating her at both ends. Otherwise our two-and-a-half pound puppy faced emergency surgery.

Shopping for a Few Essentials

You've puppy-proofed your home and have a long weekend coming up to welcome your new pet. Now it's time to go shopping. Pepe needs a few things right away.

Just look at the colorful display of dog toys, collars, leashes, food and water dishes, and even canine clothing, in the pet store. It's tempting to buy twice what you need. How will you know what's necessary and what isn't? By using a shopping list. Later I'll explain each item, so you can get the perfect one for Pepe.

Shopping list for your new Chihuahua

The shopping list below contains the essentials you'll need for your new Chihuahua:

- Two dishes, one for water and one for food
- Puppy (or dog) food
- Collar
- Leash

- ✔ Grooming equipment, including a natural bristle brush, nail clipper, toothbrush, doggie toothpaste, and shampoo. Long coats also need coat conditioner, a hard rubber comb and a mat splitter.
- ✔ Three or four toys
- ✔ Dog crate
- ✔ Dog bed (optional)
- ✔ Warm sweater (if it's chilly outdoors)
- ✔ Pooper Scooper
- ✔ Identification
- ✔ An excellent veterinarian

Practical dishes

What's a practical dog dish? It's one that's easy to clean and hard to tip over. Some of the nicer dishes are made of stainless steel; although acrylic, heavy-duty plastic, stoneware, and porcelain are good choices. Some dishes are wider at the bottom than at the top and others are weighted. These are good features because it makes them impossible to tip over, even if Pepe likes to play with his bowl.

When feeding Pepe, place his dish where it won't slide around the floor while he eats. A corner usually works well. Eating meals indoors is best for your Chihuahua, but if you decide to give him an outdoor picnic on a pretty day, pick up his dish as soon as he finishes. Otherwise, every bug in the neighborhood is attracted to your yard and the bowl.

Puppy (or dog) food

Kibble? Soft-moist? Biscuit? Pellets? Canned? Chopped or chunky? Are you confused yet? Don't be. Feeding your dog a good diet is easy and mighty important . . . so important that it has its own chapter. So instead of giving Chihuahua chow your best guess, turn to Chapter 6. It tells you how to meet Pepe's nutritional needs during every stage of his life.

If you buy ceramic dishes for your Chihuahua, make sure they were made in the good ol' USA. Look for ceramics that are well glazed (read: glossy). Remember some foreign glazes still contain toxic stuff, including lead.

First collar and leash

Wait until you bring your puppy home before buying a collar, so you can get one that fits his neck perfectly. Pepe's collar applies no pressure as it encircles his neck but not so loose that it easily slips over his adorable apple head.

Shop for a flat collar made of nylon webbing or leather that closes via a buckle and has a D ring for attaching a leash. Some of the newer nylon collars have a plastic clasp similar to those used on camera bags and fanny packs (but in miniature) and come in a variety of attractive designs.

Check the fit of Pepe's collar weekly. Although he won't grow much, puppies do grow fast, and the collar must be replaced right away if it feels tight. It's not unusual for puppies to go through two or three collars before they mature, so keep that in mind when pricing puppy collars.

The length of Pepe's lead is best between five and six feet. Leather, nylon, or other flexible fabric leads are preferred. Expandable leads that allow a dog to get several feet away from its owner are also available. They give dogs a feeling of freedom while still being safely under control but should be considered optional. The traditional type is still the safest choice in crowded places. To find out how to lead break Pepe, see Chapter 9.

Don't buy a leash or collar made of chain. Chain is too cumbersome and can hurt Pepe's legs if he gets tangled in it. And don't buy any type of training collar (they also come in nylon and webbing) with a ring at both ends that tightens up when you or your dog pulls on it. Commonly called choke collars, these training devices are meant to be used during obedience training only (never for everyday wear) and Toy dogs don't need them at all.

Grooming gizmos

Smooth Chis have easy-care, wash-and-wear coats, so for grooming, they can get by with a quality shampoo that is pH-balanced for dogs, a natural bristle brush, a toothpaste formulated for dogs, a soft toothbrush made for small dogs or human babies, and a doggie nail clipper. Other items like cotton ear swabs are also useful in grooming your Chi (see Chapter 7), but you probably have most of them in your medicine cabinet already.

Long coated Chis are also easy to maintain, but require a few more things. Both you and Pepe appreciate a coat conditioner formulated for dogs. Besides making his coat a cinch to comb after his shampoo, it keeps it soft and silky. A hard rubber comb is a must for keeping mats out of a Chi's coat, especially behind the ears. If you don't use the comb often enough (don't worry, it takes only a minute or two), you'll probably need a mat splitter to put Pepe's coat back in good condition again. Chapter 7 tells you how to use your grooming gizmos to keep your dog's skin and coat healthy.

Don't buy a nylon or metal comb, or a brush made with anything but natural bristles. Natural products do the least damage to a dog's coat, and if you comb your dog during the winter with a nylon or metal implement, you'll probably zap him with static electricity. He'll hate it and won't want to be groomed anymore.

Toys for toys

Toy dogs need playthings that are small enough for them to manipulate but big enough so they can't swallow them. Think of Pepe's toys as essentials, not extras. He needs something safe to gnaw on while he is teething and a couple of toys available to play with the rest of the time.

Although your Chihuahua continues chewing after he grows up, he won't wrap his fangs around everything he can reach the way teething puppies do. Be glad your mature Chi still likes to chew (for example, see Figure 5-1). Besides keeping him content, chewing promotes healthy gums and teeth.

Figure 5-1:
She may be pushing 12, but Manchita is still serious about her chew toys.

Rawhide chew toys are a traditional favorite, but on rare occasions, dogs have accidentally choked to death when a piece of rawhide got caught in their throats. You don't have to boycott rawhide altogether. Instead, let your dog enjoy it when you're with him but replace it with something safer when he is unsupervised.

Chew toys made of hard nylon are safe in Pepe's mouth even when no one is home. Chihuahua puppies, and many adult dogs, prefer the softer and equally safe gummy-nylon chews. Solid, hard-rubber toys are also safe and fun.

On the other hand, squeaky toys (featherweight rubber or plastic critters with squeakers inside) are popular with pups but are safe only when you are supervising — or better yet, joining in the fun. That's because toys of this type are easily chewed open (yes, even by a Chihuahua) and the squeaker inside is mighty dangerous when swallowed. Like rawhide, you don't have to deprive Pepe of a squeaky toy. Instead, buy him one but keep it out of his reach. Then, get it out once every few days as a special treat, and watch the fun when he play-kills it.

Don't use old leather shoes, purses or wallets as dog toys. Sure, your dog likes sinking his teeth into the well-worn leather, but it teaches him that leather objects with your scent on them are chew toys. That won't do your new accessories any good.

Flat fleecy toys (shaped like gingerbread people or other animals) are popular, and dogs like cuddling up to them. They are machine washable and safe as long as Pepe doesn't shred the edges of his toy and swallow some of the material. Just keep an eye on the toy and throw it away if it ever becomes worn enough to worry about.

The braided rope toys sold at pet stores are fun for playing games with your Chihuahua. They also help keep his teeth tartar-free. If you can't find one small enough for Pepe, check the bird toys. These toys usually last for years, but if your Chi starts unstringing his rope, don't leave him alone with it. Swallowed strings can cause serious intestinal troubles.

After Pepe owns a few toys, never let him have all of them at once. Instead, put a few away and rotate them every couple days. That way Pepe won't become bored with his belongings. Keeping at least three toys (but no more than five) in service at one time is a good rule of thumb — one in his crate, one or two in his play room (if he has one), and one or two in the room where the family gathers. While indulging an older dog is okay, an overabundance of toys scattered throughout the house may lead a puppy to believe that whatever he can reach is his to chew.

A cozy crate

Dogs descend from denning animals that spent much of their time in the relative security of their lairs. That's why it won't take long before Pepe feels comfortable and protected in a dog crate. Contrary to being cruel, as some new dog owners imagine, crates have saved dogs' lives and owners' tempers.

If you can't give Pepe his own puppy-proofed room, a crate becomes even more essential. It keeps him from stalking snakes (that's electrical cords to you) while you're away. Because they are so curious, puppies are bound to get into mischief (or danger) when left at home alone. Besides, coming home to a safely crated puppy is much nicer than coming home to teeth marks on table legs and a soiled carpet. For info on introducing Pepe to his crate, see Chapter 10.

Buy Pepe a crate that's big enough for a full-grown Chihuahua to stand up and turn around in comfortably. Bigger is not better for two reasons: Chihuahuas enjoy the cozy comfort of a just-the-right-size den, and a too-large crate loses it's potty-training potential. Because dogs don't like to soil their beds, a crate is a big help during housetraining (see Chapter 10). It also keeps Pepe out of trouble while you're asleep.

For safety's sake, always crate your Chihuahua when taking him for a drive, and secure the crate so it won't slide or roll over during turns or quick stops. A crated dog has a better chance of surviving a car accident than a loose dog does. Not only that, but you'll drive better without your Chihuahua vying for your attention.

Most crates are made of either wire or plastic (with a wire door). Both have their benefits, but plastic is the best choice for smooth coated Chihuahuas. The solid sides (except for ventilation holes) keep Pepe draft-free.

The inside of Pepe's crate is his private place within your home as well as his home away from home, so create a comfortable den. Make sure the bedding is easy to wash or change and not dangerous if chewed or swallowed. An old twin-bed size sheet does nicely. If you don't have one, use several thicknesses of newspaper (black and white, not color or glossy like the comics or ads). For extra coziness, rip one section into long, thin streamers and place them in the crate on top of the whole sections (Chis love having something to burrow under). Once Pepe keeps his crate clean (which doesn't take long if you follow the schedule in Chapter 10), give him a nicer *mattress*. A fleecy crate pad or soft rug samples are two possibilities.

The best place to put Pepe's crate is in his puppy-proofed room (if you have one). Then caring for your new puppy works on the same principle as caring for a human baby. Just visualize Pepe's puppy-proofed room as his nursery, and his crate as a combination crib, playpen, and car seat, and you can see how handy both are. Of course, you may opt to use a real playpen or a made-for-dogs exercise pen, in addition to a crate.

For the ultimate crate toy, buy the smallest sterilized bone you can find (available at many pet supply stores) and stuff it with cheese. That keeps Pepe occupied for hours.

A snug bed

If a crate doesn't satisfy your concept of interior design, let your Chihuahua graduate into an attractive doggie bed after he's housebroken. Most are made of wicker and come with a nice mattress. Place the bed in a draft-free area, and top it with a snugly blanket.

A useful sweater

Some canine couture is created just to look cute, while other clothing actually serves a purpose. Since Chihuahuas chill easily, Pepe may need a jacket or sweater that actually helps him stay warm. Look for one that covers his chest, part of his neck, and as much of his belly as possible (see Figure 5-2). If your Chi is a female, the more of her bald belly it covers, the better. When fitting your male, remember that he wears his jacket outdoors when he goes potty, and you won't want him to wet the material. Most canine clothes are machine washable, but read the label just in case.

Figure 5-2: Manchita's coat is functional.

Sharing home with dogs — an old, old story

Archeologists agree that the dog was the first animal domesticated by man. In fact, cave drawings from the Paleolithic era, the earliest part of the Old World Stone Age (some 50,000 years ago), picture men and dogs hunting together. Primitive people shared their living quarters and food with the dogs that defended their camp and helped them catch their dinner. As humans became more civilized, they found additional uses for dogs. Some dogs served man by guarding flocks. Others pulled carts. Through selective breeding, humans developed dogs for a variety of purposes from killing vermin to pulling sleds, and from hunting lions to warming laps.

All of today's domestic dogs, from Chihuahuas to Saint Bernards are related, no matter how different they look. That's because every modern breed descended from *Canis lupus,* the gray wolf.

Pooper scooper

Poop scoops are available in a variety of styles at your pet supply store. They are convenient for cleaning up your yard and for cleaning up after Pepe when you take him on walks. Most of them have long handles so you don't have to bend down.

If you don't mind bending down, you can get by without a pooper-scooper. Instead, stock up on plastic sandwich bags. Put a couple in your purse or pocket before walking your dog. Turn one inside out for a quick pick-up, then close it and toss it in the nearest garbage can.

A trusted veterinarian

Pepe's veterinarian is his other best friend, so choose one before bringing him home. How will you know which dog doc is best for your puppy? Check out Chapter 13. It covers the pet/vet relationship.

Identification

You new dog should carry identification all the time. Chapter 13 tells you all about it.

Planning the First Two Days

Let's go! You have everything you need and now it's time to pick up Pepe!

Get off to a smart start by taking your crate along so your puppy can ride in it on the way home. It's his safest sanctuary in a moving vehicle.

When you arrive home, give Pepe an opportunity to relieve himself outdoors before going in. Then take him to his puppy-proofed room, give him fresh water in his own dish, and let him explore *his room* to his heart's content. You're not depriving him by keeping him from investigating your whole home right away. Too much new territory is confusing, and besides, if he's teething and isn't housebroken yet, more space simply means more trouble. If you don't have a puppy-proofed room, keep a close eye on Pepe as he inspects his new digs. And use a crate when no one is supervising.

Make sure extra warmth is available whenever your Chihuahua needs it. Whether you use a crate, playpen, or dog bed, it needs to be equipped with a sheet or blanket that he can burrow under.

After Pepe has a drink (and some food if it's feeding time), take him outdoors again. Then put him back in his puppy-proofed room, give him a toy, and play with him quietly. No matter how excited you are, this isn't a good time to overstimulate your puppy. Chances are, he's tired from the trip home and seeing so many new places and faces. When he gives out (some puppies go from playing to sleeping so quickly they appear to have passed out) crate him, or put him in his bed, and let him take a nap. He loves sleeping on your lap, of course, and it helps both of you bond . . . but don't put him on your lap for every nap. Pepe has to learn to sleep alone, too.

For the first couple of days, try to keep household activity normal . . . even low key. This isn't the time for Junior to jam with his band or for Julie to invite her friends over to practice for cheerleading tryouts. Don't start spring cleaning or get out the vacuum cleaner either. And remind enthusiastic family and friends not to rush at Pepe. Unfamiliar surroundings and strange voices are enough for a puppy to get used to during the first 48 hours. After that, household activity can gradually return to normal.

Picking puppy up

Sure puppy Pepe fits into your palm; but you need to use two hands to pick him up anyway. One hand goes under his chest and the other cups his rear. Check your hands the first few times to make sure your fingers don't apply pressure to his front legs — either spreading them too far apart or squeezing them together. Habitual spreading could cause permanent damage to your puppy's elbows. On the other hand, squeezing them together can harm the legs and shoulders. Best bet? Place your thumb on one side of your dog and your little finger on the other, supporting his chest with the middle three fingers. After you try this method once or twice, it becomes automatic. Then hold him gently, but firmly (puppies wiggle), against your body with both hands, so no part of him dangles.

Never leave your puppy alone in a place where he could fall. For example, if you and your Chihuahua are watching TV in the recliner, and you get up to check out the fridge, place your pup on the floor until you return. When Pepe matures, he becomes able to jump on and off the furniture by himself, but that's a dangerous leap for a puppy.

Blending dogs and kids

Please don't skip this section just because you don't have any kids at home. You may have grandchildren or friends with children, and these tips assure that visiting kids and Pepe have pleasant (and safe) visits.

Sometimes kids and dogs scare each other without wanting to. Tiny dogs fear shrill sounds and fast movements (especially swooping down on them), and youngsters come well equipped for the task with high-pitched voices and jerky movements. When dogs feel threatened or cornered, they usually growl, warning the offender away. But many young children either don't recognize the warning, or simply ignore it, and that's how bites happen. On the other hand, children fear shrill noises too, and Pepe's piercing puppy bark may make them cringe.

I already told you that Chis and young children are not a good combination. The truth is, kids and dogs can hurt each other. But many people have surmounted the obstacles and succeeded in raising children and Chihuahuas at the same time. How? By being vigilant and never leaving little children and Chihuahuas (or any dog for that matter) alone together. Using careful and calm supervision every time a child and puppy are together keeps the child and the pup from learning to fear each other. Just imagine, for example, their reaction if you seemed scared.

From about the age of 3 or 4 on, children — depending on their individual self-control and emotional maturity — can *help you* care for Pepe. Examples of things kids can do (provided you have patience and won't freak out over spilled food or water) are picking up Pepe's dirty dishes and bringing them to you, and giving Pepe his water or food after you fill the dishes. Kids also get a kick out of giving Pepe an occasional treat. When children are young, helping to take care of a pet needs to be fun — a privilege, not a responsibility. Do it yourself when you're in a hurry. Chubby little fingers sometimes spill stuff.

Children who are ready to help care for a puppy are also ready to discover some simple rules. Here are a few that work on your own kids and visitors too. Of course, you may have to create others to fit your situation:

- Always sit on the floor to play with Pepe.
- Don't put your face close to Pepe.

Chihuahuas love to be loved and are true companion dogs. They need affection to thrive and socialization to cultivate their character.

Every Chihuahua should have her own snug bed, complete with a toy or two.

Although they are too little to stop a thief, Chihuahuas are alert watchdogs. If those big ears detect a stranger's footsteps, he'll race to the door, barking a warning.

The Chihuahua standard describes the breed as alert, with a saucy expression and terrier-like qualities.

This charmer's eye-catching coat comes from good breeding, good nutrition, and good grooming.

A nice thing about Chihuahuas is that they take up so little room on the furniture.

What will these puppies be like when they grow up? They will probably be a lot like their parents, so ask to meet their dam (mom) and any other family members the breeder has on the premises.

It can take several weeks for puppy ears to become erect, and they don't always do it at the same time. Occasionally, the Chi's ears refuse to stand even after the pup is grown. The result is a dog that won't win in the show ring but can still be a super pet.

Little dogs command lots of attention.

You can tell by his body language that this smooth coat wants to play.
Chihuahuas are very social animals.

What's up?

Like all dogs, Chihuahuas need appropriate chew toys to play with.

© Mary Bloom

Every Chi should know how to walk on lead and obey basic commands like sit, down, and come.

This puppy is performing a friendship dance and should soon have a partner.

© Mary Bloom

© Mary Bloom

Chihuahuas are the ultimate housedogs. They can get enough exercise indoors but enjoy going for a walk on a pretty day.

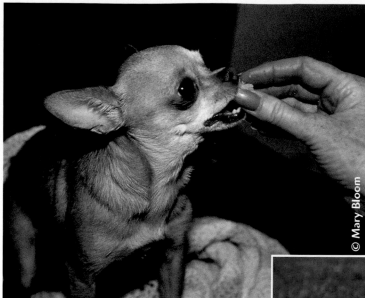

Chihuahuas have well-rounded heads, often referred to as "apple domes."

© Mary Bloom

Some long-coated Chihuahuas have more hair than others. This one sports a thick coat.

© Mary Bloom

© Mary Bloom

Playing with toys helps puppies develop both physically and mentally.

Although Chis are too tiny to associate with toddlers, they are content in the arms of gentle school-age kids (under supervision, of course).

Here's a party animal ready to howl "Happy Birthday!"

- ✔ You may pet Pepe, but don't close your hand. That keeps children from squeezing, or from grabbing a leg, ear, or tail.

- ✔ Don't tease or poke Pepe. You may have to explain what teasing is.

- ✔ Never give Pepe anything to eat or play with without permission.

- ✔ When Pepe wants to leave, let him go. Don't hang on and try to stop him. Remember, the "don't close your hand" rule.

Older children and Chihuahuas

By the time they are third- or fourth-graders, some kids become attuned to animals. In fact, older children often have better relationships with their pets than grown-ups do, because they take the time to discover the animal's body language. Responsible older kids can share in Pepe's care by feeding, grooming, and walking him. And they may surprise you by teaching him a few tricks.

Junior and Julie find out the most valuable lessons about pet care when it's a family affair. Don't expect a child (or teenager) to take full responsibility for Pepe, even if they promised they would when they begged you to buy him. Instead, give them an excellent example (yes, that's you) to follow. Most important of all, never make threatening remarks like, "If you don't do those dishes right now, I'm giving that &*%$#@ dog away!" Pepe isn't a disposable object like outgrown skates or a broken barrette. He deserves affection, care, and a permanent home, and threatening to give him anything less sends your child a sorry message.

No matter how good your children are with the family Chihuahua, keep an eye on the situation when their friends visit. Other children with little or no experience with tiny pets, may want to experiment ("What would happen if we fed him this?") or may even harbor a mean streak. And the best of kids (like yours) may find themselves helpless in the face of peer pressure.

Dog to dog

Don't bring your precious new puppy into the house, cuddle him close, and tell old Rover to buzz off and behave himself. Doing so creates the canine equivalent of sibling rivalry. And if ol' Rov is a big boy, the situation may be dangerous for Pepe. Just imagine how a 3-year-old child reacts to her new brother if she's suddenly shoved aside while the baby gets all the attention.

The best way to introduce Rover to Pepe is on neutral ground, so Rover doesn't feel the need to defend his territory from a tiny intruder. Just a half a block down the street does fine if both dogs know how to walk on leash. Pepe must stand on the ground (not in your arms) to participate in a proper doggie introduction, so if he isn't leashbroken, borrow a fenced-in yard for the opening ceremony. The easiest way to accomplish a successful meeting is to ask a helper to take Pepe to the designated place. Then you take Rover for a walk, on leash, and meet them there.

As the dogs near each other, start a conversation with your helper, but watch while the dogs go through the motions of meeting. Give Rover just enough slack in the lead so he can sniff Pepe all over, but maintain complete control of the situation. Act nonchalant so the dogs don't sense any anxiety in you, and don't pet either dog. As soon as Rover displays gentleness toward Pepe, praise him verbally. In most cases, dogs are civil, even friendly, to each other. In rare cases, where Rover appears threatening or overly excited, give an immediate jerk on the lead and walk away with him. Then try again when he simmers down.

Once the dogs seem comfortable with each other, walk them home together if both dogs walk on leash. Otherwise, let your friend carry Pepe, and you walk Rover, praising him occasionally along the way. When you get home, try to make Rover think that inviting his little friend in was his idea. Inside, put Pepe on the floor in the same room with Rover, and supervise closely. Most big dogs treat little puppies gently as long as they don't suddenly feel unloved. Remember to give Rover at least as much attention as you ever did, and don't leave the dogs alone together until you're sure they get along. Use their crates, or keep them in different rooms, when no one is home.

If you have more than one dog, introduce them to your new dog or puppy one at a time. Start with your calmest canine and work up to your most excitable.

Cats and other critters

Dogs and cats in the same household usually get along, and some become best buddies. If Pepe isn't especially agitated at the sight of Tabby, she may become curious and try to sniff noses with him. If he sniffs back, that's good. Chances are they'll be friends in no time (see Figure 5-3). While waiting for that to happen, keep a watchful eye on them when they're together. Some dogs, even little ones, have an undeniable urge to chase cats. And while some cats run from Chihuahuas, others may take a swipe at the tiny tormentor, damaging your Chi's eyes and nose.

Furry and feathered caged pets, such as hamsters, birds, rabbits, and mice, may appear to be prey to Pepe. Dogs (yes, even little ones), instinctively catch and kill prey. The best solution is to keep these critters out of Pepe's reach and correct everything from too much interest to a menacing growl with a firm "No!" Pepe doesn't have to make friends with these animals. It's fine if he learns to ignore them. Most dogs lose interest in caged pets once they get used to seeing and smelling them on a daily basis. But until then, supervise Pepe every time he's in the same room with your caged critters.

Figure 5-3:
Boudreux
and
Manchita
have been
buddies for
years.

Protecting Your Dog from Total Freedom

Some dog owners think their dog somehow misses out on something if he never experiences absolute freedom. In fact, more than 7 million dogs die every year from accidents encountered while roaming free. In addition to being crushed by cars, or picked up by animal control officers, loose dogs lick poisonous substances; like tasty drops of deadly antifreeze (it's sweet) or lawn herbicides. Besides being a menace to your neighbor's flowerbed, a loose Chihuahua faces dangers like being stolen, attacked by a bigger dog, or even snatched by an owl or hawk (it happens). He may also be handled roughly by a small child. And if the child frightens or hurts Pepe, your dog may bite during his efforts to escape. Now you're in danger of a lawsuit.

Putting Pepe in a position to become a statistic isn't doing him a favor. A Chihuahua is more than a domestic animal — he is the ultimate house dog. Instead of freedom, give him what he really wants: your companionship.

Chapter 6

Feeding Your Chihuahua

*J*ust look at the pet food aisle at any major supermarket. It's stacked high with an array of kibble, meal, biscuit, semimoist, and canned canine cuisines — some for puppies, some for adult dogs and some for seniors — all claiming to offer optimum nutrition. And that's only the half of it. Pet supply stores stock several higher-priced but more-concentrated brands, each proclaiming its advantages. Are you confused yet? Don't be. Selecting a healthy diet for your Chihuahua is easy. In this chapter, I help you choose the right meals for Manchita, and tell you how to feed her though every stage of her life.

Feeding for the First Few Days

The only right food to feed Manchita for the first few days after you bring her home is the one she was eating before you got her. Even if your new Chihuahua is an adult dog, make only gradual changes in her diet. She's experiencing enough newness in her life right now without changing her dog food. Many breeders give you a small amount of puppy or dog food and a written schedule to help you get started, but if nothing is offered, ask three questions about your new dog's eating habits:

 ✔ What brand has she been eating?

 ✔ What is her feeding schedule (how frequently is she fed and at what hours)?

 ✔ How much does she eat at each feeding?

Besides using the same food, sticking to the feeding schedule Manchita is used to is best at least for the first three days. After that, it's okay to gradually change chow time until her schedule blends into your household routine.

Dogs are omnivores. That means they eat both meat and plant matter.

What if you already decided on a dog food and it isn't the one Manchita was raised on? No problem. After a few days of feeding her the brand she is used to, introduce the food you selected by adding just a little bit of it to her usual diet. Watch to make sure she eats it and check her bowel movements. As long as everything is fine (no constipation or diarrhea), add a little more of the new food and take away a little more of her old food every day. You can complete the transition by the end of a week.

Should you change dog foods?

Now that you know how to change dog foods, are you sure you want to? Look at Manchita. Is her weight right for her height? Does she have enough energy? Does her coat have a healthy glow? Gee, her breeder must have done something right. As the old saying goes, "If it ain't broke, don't fix it." If Manchita eats most of her meals and has regular bowel movements, an upbeat attitude, and a healthy coat, then the best dog food for her (at least until she reaches another stage in her life), may be exactly the one she's eating. See Figure 6-1 for an example of a healthy-looking properly fed Chihuahua.

What if Manchita is too thin or too fat, lacks energy, has a dull, dry-looking coat, or suffers from constipation or diarrhea? First, see your veterinarian. If he or she rules out parasites or an illness, consider changing dog foods (gradually). You may also want to change Manchita's diet if the one her breeder recommends is too time-consuming to concoct. Some breeders create their own formulas, and many of them are way too complicated for working pet owners. Besides, quality commercial food is probably better for your dog in the long run — provided you opt for an excellent brand. This section helps you understand the countless choices you see on the store shelves.

Figure 6-1:
A glossy coat, bright eyes, and an alert attitude are signs that Maxie is eating a healthy diet.

Using Commercial Dog Food

Good nutrition is essential to prevent dietary deficiency diseases, and it helps your Chihuahua fight off infections and reduces her susceptibility to organic ailments. The best (and easiest) way to feed your dog a balanced diet is to choose an excellent commercial brand and stick with it. Always make sure fresh water is available, too.

Beware of bargain brands

Let's start with the don'ts. Don't buy a bottom-of-the-line dog food for Manchita. Bargain dog food is seldom a bargain. The nutritional info on the package may say it has the same percentages of protein (or other nutrients) as the better-known brands, but it's the amount of usable (digestible) nutrients that's important. For example, an old leather purse is protein, but it has no nutritive value at all. The truth is, generic and economy brands are made of the cheapest ingredients available, and tests have found that many of them do not contain what their labels proclaim. In fact, they are downright dangerous for Toy breeds. Why? Because smaller dogs have higher energy requirements per pound of body weight than large dogs, but because of their size, they eat only a little at a time. Consequently, they need high quality, easily digestible dinners . . . not cheap empty calories.

So many nutritional deficiencies have shown up in dogs fed a diet of economy or generic dog foods that the Veterinary Medical Teaching Hospital at the University of California, Davis, has labeled the syndrome *generic dog food-associated disease.* The more common evidence of the syndrome is abnormally slow growth, coat and skin problems, and skeletal abnormalities.

Choosing your Chihuahua's chow

A good-quality commercial food likely contains all the nutrition Manchita needs to glow with good health. The better brands of commercial dog food are balanced, providing your dog with the best canine nutrition known to modern science. That's why they're healthier than anything you can create at home for twice the price. The right balances of protein and carbohydrates, fats and fiber, and vitamins and minerals are too important (and complicated) for our guesstimates and are best left to the test kitchens of the major dog food companies. Feeding a quality commercial food also protects puppies from our dangerous, but all-too-human tendency to believe that if a little of something is good, then a lot is even better. Not only does nutrition not work that way, but also more of some substances actually are toxic.

Do you remember a Hill's Pet Products commercial from back in the early 1980s? It showed a *guaranteed analysis* just like the ones displayed on dog food cans. Protein was listed at 10 percent, fat at 6.5 percent, fiber at 2.4 percent and moisture at 68 percent — all typical numbers for those nutrients. Finally the ad displayed the actual ingredients: eight worn out leather work shoes, a gallon of used crankcase oil, a bucket of coal (crushed) and 68 pounds of water. When analyzed, the items equaled the guaranteed analysis, but imagine how much nutrition your Chihuahua receives from such a concoction!

Regular or premium?

Now that you know not to go bargain hunting, you still must consider two qualities of dog food. Let's call them the regular brands and the premium brands. The regular brands are the well-known names you've seen on supermarket shelves for years. Their ingredients are more digestible and made from higher quality ingredients than the economy foods. Costwise, they're the middle-of-the-road brands — neither the cheapest nor the most expensive.

Premium brands are the highest-priced dog foods, and seldom are they seen in supermarkets. Instead, they're sold at pet supply stores, pet shops, and some veterinarians' offices. What sets them apart from the regular brands? While regular brands usually use wheat, corn, or soybeans as their primary ingredient, many premium foods use a meat source as their main ingredient. Likewise, because premium foods contain only top-quality, highly digestible ingredients, they're considered concentrated. That means dogs eat less of them and still get optimum nutrition. So even though they cost more, premium brands go further than regular brands. Another advantage is that concentrated food makes for smaller, more compact stools, which makes for easier cleanups. Of course, that's more important to a St. Bernard owner than it is to you, but I thought I should mention it anyway.

I bet you think I'm going to tell you to run right out and buy a premium brand. But it isn't that simple . . . at least not with Toy dogs. Yes, I know you want the best for Manchita, and yes, premium food is the way to go if it agrees with her. But it may not. If you try a premium brand for a few weeks, and Manchita starts to show signs of constipation (straining to eliminate), gradually change back to a grain-based brand. Some small dogs do best on less-concentrated food and stay more regular when eating dog food containing corn. If Manchita is one of them, find a reputable brand that keeps her bowels regular and stick with it.

Many dog foods are specially formulated for different stages of dogs' lives and labeled accordingly. I'll tell you more about them later, but first let's talk about the three major types of dog food: dry, canned, and semimoist.

The ingredients on a container of dog food are listed in descending order, by weight. But just because chicken is the first ingredient doesn't mean the food is mostly chicken. The next four ingredients may be wheat flour, corn meal, barley flour, and wheat germ. When combined, the plant-based ingredients probably weigh a lot more than the chicken.

Dry dog food

Dry dog food, sold in bags or boxes, is the more popular commercial-style feed. When choosing a dry food for your Chihuahua, check the size and texture of the pieces before buying. Manchita prefers small pieces she can easily chew as opposed to large, extra-hard chunks that make it hard for her to close her little mouth.

The plus side of dry food: It's easy to feed and store, has a decent shelf life (three to six months), has little odor, and is good for your dog's teeth (when fed dry). On the minus side: Chihuahua puppies may not consume enough dry dog food to meet their energy needs. They eat larger servings when the nuggets are soaked and softened, but that removes the teeth-cleaning bene-fits. Read the labels on dry food carefully, because some are meant to be con-sumed dry, others form gravy when moistened and are meant to be eaten slightly wet, and still others may be consumed dry or moistened.

Canned dog food

The best canned foods are made mostly of meat products, have a high mois-ture content and usually contain some vegetable products too. If you're plan-ning to use canned food exclusively, read the label carefully. Some canned foods provide total nutrition, while others are formulated to be mixed with dry food. If the canned food alone provides every nutrient a dog needs, the label says something like "100 percent complete," or "complete dinner." Personally, I choose cans with complete nutrition even though I mix the canned food with dry. Some brands provide a choice of either chopped or chunky. The nutritional values are the same, but Chihuahua puppies, and most adult Chis, prefer the chopped version.

The best thing about high-quality canned foods (those made mostly of meat) is that Manchita likes them. In addition, they are easily stored, have long shelf lives, and some of the top brands for Toy dogs are conveniently avail-able in the supermarket.

The downside of canned dog food is that the best brands (the only ones you want for Manchita) are expensive when compared to dry food. They also have an unpleasant smell (to some people) and won't help scrape tartar from your dog's teeth like dry foods do. In addition, they have to be covered and stored in the refrigerator after opening.

The freshest food is the best food. After you choose a brand of dry dog food, buy it in the smallest bag or box you can find. And as you get down toward the bottom of the bag, check to make sure it still smells fresh, like biscuits, rather than stale or moldy.

Semimoist or soft-moist foods

As their name implies, the moisture content of semimoist foods is higher than that of dry food and less than canned. The result is dog food with a chewy texture. The best thing about semimoist food is its convenience. It is usually packaged in individual servings; however, that helps owners of average-sized dogs more than it helps you. Because the serving size is probably more than Manchita eats at one time, you still must put the left-overs in an airtight bag so they don't dry out before the next meal.

Semimoist foods are usually priced higher than dry food but lower than quality canned dinners. Many dogs like semimoist food, but the reason they eat them so eagerly makes them a minus rather than a plus in the nutrition department. The truth is semimoist foods contain more sugar (or sweeteners such as corn syrup) than your dog should eat. Besides, they often contain too much salt, and a variety of artificial colors and preservatives. In short, I don't recommend them.

What's the solution?

Now that you know a little about the three popular types of dog food, which one should you choose for Manchita? Many long-time Chihuahua owners say their dogs do best when they're fed a diet of dry and canned food mixed together. A popular ratio is one-fourth canned to three-fourths dry, mixing well before serving.

Loaves of frozen dog food are available in some locales. The best ones have a high percentage of meat. Dogs like them, and they are stored in the freezer so they seldom spoil. Check the date on the package before purchasing, and thaw your dog's portion thoroughly before serving. Use them alone, or mix them with dry food.

What about treats and table food?

High-quality biscuits are a good treat because they help scrape tartar from Manchita's teeth. Just don't give her too many. Little tummies can only hold so much food, and most of Manchita's calories should come from her regular meals. Many companies make miniature dog biscuits just the right size for Toy dogs. One company even offers dog cookies shaped like tiny postmen.

Some dogs enjoy an occasional vegetable or fruit treat such as a slice of carrot or celery, peas, or a seedless grape. Treats that are good for training include tiny pieces of cheese or chicken.

Don't give Manchita food directly from the table or she becomes an accomplished beggar. If you have healthy leftovers like chicken or pot roast (not scraps like the fat you trimmed off your steak), you can serve them mixed with Manchita's dinner. First chop or mash them well and then mix them in with her regular ration. If you get lazy and leave them chunky, she'll inhale them first and walk away from the rest of her meal.

Matching Food Formulas to Your Chi

Many of the major dog food companies offer special formulas (dry or canned) for every stage of your dog's life. And that's a good thing. Dogs have different nutritional requirements at different times, just like people.

Grub to grow on

Whether you choose dry, canned, or a combination of the two, Manchita needs to eat a diet formulated for puppies (often called a growth formula) until she's a year old. Growth formulas contain more protein and fat than adult diets. Puppies need extra protein for growth and extra fat to keep up with their energy levels.

Maintenance meals

After Manchita celebrates her first birthday, switch gradually to an adult (maintenance) food. You can use it until she's an oldster, provided it keeps her healthy inside and out. A poor coat is usually the first sign that your dog's diet is letting her down. Depending on her activity level, you may want to adjust amounts a little bit over the years to keep her from gaining or losing weight.

Provisions for performers

If you decide to enter Manchita in dog shows, or train her for high-energy events such as obedience or agility competitions, consider feeding her a performance (sometimes called stress) formula. Most performance foods have higher protein and fat percentages than maintenance foods. They are similar to puppy food. In fact, some exhibitors simply keep their dogs on top-quality puppy food as long as they're competing.

Assuming you feed Manchita in the kitchen, you may want to put a carpet sample under her bowl. Many Chihuahuas (and other dogs too) like to eat on the rug. They accomplish this by putting a few morsels in their mouths, trotting off to the closest carpeted area, and munching them there. If your Chi is determined to eat dinner on a comfy carpet, an area rug may (notice I'm not promising anything) keep her in the kitchen.

Low-calorie lunches

When it comes to losing weight, prevention is the best policy. Make sure Manchita exercises enough, eats a regular diet of dog food (not table scraps), and don't indulge her each and every time she begs for a dog biscuit. If she starts getting pudgy anyway, a variety of reduced calorie dog foods are available to help her slim down. Most of them contain lower percentages of protein and fat and higher amounts of fiber than maintenance formulas. While the fiber helps Manchita feel full on less food, and a lower fat content helps her lose weight, other weight-loss options are usually healthier. The best option is increased exercise. If that doesn't do it, try feeding her a little less of her regular food at each feeding. Start by giving her 90 percent of her normal ration for a month. After that, if you don't see any improvement, talk it over with your veterinarian.

Senior cuisine

Diets for geriatric dogs contain less protein than maintenance foods, and this may or may not be a good thing. If your Chi is a healthy oldster, changing chow may not be necessary. But if she suffers from kidney disease, your veterinarian may recommend a senior formula because less protein puts less stress on her kidneys.

Prescription dog food

If your Chihuahua has a specific problem, such as diabetes, heart disease, renal failure, pancreatitis, or certain skin ailments, your veterinarian may prescribe a diet formulated especially for dogs with the specific disease. Prescription diets are available only through veterinarians, because the formulas are so different that they aren't good for normal dogs. If your veterinarian puts Manchita on a prescription diet, he or she wants to monitor her progress — at least during the first few months.

Feeding a Puppy

Depending on Manchita's age, her breeder probably fed her between three and five times a day. The younger and tinier the puppy, the less she can eat at a time and the more often she needs nutrition. As she grows older, she chows down on larger amounts at a time and therefore needs less frequent meals.

Most Chihuahua puppies need four meals a day when they move into their permanent homes, but they don't have to eat that often forever. How do you know when to cut back to three feedings? It's easy. Manchita tells you, She simply starts ignoring all or most of the food at one of her meals (usually when she is around 3 months old). After she leaves most of one meal several days in a row, cut out that feeding. Give her slightly larger portions than before, but offer food only three times a day.

At around 6 months old, Manchita loses interest in another meal (usually the middle one). Then its time to increase the portions again and feed her two meals a day, between 10 and 12 hours apart. Many large dogs wolf down a big dinner once a day and do just fine, but that doesn't work with a little dog. Manchita's energy requirements are big, and her belly is small, and too much elapsed time between meals can cause a dangerous drop in blood sugar.

As a starting point, offer your puppy a minimum of half a cup of food at every meal. If she finishes it quickly, licks the bowl, and looks for more, increase the amount. No tried-and-true rule exists for how much a puppy needs to eat, and appetites vary. Your eyes are your best gauge. They'll tell you if your pup is gaining or losing weight, or staying just right.

Feeding a Mature Manchita

Adult Chihuahuas do best on twice-a-day feedings, but the meals don't have to be identical. After Manchita is a year old, you may try giving her dry food served dry in the morning (good for the gums and teeth), and dry food slightly moistened and mixed with canned food in the evening (or vice versa).

If you feed a healthy, parasite-free Chihuahua properly, she maintains the same weight month after month, along with bright eyes, a shiny coat, healthy skin, steady nerves, and enough energy. If something is missing from Manchita's diet, or if she consumes too many calories, you'll see it. Poor nutrition displays itself through coat and skin problems and sometimes a lack of energy, while excess calories lead to obesity. Please don't let Manchita get fat. It's bad for her bones and organs, and does as much damage to dogs as it does to people. Obesity is a major health problem in American dogs. In fact, an estimated 41 percent of the dogs in the United States are overweight.

After you find a high quality dog food that Manchita enjoys and obviously does well on, you have no reason to change. Dog foods have eye appeal to attract people, not dogs. Manchita won't get bored with the same food every day like you and doesn't need to discover new shapes, colors, and sizes in her bowl at frequent intervals. As long as you feed her a quality food and she thrives, it isn't likely that any change is for the better.

Supper for seniors

When Manchita is a golden oldie, try feeding her so she maintains the same weight she carried in healthy middle age. You can adjust amounts, or even how the food is presented, to keep your senior Chi in top condition.

If Manchita has less appetite than she used to, try tempting her with a few easy options. For starters, warm up her food. That's often all it takes to stimulate an old dog's appetite. Another option is treating her as though she's in her second puppyhood by feeding her small meals at frequent intervals. If that doesn't help, try soaking her dry food until it softens. That makes a difference when sore teeth or gums are the problem. The final option is mashing tasty goodies, like boiled chicken, cooked ground beef, or cottage cheese, into her regular dinner. It's only fair to tell you that special foods spoil your pet and make her expect the same treatment at every meal. But then that isn't so terrible. If your Chi is well into her teens, a little spoiling may make both of you feel better.

When is Manchita a senior by Chihuahua standards? When she's around 10 or 11. Most breeds are considered seniors when they are older than 7, but because Chihuahuas are so long-lived (usually well into their teens), they aren't oldsters until their ages reaches double digits.

Special situations

Supplementation may at times in Manchita's life be good idea. Show dogs stressed from constant travel, performance dogs competing in obedience or agility, dogs recuperating from illness or injury, and dogs used for breeding may benefit from dietary supplements. If you think Manchita needs a little extra help nutrition-wise, check with your veterinarian. He or she may recommend a prepared vitamin-mineral powder or tablet, or simply suggest the addition of cottage cheese, hard-boiled (never raw) eggs, or a little fat to her diet.

Over supplementation with vitamins and minerals can be dangerous — even toxic. Check with your veterinarian before adding supplements to a balanced dog food.

Warning: Don't feed your dog any of these

Some of the forbidden foods in the following list may surprise you.

- ✔ Don't feed your Chihuahua chocolate, onions, or any highly spiced, greasy, or salty foods. Chocolate is deadly to some dogs, onions (raw or cooked) can also be toxic, and spicy sauces and junk food lead to upset stomachs.

- ✔ Don't believe ads that encourage you to vary your dog's diet. Dogs do best when they are fed the same brand of food daily at regular hours.

- ✔ Don't fill your puppy with table scraps. Tiny dogs (especially puppies), can't hold much food at a time, and no matter how nutritious your dinner is for humans, chances are your puppy's food is better for her. Likewise, dogs that eat table scraps usually lose their taste for dog food completely.

- ✔ Don't give Manchita any bones. Chicken, turkey, and pork chop bones, for example, can shatter and slice open her intestines with their sharp points.

- ✔ Don't let Manchita keep her food dish longer than 15 minutes. If she hasn't finished her meal by then, remove it until the next feeding. That helps her learn to eat when she's fed.

- ✔ Don't try to teach her to clean her plate by giving her the same stale meal at every feeding until she finishes it. That won't teach her a thing and may make her sick. She needs fresh food in a clean bowl at every meal.

- ✔ Don't give Manchita a sip of beer, wine, or any other alcoholic beverage. Alcohol poisoning is deadly, and it doesn't take much to do in a little dog.

Chocolate is dangerous to dogs, but they don't know it and are attracted by the aroma. Don't give your Chihuahua any chocolate no matter how much she begs — not even a tiny tidbit. Too many dogs have died from it already.

Understanding What Nutrients Do

If you understand human nutrition, you can skip this section. Nutrients serve practically the same function in dogs as they do in people, so you already know how your dog utilizes them. For those of you who were daydreaming when your fifth-grade teacher talked about the body's building blocks, here's what some of the more important nutrients do for your dog.

Building healthy Chihuahuas

✔ Carbohydrates are starches, sugars, and fiber. They aid digestion and elimination and provide energy and the proper assimilation of fats. Excess carbohydrates are stored in the body for future use.

✔ Protein can come from meat or vegetable sources. It is not stored in the body, so your dog needs to eat it every single day. Protein is used for bone growth, tissue healing, and the daily replacement of body tissues burned up by normal activity.

✔ Fats are necessary as an energy source. They also add suppleness to your dog's skin and luster to her coat. But excess fat is stored under the skin and can lead to an overweight dog. Fat balance is important. Too much fat leads to the same obesity problems that humans suffer, while too little robs your Chihuahua of necessary protection from changes in temperature, and can make her overly sensitive to cold (as if she isn't sensitive enough to cold already).

Vitamins and minerals

✔ Vitamin A is used by the body for fat absorption and is necessary for a healthy, shiny coat. It is also essential for normal growth rate, good eyesight, and reproduction.

✔ The B vitamins protect the nervous system and are necessary for normal coat, skin, appetite, growth, and vision.

✔ Dogs synthesize Vitamin C in their liver, so it isn't often mentioned in an analysis of commercial dog food or vitamin supplements. Some breeders add it anyway.

✔ Healthy bones and teeth and good muscle tone are dependent on Vitamin D, but the vitamin must be ingested in the correct ratio with calcium and phosphorus.

✔ Vitamin E is associated with the proper functioning of the muscles and the internal and reproductive organs.

✔ Most dogs are able to synthesize Vitamin K in their digestive tract, and this vitamin is essential to normal clotting of the blood. If Manchita seems to bleed too long from a minor cut, mention it to your veterinarian. It could indicate a deficiency of Vitamin K.

✔ Calcium and phosphorus must be fed in the correct ratio to provide puppies with protection from rickets, bowed legs, and other bone deformities. They also aid in muscle development and maintenance.

- ✔ Potassium is necessary for normal growth and healthy nerves and muscles.

- ✔ Sodium and chlorine boost your Chihuahua's appetite and enable her to enjoy a normal activity level.

- ✔ Magnesium is necessary to prevent convulsions and nervous system disorders.

- ✔ Iron is needed for healthy blood and prevents fatigue from anemia.

- ✔ Iodine prevents goiter in dogs the same way it does in people.

- ✔ Copper is necessary for growing and maintaining strong bones. It also helps prevent anemia.

- ✔ Cobalt aids normal growth and keeps the reproductive tract healthy.

- ✔ Manganese also aids growth and is necessary for healthy reproduction.

- ✔ Zinc promotes normal growth and healthy skin.

Chapter 7

Grooming the Body Beautiful

*L*ess than five minutes of daily grooming keeps Pepe squeaky clean, but its benefits go way beyond that. Brushing helps his skin and coat stay healthy by stimulating circulation and the secretion of natural oils. It also removes dirt, dead hair, loose skin particles, and dandruff.

Grooming also makes Pepe more lovable. After all, whether his coat is sporty smooth or luxurious long, nice clean hair is mighty inviting for petting and hugging. On the other hand, no one likes to snuggle with a smelly, matted dog that is frantically scratching itself. Smelly! Oh yuck! Not your Pepe! Don't worry. In this chapter, I talk about how just a few minutes of your time can keep his coat enticing to the touch.

Taking Care of a Chihuahua's Coat

Grooming your dog daily (remember, it only takes a few minutes) is ideal, but if that isn't possible, make three times a week the bare minimum. Just before brushing, give him a full-body massage. He loves it because it feels good, but you're actually stimulating his skin and examining him from head to toe at the same time. Figure 7-1 shows a Chi undergoing such an examination. Look for lumps and bruises, scratches and skin infections, and for signs of external parasites like fleas and ticks. Everything is easier to treat when discovered early.

While most ticks are easy to spot on a smooth's sleek coat, they are a little harder to find on a long coat. Favorite hiding places are in the ears, between the toes, in the thick neck hair or in the rump area just before the tail. To uncover fleas, rough your Chi's coat the opposite direction from the way it grows. You may not see any of the minuscule pests move, but tiny black specks on the skin tell you that fleas are having a free lunch courtesy of Pepe. If you see the telltale specks, ask your veterinarian to recommend a treatment program (see Chapter 15) and use the products exactly as recommended on the label.

Starting early

How soon do you start grooming your pretty puppy? As soon as he settles in — just a day or two after you get him. Condition Pepe from puppyhood to accept grooming as a fact of life and he soon learns to like it. Talk to him softly as you work on him (go on, tell him what a handsome fellow he is). If he becomes fidgety about being handled on any part of his body, say "No!" sharply and firmly (but not loudly or in a threatening tone) and continue grooming gently. Soon the sessions become routine.

Grooming tables

You can groom your Chihuahua on your lap, but some Chi owners prefer placing their dogs on tables. Special tables just for grooming dogs are available through pet supply stores, booths at dog shows, or animal supply catalogs. They even come in small sizes for toys. You can also create your own. Any tabletop does well, as long as it's the right height for you to work on and stands absolutely steady, without even a hint of a wobble. Provide traction by attaching rubber matting to the top. And never — ever — turn your back when your dog is on the table, not even for an instant.

Your Chihuahua's coat grows in cycles. As it grows, it should look glossy, but eventually it stops growing, dries out (doesn't look quite as shiny), and finally, is shed. The cycle takes a little more than one-third of a year, or about 130 days, but it varies considerably between Chis. In fact, smooth coats shed some hair all the time. Dogs that spend a lot of time outdoors always shed their winter coats in the spring, but since Chi's are house pets, and don't always grow winter coats, they tend to shed on their own personal schedule.

Brushing

Whether Pepe is a smooth or a long coat, you wear less of his hair, and he stays cleaner and needs fewer baths if you brush him regularly. Use a natural bristle brush and place Pepe so he faces away from you on your lap or on a nonslip grooming table. A few strokes in the opposite direction of hair growth is the quickest way to loosen dead hair. Start brushing his body against the lay of the hair, from just in front of his tail to the top of his neck. Next, do the same along each side. Now brush Pepe's back, sides, neck, and legs in the same direction as his hair grows. Finished? Then it's time to turn him upside down.

Figure 7-1: During grooming, examine your dog from head to toe.

Gently turn Pepe upside down in your lap or on the table and brush his chest, belly, and the underside of his neck. Now place him right side up and, if he's a smooth coat, finish by brushing his tail. Then praise him for being such a cooperative boy and give him a treat. That's all there is to it unless it's teeth-cleaning or toenail-trimming day. I tell you how to handle those procedures in the "Keeping Those Pearlies White" and "Trimming the Toenails" sections later in this chapter.

Long coats have their own lingo. The hair on their legs is called *furnishings,* the tail hair is *a plume,* and the fine hair falling from their ears is called *fringe.*

If your Pepe is a long coat, you'll need a rubber comb for the finishing touches. With him right side up, comb his ear fringe and the long hair on his legs. Be gentle, but make sure you get all the way to the skin. Next, brush his tail and then comb it. That's all there is to it, unless his coat is (horrors!) matted.

Mats (balls of hair you can't get a comb through) seldom occur on a dog that is groomed daily, but when they do, they usually show up just behind the ears. Of course, leg hair and tail hair is also susceptible to matting. Minor mats can be loosened with your fingers, by separating each hair patiently until the mat is gone. An implement called a *mat splitter* (available at pet supply stores) is usually necessary for major mats. Using it gently, it loosens the mat while removing the worst of it.

If you have a long coated Chi that has gone ungroomed for months, your best bet is to take him to a professional groomer. The pro bathes Pepe, removes the mats, trims the toenails, and puts your Chi's coat back in shape so you can easily care for it yourself.

Do your clothes and furniture look furry? Don't blame poor Pepe. All that dead hair would be on your grooming brush instead of your navy suit if you brushed him daily.

Giving the Ears a Look

Don't forget Pepe's perky ears when giving him the once-over. Healthy ears are pinkish on the inside and their edges are smooth. They don't have nicks, splits, or places along the edge where the hair is stuck together as if with dark glue. When something is wrong, your nose may be the first to know. That's because nasty odors or discharges are early signs that *ear mites* have set up camp. These pests live in the ear canal, irritating your Chihuahua's sensitive ears and producing a dry, rusty-brown-to-black discharge. Even if no unusual odor or discharge is present, suspect something if Pepe paws at his ears, shakes his head often, or stands with his head unnaturally cocked to the side. Ear mites are easily banished, and ear infections are quickly cured, when discovered early, As soon as you see signs of trouble, visit your veterinarian.

Are Pepe's ears driving you crazy because they're erect one day and flopped over the next? It's probably because he's teething. His ears generally stay up by the time he's 6 months old, but if they're still hanging like a *hound dawg's* by the time he's 8 months old, you may as well learn to like it. They're going to stay that way.

Keeping Those Pearlies White

According to the American Veterinary Medical Association (AVMA), 80 percent of adult dogs develop *gum disease* by the time they are 3 years old. Not only is that outrageous, but unnecessary, too. If you brush Pepe's teeth three or four times a week (no, I'm not kidding — they make toothbrushes and toothpaste just for dogs), you can keep plaque under control.

Start when Pepe's a puppy, and he becomes accustomed to having his teeth brushed. Begin by getting him used to you lifting up his lips and gently touching his teeth and gums with your finger. The more matter-of-fact you are about it, the sooner he learns to live with it. When he stops pulling away from your finger, introduce him to a soft toothbrush; either the smallest one made for dogs or one made for human babies. At first, just touch his teeth with it, but gradually apply a little pressure. When he tolerates that, move the brush so it touches his back teeth, gradually add pressure, and finally a gentle up and down brushing motion. It won't be long before you're able to clean all his teeth with relative ease.

Pet supply stores sell toothpaste for dogs in a variety of flavors and you may even find one that makes Pepe look forward to his brushing. But don't count on it. If he hates them all, plain warm water is better than no brushing at all.

At least once a year (twice is better), ask your veterinarian to check Pepe for plaque or early signs of gum disease. A professional cleaning may be necessary if his teeth have been neglected for years.

Never use a toothpaste meant for people on Pepe. It's bad for dogs and probably upsets their stomachs.

Retained puppy teeth

Dogs, just like people, have two sets of teeth during their lifetimes. The puppy, or *deciduous teeth,* should all be gone by the time Pepe is 6 months old and replaced by *permanent teeth*. But that isn't always what happens. Toy dogs often have a problem with deciduous teeth refusing to fall out to make room for the emerging permanent teeth. That creates havoc in a dog's mouth. After all, when permanent teeth can't slip into their slots because baby teeth are blocking them, they grow in whatever direction is the can. The result is a mouthful of crowded teeth pointing every which way.

Now that you're aware of the possibility, it won't happen to Pepe. Just look at his mouth and you can to tell if a new tooth is trying to emerge before a baby tooth falls out. It's an old story to your veterinarian, who has probably removed hundreds of retained baby teeth so that permanent ones come in strong and straight.

Symptoms of gum disease

If Pepe was an adult when you got him, he may already have gum disease. Symptoms are bad breath, swollen, bright red or bleeding gums, tartar against the gum line, loose teeth, and infected teeth. Sometimes dogs that appear to be finicky eaters actually are hungry, but they have such sore mouths that they chew only enough to survive. So if Pepe has any symptoms of gum disease, see your veterinarian right away.

Most adult dogs have 42 permanent teeth, but Toys, with their tiny mouths, often have fewer than that.

Trimming the Toenails

Pepe's toenails are too long if they make clicking noises on the floor when he walks or touch the ground when he stands still. Dogs with too long nails are forced to walk on the backs of their feet, leading to *splayed* (that's dog lingo for "spread") toes and an awkward gait. When untrimmed for months, toenails and *dewclaws* (the higher, useless extra toe that your dog may or may not have) eventually curl under the foot, circling back to puncture the pads.

Are you wondering how come wolves, coyotes, and even stray dogs trot along just fine even though no one trims their toenails? In their quest for food, they cover enough ground to wear their nails down to a practical length — something that won't occur during Pepe's stroll from the carpet to the linoleum. Trim your dog's toenails a minimum of once a month, although once every two weeks is better. My favorite type of *toenail clipper* for Chihuahuas is the smallest guillotine-style implement, although others on the market work just fine.

Some people use a grooming table when trimming nails, while others do the clipping when their Chihuahuas are on their backs in their laps. You pick the place and posture that works best for you and your dog. Start the job by lifting Pepe's foot up and forward. Then hold it firmly but gently in your left hand so your right hand can do the trimming (reverse this if you are left-handed). If Pepe has white or light nails, your job is easier than if his nails are dark. That's because the blood vessel inside each nail (called the *quick*) is easily seen through light colored nails. Avoid cutting the quick by trimming the nail just outside of it. You won't be able to see the quick in dark nails, so trim just the tip, at the point where it starts curling downward.

Trim his nails properly and Pepe feels nothing more than slight pressure, the same as you feel when trimming your own toenails. But if you accidentally cut the quick, Pepe's nail hurts and bleeds. Stop the bleeding with a *styptic pencil* made for people, or use the styptic powder sold at pet supply stores. In an emergency, pressing the bleeding nail into a soft bar of soap for a minute or so also stops the bleeding.

Without a doubt, Pepe prefers prevention. Work under good lighting so you can cut his nails without a mishap. Your dog may forgive a cut quick if it's a rare occurrence; but if you hurt his toes often, he struggles and screams when you try to work on his feet. Wouldn't you?

Don't trim your Chi's toenails during the first week you have him. Instead, get him used to having his feet touched first (see Chapter 10).

It's only fair to warn you that Chihuahuas that are terrified of having their toenails trimmed morph into monsters at the sight of a toenail clipper. If yours is one of them, it may take two people to accomplish the mission — one to hold him and the other to wield the clipper. But remember, regardless how frustrating the job becomes, no rough stuff. That tiny leg you're holding in your hand is breakable. If you can't do the job safely at home, don't hesitate to take Pepe to the veterinarian or a professional groomer.

The Eyes Have It!

Oh, those big, beautiful eyes, the mirrors of Pepe's semisweet soul. To keep them sparkling, all most of you will have to do is occasionally wipe a bit of *sleep* out of the corners with a clean, damp cloth.

Does Pepe have stains under his eyes that make him look like a woman leaving a tearjerker with mascara traces on her cheeks? Those really are *tearstains,* even though your dog didn't cry when Leonardo died. When a Chihuahua has too-small tear ducts, the overflow trickles down his face. Wipe the area every morning with a soft cloth dipped into distilled water (it becomes a habit like washing your own face). Although no treatment for tiny tear ducts exists, check with your veterinarian anyway. Sometimes tearstains are caused by an infection called *conjunctivitis,* by *entropian,* a genetic condition where the eyelashes turn in and rub the cornea, or by *ectropia,* a condition where a lower eyelid sags and lets in foreign matter. The good news is that these problems are not common in the Chihuahua.

If Pepe's doesn't have tearstains, his eyes won't need any special care unless he develops a problem (see Chapter 15). Just use common sense. Don't get shampoo in his eyes (even the tear-free type), never spray pesticide near his head, and don't let him put his curious orbs out of the car window. I bet some of you have had windshields shatter when a pebble flew off the tire of a passing car (it happened to us last year). If a small stone hit Pepe full in the face with that much force, the consequences would be tragic.

Bathing Your Beauty

Your Chihuahua seldom needs a bath if you brush him briefly every day. And that's a good thing. Shampooing washes away the natural oils that moisturize his coat and skin, so bathe Pepe only when necessary — no more often than once a month unless he rolls in something smelly. Actually, many experts say a bath only every two months is best.

The well-equipped bath

Gather up all Pepe's bathing equipment before you get started. That way you won't have to turn your eyes away from your soapy-slick dog once you begin. Here's what you'll need:

- ✔ Old clothes for you. When Pepe shakes, you'll get wet too.

- ✔ A tub, preferably with a drain, so your Chi won't have to stand in soapy water. Many Toy dog owners use the sink, because it's much easier on the back. But if you put Pepe in the sink, don't take your eyes or hands off of him for even an instant. A leap to the floor could be fatal.

- ✔ A rubber bath mat for traction in the tub or part of a rubber mat to line the sink.

- ✔ An unbreakable cup for dipping water or a spray-nozzle hose attachment.

- ✔ pH-balanced *dog* shampoo, or insecticide shampoo or dip, if necessary (see Chapter 15).

- ✔ Coat conditioner for dogs (optional but nice, especially for long coats).

- ✔ Cotton balls.

- ✔ A washcloth.

- ✔ Mineral oil.

- ✔ A nice fluffy terry-cloth towel (100 percent cotton).

Let's get wet!

Wait! Before putting Pepe into the tub or sink, take him for a walk outside and give him time to relieve himself. Otherwise the excitement of bathing may make him want to or have to rush outdoors immediately after his bath, and that's a bad idea. Pepe needs to stay inside until he's thoroughly dry, because Chis get chilled easily.

Begin by placing a cotton ball inside each of Pepe's ears (gently, don't push it too far down) to keep the water out. Now spray or pour warm water (temperature test it on the inside of your arm) over his whole body with the exception of his face and head. Massage him gently as you wet him, helping the water soak in to the skin.

Put a few drops of shampoo on Pepe's back, spread it around and massage the lather into his coat. Add a drop or two as needed to soap up his legs, underbelly, tail, and neck. All done? Now you've reached the most important part of the procedure — the rinse. Never rush this step. If shampoo dries in Pepe's coat, it can make him itch like crazy and rob his hair of its shine. Following the rinse, use coat conditioner (optional), following label directions and rinsing it out well.

After Pepe's body is rinsed, wet a washcloth in warm water, wring it out well, and wipe his face and head. Remove the cotton balls from his ears and clean each ear gently (again, not far down) with a fresh cotton ball dipped in a tiny bit of mineral oil. Now wrap him in a towel and dry him thoroughly — from his ear tips to his toes . . . paying special attention to his easily chilled chest and underbelly.

Finishing touches for your long coat

After towel drying your long coat (see Figure 7-2), its best to finish the job with a hand-held blow dryer. Don't spend much time on the same spot, or hold the dryer too close to his body, because the hot air can burn Pepe's coat and skin. Use the warm setting if your dryer has one, and blow his coat in the direction it grows, starting at his neck and working toward his plume (yup, that's the tail).

Figure 7-2: Cindi Zablocki grooms her long coats outdoors during nice weather.

When Pepe is dry, brush him with a natural bristle brush. Then use your hard rubber comb on his ear fringe, furnishings (the long hair on his legs), and plume. Wow! I bet he's gorgeous. And he knows it. Just watch him strut when you put him down.

Is the thick hair around Pepe's anus often dirty? Use a sharp scissors and trim away just a little bit of hair from each side of the anus and just below it. That keeps it from becoming soiled during bowel movements.

Chapter 8

Chirobics: Getting Some Exercise

Although Chihuahuas are small enough to get a good workout in a one-room apartment, many become obese because their owners don't encourage them to be active. Poor owners. They don't know how much fun they're missing! Sure exercise is essential to your Chi's health, but it doesn't have to feel like work. In this chapter, I tell you how to make Manchita's body-building breaks so much fun you'll find yourself looking forward to them.

Making Exercise a Habit — and Fun

The muscles rippling beneath Manchita's coat are not the only ones that exercise strengthens and tones. Her heart is almost entirely muscle, and even her intestine contains muscle tissue. Regular exercise keeps a healthy supply of blood circulating through these vital muscles. So if Manchita leads a moderately active life, instead of becoming a couch puppy, she looks better and lives longer. Chances are, she behaves better too. Simply giving a problem puppy more exercise cures countless behavior problems.

What's the best way to exercise Manchita? A brisk walk, an indoor game, or playing with your friend's Chihuahua all help keep her fit. Although your Chihuahua may play with a variety of small dogs, most Chis prefer their own kind.

When it comes to exercise, variety is best. I know a professional trainer whose motto is, "Never let your body know what you are going to make it do next." According to her, if you get on an exercise schedule and stick with it day after boring day, your body gets so used to it that the workout stops being as beneficial as it should be. She recommends varying your regimen so your body has to stay fit to handle an assortment of activities. Now doesn't that make exercising Manchita easy? You may try a walk around the block one day (see Figure 8-1) or an indoor game the next. You can even exercise Manchita from your recliner (or lawn chair if you have a fenced yard). Organized activities like obedience and agility (see Chapter 11) also provide exercise for dogs (and their owners).

Figure 8-1:
When it comes to exercise, nothing beats a brisk walk.

Make exercise a habit, even though its form changes from day to day. Otherwise, your puppy may become the pudgy and pooped type. If Chihuahuas were people, you'd find them in the hammock on sunny summer days, instead of hiking, canoeing, or swimming. Lots of them become lazy while still young in life.

Let's keep it simple. Any form of exercise you and Manchita feel like doing is fine, as long as it keeps her moving and isn't too much for her. Too much? Yes, it's easy to overdo exercise with a tiny dog. Compare a Chihuahua's stride to the stride of a Labrador Retriever, or any of the other breeds that need a chunk of time and a lot of space to get a good workout. See the difference? It isn't that tiny dogs don't need as much exercise as big dogs — they do — but they can satisfy their exercise needs in much less time, using much less space.

The next time you take Manchita for a walk, notice how many strides she takes to keep up with just one of yours. Sure she can do it, and it's good for her too, but within reason. If you stroll too far, or the day is hot and humid, give her a rest in the shade and a drink of water at the halfway point, or simply carry her home.

Although the type of exercise you give Manchita isn't important, consistency is. She needs exercise in some form all her life. When she's young, Manchita may help you invent games that provide excellent exercise. When she's a senior, you may have to initiate play. In the next section, "Teaching Games to Your Chihuahua," I give you some ideas for indoor exercise. Some of the games are so much fun you'll forget that their main purpose is Manchita's health.

Teaching Games to Your Chihuahua

Show Manchita how to play these games when you're in a good mood, and always stop playing before she wants to. No matter how much fun a game starts out to be, it feels like work if you keep at it until she's bored or tired. But if you quit while your Chihuahua's still having fun, she'll always be eager for the next round.

Most healthy, well-adjusted puppies learn physical games in a jiffy, but adult dogs that never have played take a lot longer. If your mature Chihuahua isn't interested in playing games after a week or two of opportunities, don't give up. First, check your attitude. Perhaps you're trying too hard and making it look like work instead of fun. Next, check your timing. Was Manchita full from dinner or even sleeping when you tried to excite her? A change of attitude, or timing, may be all it takes to turn her into an avid player (see Figure 8-2).

 Even if you have a Chihuahua-safe fenced-in yard, putting your dog outside for an hour or so during nice weather doesn't guarantee her a good workout. Chihuahuas don't like to exercise alone any more than people do. Indoors or out, Manchita won't get active without a companion. And that's you, unless you have more than one dog.

Figure 8-2:
Cricket travels the nation in a motor home and prefers being a couch puppy. Her owners encourage her to exercise by playing games with her, and providing her with soft toys to play-kill.

When playing games with Manchita, treat her like the healthy animal she is, but don't overwhelm her with your physical superiority. Since food is one of the rewards in many games, play before her meal so she wants to earn a tasty tidbit. Is she a little chunky? Then give her a smaller supper if she eats several treats during play time. The games I describe in the following sections are fun for Toy dogs of all ages.

Tile and other hard slippery floors make maneuvering difficult for dogs. Exercise your Chi on flooring with good traction, or on the rug.

Hide'n'seek

Some physical games are also educational. This one may enhance Manchita's memory and scenting ability.

Start playing hide-and-seek by putting Manchita in another room and closing the door. Then hide a treat in a different room, perhaps beside a table leg or under a chair (the type she can easily walk under). Open the door, and when Manchita comes into the room tell her to "Find It," in an excited voice. Of course Manchita won't know what you mean at first, so keep repeating the words while encouraging her toward the treat. Help her locate the goodie, but let her make the actual find. In other words, she must pick up the treat from the floor, not your hand. When she does, tell her "Goood Dooog," (dogs love words with stretched out oo sounds) while she eats it — a double reward.

If Manchita is mature and new at your house, you can expect her to get off to a slow start when it comes to playing games. She's probably insecure, and won't be in a playful mood until she adjusts to her new home. Keep trying at intervals. One day she'll surprise you and join in.

Now put Manchita back in the other room and place another treat exactly where the first one was. Open the door, say "Find it," and watch what she does. You'll probably have to help Manchita find the treat a few times before she goes straight to it on her own. When she succeeds by herself, repeat the game one more time and quit for the day. (No, that wasn't enough action to count as exercise, but later on this game gets lively).

Use the same hiding place for the next few days and soon Manchita races to the treat all by herself on the first try, with you cheering her on, of course. When she does, throw her a curve. Put the treat in a new hiding place, farther from the starting point, and start over by helping her find it.

Don't tell Manchita "No!" when she goes back to the original spot. She's finding out how to use her memory and that's good. Instead, have a treat waiting in the old hiding places every so often (once every five to ten times). Eventually Manchita remembers several rewarding locations (from one end of the house to the other) and sprints from room to room until she finds her treats. Continue adding new hiding places (once she is familiar with all the old ones) as long as she enjoys the game. Chances are she may start exercising her sense of smell as well as her body and her memory.

Variations of this game are easy to create. Adding a second person, perhaps your spouse or child is one way. Have the person hide behind the drapes, or in a closet with the door slightly ajar. Then instead of saying "Find it," ask Manchita "Where's Tom?" Meanwhile Tom's waiting to reward her with a treat.

Catch'n'release

Make yourself a Chihuahua fishing rod and bait it to catch Manchita. Take a piece of string about five or six feet long and tie one end of it to a stick. Then bait the other end by tying on a small stuffed animal or a squeaky toy. Now sit down and start fishing. Puppies usually can't resist little twitches, but try a variety of *casts* to see what movements attract Manchita.

Tiny dogs running free in Aztec palaces!

During the 500 years that the Aztecs ruled Mexico, tiny dogs were pampered by the rich but ignored and sometimes even eaten (according to some historians) by the poor. *Montezuma II,* last Emperor of the Aztec nation, supposedly kept hundreds of our Chihuahuas' ancestors running free in his palace to assure him of a smooth journey after death. Another legend describes an Aztec princess who kept more than a thousand tiny dogs and each one had its own servant. When a dog died, its servant was slain so he or she could take care of the dog in the next world.

The Techichi's fortunes fell when the Conquistadors conquered the Aztec nation, led by Hernando Cortez, early in the 16th century. It is said that the Spanish conquerors used the Indians' pet and holy dog for meat. In fact, some historians believe the Conquistadors ate so many Techichis that the tiny dogs nearly became extinct. And for the next 300 years, nothing much is known about Chihuahua history.

Read your dog and make adjustments for her temperament when teaching and playing games. Some Chihuahuas love to hear you clap and cheer, and play all the harder to keep excitement in the air. Others tend to be timid, and owners who double as a Dallas Cowgirls may spook them under their couches.

Munchkin in the middle

This game takes two people and a rubber ball that is small enough for Manchita to hold in her mouth but too big for her to swallow. Use the ball only for playing games together, and put it away when fun time is over.

To play the game, both partners sit on the floor facing each other with about eight feet separating them and roll the ball back and forth. You may want to put on a show to entice Manchita to join in at first, so laugh and act like scooping up the ball is a really big deal. If your partner is a child, remind the youngster to roll the ball gently, so your Chi doesn't shy away from it.

Manchita may get curious about all the fun on the floor and try to intercept the ball. When she captures it, clap and cheer her on for a few seconds while she parades her prize (lots of dogs strut with pride when they capture a ball). Then say "Out," take the ball from her by trading it for a treat, and start over. Gradually increase the distance between the players so Manchita must run farther when chasing the ball and keep her interested by letting her win sometimes (but not all the time).

Fetching fun

Fetching (retrieving) games are favorites with some Chihuahuas, while others have no interest in them at all. Any number of objects, from sticks, to small balls, to miniature flying discs, are suitable for fetching, as long as their diameter and weight are compatible with a Chihuahua's size. Always roll the object away from (never toward) your dog. You want to awaken her chasing instinct, not spook her into thinking that a strange object is heading for her. Make your tosses short at first, and increase the distance gradually as Manchita catches on.

If Manchita learns to fetch well — bringing her ball all the way back to you every time — you'll be able to exercise her the lazy way, right from your recliner.

When rolling or tossing something for Manchita, seeing it leave your hand is important, especially when she's a rookie. If she chases the object and brings it all the way back to you, give her a treat and rejoice — she's a natural. But if the more likely scenario occurs — Manchita chases the object, picks it up, and parades it triumphantly without bringing it back — attach a long leash to her collar before the game begins. Then, after she chases and picks up the object, you can reel her gently in while encouraging her in a happy tone. When she brings the object all the way back to you, trade it for a treat. If she drops it long before she reaches you, don't give her anything, but don't be upset either. Many Chihuahuas don't have a strong retrieving instinct, but that doesn't mean you give up. Keep trying occasionally even if Manchita shows no desire to retrieve. Chis have been known to change their minds.

If retrieving excites Manchita, keep her in that state of mind by limiting the number of times you play Fetching Fun to four or five in a row, which is plenty. After that, play something else. If Manchita becomes a fetching fanatic, add variations by rolling a ball a little faster and a lot farther; rolling it so it rebounds off a wall; and throwing it (not hard) so it bounces (instead of rolls) away from her.

The word retriever is part of some dogs' breed names. The Labrador Retriever, the Golden Retriever, the Chesapeake Bay Retriever, and the Flat-Coated Retriever are a few of the breeds that are born with the inclination to retrieve. And even they need training to hone their natural talents.

Play-killing a critter

Play-killing a squeaky toy is also good exercise and most Chihuahuas love this sport. If Manchita starts playing this game as a pup, she always gets excited when you bring out her mousie, hedgehog, or whatever critter she *kills.* But if you acquired her as an adult, and she never learned to play, she may be clueless about what to do with her critter.

First, give Manchita time to settle into her new home and actively seek out your attention. Now that she trusts you, its time to uncover her sense of humor. To do it, you need to set an example by acting silly first (try it, you'll like it) and encouraging her to follow suit.

Choose an exciting squeaky toy with lots of appendages so her small mouth easily grips it. Then play with the toy yourself, while Manchita watches. Throw it, catch it, drop it, and chase it, amid lots of laughter. That gets her attention. As Manchita watches you enjoy the toy, occasionally and only briefly tease her with it, but don't give it to her. As another family member joins in, you can roll the toy to each other, squeak it, and shake it — but don't get wild enough to frighten an insecure dog. After two or three minutes of fun, *accidentally* drop the toy near Manchita to see if she shows interest in it. If she ignores it, pick it up and continue playing for another minute. Then put the toy away until another day.

The first time Manchita takes the toy, allow her to play with it without inter-ference for about 20 seconds. Then trade it for a treat, play with it yourself for a few seconds, and put it away. Soon Manchita wants a longer turn, so she'll probably amuse you by tossing and pouncing on the toy and shaking it as hard as she can. Let her play huntress for awhile, then trade the toy for a treat and put it away. Bring it out only for this special game because toys with squeakers aren't suitable for everyday use.

If your Chihuahua loves chasing balls but won't retrieve them, play ball with three or four balls at a time. Roll one in a straight line. Roll the next one side-ways, so it rebounds off the wall. Toss the next one so it bounces gently. You get the picture. Soon Manchita runs in all directions.

Exercising an Old Dog

One of the wonderful things about dogs is that deep down inside they're always puppies. They don't outgrow their toys or become too serious to act silly. So if your old dog suddenly ignores her favorite toy, refuses to play the games she always loved, or doesn't get excited about going for a walk, see your veterinarian. Your dog needs exercise all her life. An old dog may amble instead of trot, but that's okay, she doesn't need to lose her sense of humor or her desire to participate in activities.

Part III
Training Your Chihuahua

The 5th Wave   By Rich Tennant

"I think the Chihuahua's been up on the counter again. There are several distinct paw prints in the butter tub."

In this part . . .

Everyone loves a confident, well-mannered dog. That's the topic of Part III — giving your Chihuahua a solid base for a happy life. Even if you have never trained a dog before, just follow my time-tested methods and your precocious pet can mature into a mannerly, responsive member of the household. Good dog!

Chapter 9

Helping Your Chi Face the World

A puppy can be raised only once, so if you are lucky enough to have the opportunity, make the most of it. In this chapter, I tell you how to bond with your Chihuahua, read her body language, and help her gain confidence. Both of you'll have some mighty good times as Manchita learns to share her Chi charm with an admiring public.

Bonding and Communicating

Bonding can be relaxing for you and Manchita. Chihuahuas love attention and body warmth, so holding your puppy in your lap is one of the better ways to bond with her. And she won't mind if you read or watch TV at the same time.

While you're holding Manchita, you can condition her to be tolerant of touch. If baby Manchita lets you handle every part of her body, from the tip of her nose to the pads of her toes (see Figure 9-1), it becomes easier to groom or medicate her. Besides, all that touchy-feely stuff lowers your blood pressure (honest, petting dogs does that).

Is Manchita sensitive about having her tootsies touched? Many puppies are, but she gets over it if you deal with it right away. No, don't force the issue. Instead, pet your puppy in places she enjoys until she's nearly asleep. As she becomes limp, continue stroking her body but include her feet as well. If Manchita tenses up, go back to petting only her body until she's sleepy enough so that you can try her feet again. After she falls asleep (and she will), gently massage the toes of all four feet. Soon your puppy will relax and let you touch her toes when she's awake too, and that makes toenail trimming much easier. If she resists being touched on other parts of her body, use the same method to overcome that aversion.

Figure 9-1:
Pet your puppy from her ear tips to her toes.

Be yourself around your new puppy and incorporate her schedule into your routine. If your pup is napping and you want to watch TV or play the piano, do it. Your puppy can sleep through normal household noises.

Interpreting a Dog's Body Language

Dogs may not talk (except on Taco Bell commercials), but if you watch Manchita's body language, you soon find out how to read her needs and even predict her next move. Your Chi communicates through her facial expressions, including her ears, eyes, brows, lips, nose, and mouth. She also talks through her tail, coat (hackles), and body position, and emits a variety of sounds.

Communicating with dogs comes naturally to many youngsters, but as adults, we need to concentrate on it, because we seldom take time to sit back and use our powers of observation. In fact, the older we get, the more we rely on verbal communication and lose our nonverbal skills. To get the most fun from Manchita, sit back and study the differences in her body language and facial expressions when she is happy, curious, anxious, proud of herself, and sleepy. Soon you're able to *read* your dog.

To start you off, here are some descriptions of general canine body language:

- ✔ A relaxed dog wags her tail in a methodical, neutral position — not high, tucked under, or stiff. Her mouth may be slightly open, and her ears look relaxed (rather than fully alert). Eyes appear soft, without a trace of threat or tension, and weight is evenly distributed on all four legs.

- ✔ A submissive, shy, or frightened dog makes herself smaller by contracting her body. She tucks her tail, flattens her ears, averts her eyes, and appears to shrink slightly.

- ✔ A dominant or aggressive dog tries to appear larger. She stands absolutely erect, holds her tail either straight out or up, and raises her hackles (fur on top of her back). Her mouth is usually closed and she makes eye contact with her adversary.

- ✔ When a dog greets you with her rear-end up, front end low, a wagging tail, and lively eyes, she's *play-bowing*. It's dog language for, "Let's play."

- ✔ If Manchita flicks her tongue up to lick her nose over and over, she's uneasy about something. Maybe she's checking out your new friend, or concentrating hard to learn a new trick. In a few cases, tongue flicking precedes snapping.

- ✔ Does Manchita ever mount another dog, or stand on her hind legs with her paws on another dog's back? Sure she's a she, but in *dog-think* mounting has more to do with dominance than sex. It's her way of saying, "I'm top dog here, and don't you forget it."

Okay, you take it from here. While the body language above is universal, Manchita's going to have many unique mannerisms all her own. Enjoy.

Understanding where "the jitters" come from

Some dogs are born nervous because of poor breeding. But most scaredy pups act that way because they weren't socialized at the right time. Let's forget dogs for a minute and think about children:

Imagine how a child (let's call him Bobby) reacts on his first day of school if he had been so overprotected by his parents that it was also his first experience away from home. Bobby's anxiety increases during the walk or drive to school. Traffic sounds other children take for granted startle him, and the sight of so many strange buildings, vehicles, and people confuses him. When he arrives, the big school building intimidates him, especially if he doesn't know how to navigate stairs. In the classroom, Bobby's fear of the strange adult called Teacher keeps him from focusing on the lesson. On the playground, he doesn't know how to respond to his high-spirited classmates. Feeling vulnerable and uncertain, he may back into a corner, too terrified to talk, or become defensive and try to fight off the first child who approaches.

Now let's add another wrinkle. What if Bobby goes on two outings before starting school? Both times, he visits his pediatrician for vaccinations. In his mind, leaving home, entering a strange building, and meeting a stranger, all correlate to pain. Now how long does it take Bobby to trust his teacher and be able to relax, let alone learn? A classroom observer who didn't know Bobby's history probably labels him as shy or stupid, perhaps even stubborn.

Luckily for children, scenarios like that seldom occur. Most parents take their kids out often and by the time the youngsters enter kindergarten, they adjust quickly. Puppies, especially Toy breed puppies, don't have it so good. They're often raised like poor Bobby.

Good breeders socialize their puppies before selling them, and some of the best refuse to sell a puppy before it is 3 months old. Don't worry. Even though the puppy loves its breeder, it transfers that love to you in no time. Besides, socialization is ongoing, and plenty of fun stuff is left for you and your puppy to do.

Using the first 16 weeks wisely

The first 16 weeks of your dog's life are critical to her social development. What a puppy discovers during that short time shapes her personality, making her outgoing or shy, happy-go-lucky, or cautious. The brief time correlates to when wild pups or cubs explore outside the den for the first time, quickly learning lessons in survival. Absorbing everything in a hurry is a necessity because a cub that makes a mistake in the wild rarely gets a second chance.

Although domesticated for centuries, dogs still arrive in the world programmed to relate to their surroundings during their first four months of life. In an ideal situation, a pup finds out how to behave around dogs during her first two months. That's one reason why a good Chihuahua breeder keeps the litter together until the puppies are at least 8 weeks old. Between 8 weeks and 12 weeks, the youngsters are mentally mature enough to leave their canine family, and are the ideal age to settle into human families. From then on, their people shape their personalities.

I didn't invent the term *critical periods*. Animal behaviorists did. What makes these periods critical? If a dog isn't socialized during it's puppyhood, it never becomes as confident a companion as it can be. Breeding also plays a part. Pups from nervous parents tend to be nervous too — unless the parents got that way through a lack of socialization.

If you are lucky enough to acquire Manchita when she's still a young puppy (under 4 months old, you can help her establish (or keep) her outgoing attitude. Introduce her to a friendly world and she grows up confident — a canine clown that shows off for your friends and likes finding out new things. But keep her secluded, and Manchita begins to fear anything unusual. Later she develops tendencies to cringe in unfamiliar places and hide behind your legs when your friends visit.

Inviting People Over: It's Party Time

Socializing has one dilemma. Manchita needs to meet lots of people before she's 12 weeks old, but is prohibited from going out in public until her series of vaccinations is complete. And that usually takes between 12 and 16 weeks. Breeders who keep their puppies for 3 months or more have their own socializing programs, but many of you can expect to bring home a younger pup than that. No problem. The solution is simple — and fun. Let Manchita meet new people right in your home by throwing a few puppy parties.

Introduce Manchita to men, women, and well-supervised children by inviting a small group of friends over for dessert, or a video. Place a bowl of her dry food on the goodie table so your friends can hand feed her. Then show your helpers how to hold a puppy and ask them to take turns holding, feeding, and petting Manchita. Try to have several of these informal get-togethers before Manchita turns 12 weeks old, making sure you include children of various ages (supervised, of course) and as many men as possible.

Going for a short drive every so often keeps Manchita from associating riding in the car with receiving a shot. By the time she's vaccinated and ready for real outings, she feels secure around strangers and comfortable in the car. In other words, she's ready to experience the world.

When your puppy is between 4 and 6 months old, she's fully developed mentally but not physically or emotionally, and she hasn't yet achieved an adult attention span.

Leaving Home: Hello, World!

Every time your puppy meets someone new or leaves the house, she is socializing. Taking Manchita with you when you visit a friend socializes her. So does meeting someone while out for a walk, playing with another puppy, or examining a beach ball.

The world is Manchita's playground, so she needs to get out and enjoy it as soon as she is safely vaccinated. You'll have fun too. Few people can pass up an adorable Chihuahua puppy, and your pup benefits from these admiring people. She needs to meet senior citizens and gentle kids, bearded men and ladies in sun hats, teenagers carrying skateboards and people pushing strollers.

No matter how outgoing your Chi, nor how well she walks on a leash, always keep her in your arms when riding an elevator. If it gives a sudden lurch, or people rush on without watching where they're going, she can be stepped on.

While safely outside (in your arms or on a leash), Manchita gets used to hearing motors, sirens, and the rumble of the garbage truck. Whatever you do, don't hold her all the time. She needs to walk on grass and pavement and find out how to navigate stairs. If your house doesn't have steps, find some elsewhere and show Manchita how to manage them. Start by putting her on the third step, and encouraging her to come down to you. When she gets good at that, place her at the bottom of the stairs, sit on the third or fourth step, and encourage her to climb up to you.

The more people Manchita meets and the more sights she sees before she is 4 months old, the braver she becomes. And confident Chihuahuas are the most fun of all.

Helping a pup overcome fear

Think of socialization as a game with two rules:

- Never pet your puppy when she's afraid.
- Always praise your puppy for being brave.

When Manchita appears scared, you'll want to comfort her, but that's a major mistake. Why? Because she interprets your pats and soothing words as praise. Anything a puppy is praised for she repeats again and again, so cringing behind your legs can become her learned reaction to anything new. On the other hand, never jerk her toward an object she fears. Treatment like that can turn a little trepidation into total terror.

So what do you do if Manchita is afraid to investigate a new object in your house? Leave her where she is and go yourself. Handle the object like it was a winning lottery ticket and invite her to join you. Sitting down beside the feared object works especially well. Your puppy may start creeping toward you (and it), but hold your praise until she at least touches the thing with her nose. If the object isn't breakable or too large, roll it away from (never toward) your puppy. That might awaken her chasing instinct and entice her to play with the object.

When Manchita fears a friendly person, give the person a dog treat and ask him or her to toss it near Manchita and then ignore her and chat with you. If your pup approaches, tell the person to kneel down but not to reach for her. When Manchita gets close, the person holds his or her hand low, reaching under the puppy's chin, tickling her chest. Reaching over your Chi's head may make her back away in fright. If Manchita doesn't approach the person, don't force her, but give her much more socialization. Get your friends in on the act, and set up situations enticing Manchita into approaching people on her own.

If loud noises send Manchita behind the sofa, start announcing her favorite things with sound. For example, if she's an eager eater, mix her meal in a metal pan with a metal spoon. Just keep the noise within the realm of everyday life. Its purpose is to help Manchita handle her sound sensitivity, not startle or terrify her.

Never, ever, let your Chihuahua run free — not even for a second. Always put a leash on her when she's outside the safety of your home and fenced yard.

Sudden Fear Syndrome

Suddenly becoming afraid of anything new between the ages of 8 and 11 weeks old is not unusual for happy-go-lucky puppies. In fact, that behavior even has a name — *Sudden Fear Syndrome*. If Manchita suddenly starts spooking, remember the rules of socialization. Don't try to cuddle her out of it, or she thinks you're praising her for acting afraid. But do praise her profusely when (and if) she does something brave.

Don't be surprised if your pup shies from something as silly as a fire hydrant. During the fear phase, she may see the bogeyman everywhere. While this isn't the time to take her to a Fourth of July celebration, it's best to keep taking her on regular outings. If you *don't* force her toward something she fears, or soothe her silliness, the fear phase passes.

Kindergarten for puppies

What's more fun than watching a puppy play? Watching several puppies frolic together and being invited to join in. This treat awaits you when Manchita has been immunized and can safely attend puppy kindergarten.

Often called *KPT* (Kindergarten Puppy Training), and geared to puppies between 12 and 16 weeks of age (some may vary), classes usually run once a week for 8 weeks. KPTs provide excellent socialization by helping owners introduce their pups to people, places, things, and each other.

In addition to socialization, KPT prepares puppies for further education. Gentle training techniques encourage them to earn praise for a job well done and learn respect for the word *"No."* Depending on the instructor, pups may also be introduced to basic commands such as Come, Sit, and Down, and walking on a leash. But KPT isn't just for puppies alone. It's for people too. Instructors give advice on housetraining and answer questions about dog behavior. So by the end of the course, you'll know how to solve minor problems before they become major issues.

To find a puppy kindergarten, check your newspaper or yellow pages for kennel clubs or dog obedience schools. Some offer puppy programs. You can also check with your veterinarian.

Before enrolling your Chi in any class, talk to the teacher. Find out if he or she is experienced with toy dogs and inquire about safety. For example, if the puppies are turned loose to play together, make sure Manchita's group is composed only of other small pups.

The do-it-yourself solution

If puppy classes aren't available in your area, create your own. A few fun people and their puppies are all it takes. Use your head when choosing playmates and play groups. Puppies don't know their own strength (although playing with other puppies helps them learn it), so don't overwhelm your 10-week-old Chihuahua by putting her with an 8-week-old Rottweiler. Instead, try to find other small puppies for her to play with. Sure, they'll probably be bigger than Manchita, but Chihuahua puppies can hold their own with other small-breed puppies of similar ages.

Walking on Lead

If I were asked to list the mistakes Toy breed owners make most often, lead breaking their dogs too late is definitely near the top. It's so easy to carry a tiny dog that people just don't get around to training. That never happens with a Great Dane.

Does Manchita cough when you put the slightest pressure on the lead? She may have a collapsing trachea (See Chapter 15). Relieve that problem by having her wear a harness instead of a collar.

Some breeders teach their puppies to walk on a leash before selling them. If Manchita willingly walks with you, you don't have to read the rest of this section. Instead, snap on her leash, step outside, and enjoy.

If Manchita doesn't know how to walk on lead, and isn't used to her collar, put the collar on her and play with her. Is she a chowhound? Then put the collar on her just before meals and let her wear it a little longer each time. After a few days, she will ignore it.

When Manchita is accustomed to her collar, attach the lead and let her drag it around. Keep an eye on her so she doesn't catch it on something and start struggling. When she's nonchalant about dragging the leash (or if she's too busy playing with it to drag it), pick up your end and follow your pup wherever she takes you.

When Manchita is comfortable with her collar and leash in the house (this may take a few days), put a few of her favorite treats in your pocket and take her outside wearing her leash. Carry her about a quarter block away from the house, put her down, and walk her home (it'll probably take lots of verbal encouragement and a few treats). If she pulls and rears like a baby bucking horse, wait until her tantrum subsides and try again. Keeping the experience a positive one is important, so ignore rebellion and praise her when she walks with you (any position, out in front, following behind, or beside you are all okay). Just watch your timing. Be sure to give her a treat when she's moving with you, not when she's balking like a belligerent mule. (If you live in a crowded city, save leash breaking for early on a weekend morning or whenever the fewest people are out rushing around.)

Does Manchita scream and turn herself inside out in a ploy to make you remove her leash. Just stay calm and keep trying. Whatever you do, don't give in and decide to put off training until she's older. When she's older, she's more set in her ways and can throw bigger tantrums.

After Manchita walks home with you rather well, it's time to put gentle pressure on the leash to decide the direction both of you will go. Rather than stopping in front of your house, continue past it for a few steps, encouraging her all the way. Gradually show her how to walk both toward and away from home. More important, keep your sessions short and upbeat. When leash-breaking a Chihuahua puppy, five minutes a day is enough, and more than ten minutes is too much.

Socializing an Adult Dog

Oh no! The more you read, the worse you feel. Here I've been telling you how important it is to start socializing your puppy early, and you didn't even acquire Manchita until she was an adult. Worse yet, you're sure terrible things happened to her before you got her. Is it too late? Is your Chihuahua doomed to be insecure for the rest of her life?

No way. Just as we don't have to have storybook childhoods to make a good life for ourselves, our dogs don't have to have ideal puppyhoods to become contented companions. Life may have been unkind to Manchita, but just look how her luck has changed. She has you now and the rest of her life is ahead of her. Help her make the most of it by giving her training, not pity. Pity prevents progress rather than encouraging it.

To become a well-adjusted family member, Manchita needs self-confidence. You still can help her find it. How? Show her how to please you. Begin with the basics (see Chapter 10) and then join a novice obedience class (see Chapter 11). Then you can use the commands during daily life and praise your Chi for every correct response — not by rote, but with feeling. Gradually she will gain enough confidence to stop avoiding life and start enjoying it.

Chapter 10

Teaching Good Manners to Your Pup

Do you know why Toy dogs have a bad reputation for being yappy, hard to housetrain, and possessive? It's because so many owners let little pets get away with rudeness. I'm sure glad you're not one of those owners. How do I know? Because you're reading about manners. After you train your Chihuahua, he can become a good ambassador for this bright breed.

In this chapter, I help you raise Pepe to be a polite pup, while you discover how to housetrain him, introduce him to simple commands, and nip problem behavior in the bud before it becomes a nasty habit. Not only does Pepe love the positive attention that comes with training, but his well-behaved nature also makes him welcome in many more places. And going places together is one of the best parts of having a canine companion.

Accepting the Crate as Home Base

Besides serving as Pepe's private den, and his home away from home, Pepe's crate is your best *housetraining* tool. But before getting to that chore, let's teach your Chi to accept, and even enjoy, being crated.

Every time you put Pepe in his crate, toss a favorite toy or special treat into the crate ahead of him. Then say *"Crate"* or *"Kennel up"* and gently, but firmly, put Pepe inside and shut the door. Now walk away. Don't wait around to see how Pepe responds, because that entices him to react. It won't be long before your Chi learns what the word Crate means and enters his little den on his own.

Pepe may cry the first few times he's introduced to his crate, but if you leave the room and don't retrieve him until he settles down, he soon learns to relax in it. The worst thing you can do is rescue him when he cries, because that teaches him to control you by whining and howling. If Pepe still complains in his crate after a week or two, help can be found in Chapter 13.

Never punish your Chi for something he did when you weren't supervising. He won't know why he's being punished and that leads to all sorts of anxiety problems. If you didn't catch him in the act, let it pass. Keep it from happening again by using prevention, not punishment.

Using the crate as a bed

At night, make sure Pepe relieves himself before crating him and putting his crate in your bedroom, right beside your bed. No, he won't make it through the night, but he should be okay for three or four hours. If he cries in his crate as soon as the lights go out, speak soothingly to him (to let him know someone is near) but don't take him out of the crate. The first few nights are hardest on him, because your place won't feel like home yet. Pepe's used to snuggling with his dam and littermates and misses them most during the wee hours. So you're going to lose some sleep.

Eventually, Pepe falls asleep and so do you, but expect him to wake you with his cries after a few hours. Like it or not, you must get up quickly and take your puppy outside to relieve himself. Dogs don't like to soil their sleeping quarters. That's why a crate is such a good housetraining aid. But if you ignore Pepe's plea to go potty, he'll have to soil his crate. Puppies just don't have much holding power. If that happens too often, he adjusts to living with filth instead of maintaining the clean habits he was born with. And, believe me, that's the last thing you need.

When housetraining your Chi, take him to the same outdoor area to Go Potty every time and repeat the same words "Go Potty" as he eliminates. Routine is so important that taking the same route to the potty place every time is a good idea (for example, go out the same door and turn the same direction).

Crate expectations

Never use the crate to punish Pepe and be careful not to use it too much. Your dog doesn't need to spend the majority of his time in a crate. How do you know if you're doing it right? Watch Pepe's reaction as he matures. Eventually his attitude toward his crate becomes neutral. If he either resists going into it, or loves it so much it's hard to get him out of it, something is wrong.

When your Chi matures, you may want to leave a crate in a corner of your living room with the door always open. Pepe may appreciate a private place of his own where he can chew a toy or take a nap when he needs one. Let your kids know that when he curls up in his crate, he's tired and wants to be left alone.

Housetraining — Avoiding Problems

Dogs are naturally clean critters, yet *accidents* in the house are considered one of the biggest behavior problems in the Toy breeds. Wait. It's too soon to worry. I'm going to tell you why Toy dogs have an undeserved bad reputation when it comes to housetraining and how to avoid the problem. The truth is Toy dogs are every bit as bright as larger breeds (okay, often brighter), and can control themselves just as well as big dogs. Thousands of toys are extremely reliable in the home, and yours can be one of them if you follow the guidelines in this chapter.

 Even if you're lucky enough to get your puppy while you're on vacation, introduce him to a schedule you can live with and stick to it. Don't confuse him by putting him on one schedule during weekends and vacation days and another schedule on workdays.

Establishing good habits from day one

Do Toy dogs have poor *plumbing* systems? Not at all. Toy dogs are considered hard to housetrain, because so many owners don't get around to it until the dog has already developed bad habits. Then they face the enormous job of breaking a bad habit, rather than the much easier task of establishing a good one.

Here's why Toy dog owners let their puppies get away with leaving puddles and poops on the floor:

- ✔ Because the *accident* is so tiny that it can be cleaned up quickly.
- ✔ Because Sassy is so small, she probably doesn't understand.
- ✔ Because the Muffster hates to get her feet wet and it's drizzling outside.
- ✔ Because no one feels ambitious enough to walk the dog right now.

Yes, those are answers people give for letting their little dog *do it* on the floor just one more time. Bet they wouldn't think that way if a Saint Bernard just did it on the floor!

To clear your head of that kind of thinking, remember:

- ✔ The accident may be easy to clean, but do you want to clean up accidents several times a day for the next dozen or more years?

- ✔ Being small is not the same as being stupid. Chihuahuas are smart. Sassy understands if you take the time to teach her.

- ✔ Toy dogs are still dogs, and Muffy needs to learn to relieve herself in the right place, rain or shine. Most dogs do their duty real fast during bad weather.

- ✔ To housetrain a dog, you must train yourself.

Pepe may take longer to be reliably housebroken than your big dog did. That's because Toy dogs see the world differently than large dogs do. As far as they are concerned, it's a long way from the kitchen to behind the living room sofa, so they can squat there and still be clean critters. Keep Pepe close to you until he understands exactly where he is supposed to go potty. And keep in mind that Toy dog puppies have to relieve themselves a little more often than large dog pups.

Establishing a routine — same times every day

The keys to housetraining are a regular routine and an alert trainer. A housebroken dog is simply a dog with a habit — the happy habit of eliminating outdoors.

Simply put, Pepe needs to be fed, watered, exercised, and taken outside to eliminate at the same times every day. Besides being healthier, a routine makes housetraining easier. Dogs are creatures of habit, so sticking to a schedule right from the start helps Pepe make sense of his new environment. As he begins to recognize his daily routine, he learns to understand your expectations. And because puppies love to please, the habits he forms are good ones.

If you live on the 20th floor, or where the snow drifts as high as a Chihuahua's eye, try the litter-box method. Instead of cat box filler, line the box with several thicknesses of newspaper. Use the housetraining routine recommended in this section, but when I tell you to take your dog outside, take him to the litter box instead. Soon your Chi is litter-box trained. Pet shops also sell chemically treated pads that attract dogs and help them decide to squat in the area you choose.

Chihuahuas are basically clean creatures and don't want to soil their living quarters. When housetraining Pepe, take advantage of that trait by confining him to a dog crate every time you're away or he's left unsupervised. Then, as soon as you arrive home, take Pepe outside and praise him for eliminating. If Pepe soils his crate, clean it up immediately. Besides being dangerous to his health, leaving Pepe in a wet or dirty crate teaches him to live with his mess. And that attitude hinders the housetraining process.

Training yourself first, a.m. to p.m.

Staying on schedule makes or breaks housetraining, so plan ahead. You may need to get up 15 minutes earlier; come home for lunch (or hire a dog walker); and come straight home from work; until Pepe is a little older. Here's a tentative schedule for a young puppy:

Morning

- ✔ First thing in the morning, take Pepe outside for several minutes, and praise him for a job well done.
- ✔ When you bring him in, feed and water him.
- ✔ Take him outside again after he eats breakfast. Young puppies almost always have to relieve themselves soon after eating. Now Pepe can spend time with you, or have the run of his puppy-proofed room (see Chapter 5), if you're at home but unable to supervise. If you're leaving, confine him to his crate.
- ✔ Take Pepe outdoors mid-morning if you are at home.

Afternoon

- ✔ Take Pepe outside as soon as you get home at lunchtime.
- ✔ Give Pepe lunch and fresh water.
- ✔ Take Pepe outdoors after he finishes eating. Then confine him if you can't keep an eye on him, or won't be home.

Evening

- ✔ When you arrive home in the evening, take Pepe outdoors right away and enjoy a nice walk (weather permitting). Then let him watch you fix dinner, or join you for the evening news.
- ✔ Feed and water Pepe for the last time each day between 6:00 p.m. and 7:00 p.m.; then remove the water bowl until morning.
- ✔ Take Pepe outside when he finishes eating. After he relieves himself, enjoy his company for the evening.
- ✔ Take Pepe outside just before you go to bed. Confine him for the night.

Buy a good odor neutralizer and stain remover (without ammonia). Removing the evidence of Pepe's mistakes immediately keeps your house looking and smelling like home, not a kennel. An odor-free floor is an important part of housetraining. Dogs tend to eliminate where their noses tell them they went before, so quick cleanups help prevent accidents.

Recognizing the signs of need

Sometimes (possibly many times), Pepe must relieve himself more often than the sample schedule says. When housetraining, prevention works wonders and correction makes things worse, so watch him closely. Take him outside immediately if he begins walking in circles and sniffing the floor, if he starts panting when he hasn't been exercising, or if he suddenly leaves the room. Play, heavy exercise, and a nice massage also act as *on* switches for puppy plumbing. So if you just finished a playing or petting session, it's a good idea to take Pepe outside.

Does it sound like you'll be running in and out as often as a confused cat? Well, for awhile, you will. But it isn't a life sentence. As Pepe gets older, he needs to eat only twice a day and his holding capacity increases, so he needs fewer trips outdoors.

Dealing with accidents

All puppies make mistakes. If you get home too late and Pepe already had an accident, don't make a big deal out of it. Your puppy won't understand why you're so angry with him when he was so glad to see you, and that leads to far worse problems. No, pointing at the poop while screaming at him won't help. It'll surely scare him, and may lead to anxiety-related problems. Bottom line: It won't teach him a thing.

If the dirty deed was done before you got home, take Pepe outside anyway. Eventually he learns to expect the opportunity to go outside and to wait for it. Have patience and understand that Pepe may still be too young to control himself for the length of time you were away. Clean up the soiled spot as soon as you can, using an odor neutralizer or plain white vinegar.

Never use anything containing ammonia, to clean the crate or carpet. The odor of ammonia makes dogs seek out the same spot to go potty again.

If you catch Pepe in the act, you may be able to stop him mid-squat with a firm "No!" or a loud noise like clapping your hands. Then pick him up, hurry him outside to the right spot, and praise him if he finishes what he started.

Contrary to old wives' tales, swatting Pepe with a rolled up newspaper or putting his nose in his mess won't work. Punishment teaches a dog to eliminate behind the sofa where he thinks you won't find it, not to go outside and do it proudly in front of you.

Teaching Words that All Good Dogs Know

Imagine how nice it is living with a dog that always comes when you call, sits and lays down on command, stays in place when told to, and respects the words "No," and "Enough." It's easier than you think. Conditioning your Chi to respond to the commands *Come, Sit, Down, Stay, No,* and *Enough* can start at any age, but younger is better.

Conditioning Chihuahua puppies (or adult dogs) requires a trainer with an upbeat attitude — one who gives lots of praise and positive reinforcement, and absolutely no punishment. If that's you, let's get going. When teaching the meaning of the following commands, praise or reward Pepe every time he gives you the correct response, and simply ignore him when he doesn't. Dogs do virtually anything for attention, so Pepe quickly learns the lingo.

Conditioning your puppy to come when called

Use bribery to teach Pepe what Come means. Introduce the word at feeding time by saying his name and then the word "Come" in a happy voice ("Pepe, come."). Show him his dinner dish; then walk backwards a few steps while holding it. When your pup follows, praise him and let him eat. Repeat the process every time you feed him.

How soon should you start training your puppy? As soon as he settles in. He loves the attention, but keep training sessions real short (like puppy attention spans) and always be cheerful and upbeat.

Puppies love to chase and chasing games also help them learn what Come means. Touch Pepe on his rump playfully, say his name followed by the word "Come," and run away a few steps while clapping (not too loud), and talking happily. Let him catch you, then play with him a few seconds before giving him another playful tap and starting over. Three times is plenty for one session.

When conditioning Pepe to come, call him only when you know he wants to come — not when he's sleepy or busy with food, a toy, or another person. Later, when your Chihuahua is older, you may want to attend obedience school (see Chapter 11). There you discover how to teach him to come no matter what the distraction. In the meantime, practice often. Call Pepe for all the good stuff — dinner, treats, and cuddles — and he soon responds happily.

Never sabotage your training by calling a Chihuahua of any age and then giving him a pill or chastising him for something. Instead, go to your dog for the upsetting stuff, and keep his Comes carefree.

Sitting pretty

To teach Pepe what Sit means (see Figure 10-1), hold a treat in front of his nose, say "Sit," and move the treat upward and back over his head. When his eyes follow the goodie upward, his head will tilt back and his rear will lower until it reaches the floor. Give the treat immediately (while he is still sitting) and praise him. Try it three or four more times, but be sure to quit while he's still having fun.

Figure 10-1:
Manchita
sits on
command.

Teaching the Down

To teach the Down command, start with Pepe in Sit position. Then hold a tasty treat right in front of his nose and say "Down." Next, make a movement shaped like a *capital L* by lowering the treat straight down just in front of Pepe's paws and then slowly pulling it forward at ground level. As Pepe reaches for the goody, the front half of his body moves downward. If it doesn't lower completely to the ground, put gentle pressure on his shoulders with your free hand, but don't mash him down. The instant his whole body is in Down position, give him the treat (see Figure 10-2).

Never train your pet when you are in a bad mood. Puppies are just learning how to learn, and your earliest teaching colors their lifelong attitude toward training.

Conditioning puppies to stay

Staying in place is not a puppy's forte, so when conditioning young Pepe, begin with two- or three-second Stays and don't try to make him remain in place longer than ten seconds (use a watch, you'll be surprised how long ten seconds actually is). If your ultimate goal is for him to Stay in place for several minutes, an obedience school is your best bet (see Chapter 11). In the meantime, let's show Pepe what the word "Stay" means.

Figure 10-2: Manchita downs for a treat.

Pepe probably bounces up from his Sit right after you give him his treat, but now we're going to prolong that process. Stand on Pepe's right side, with both of you facing the same way, and hold a treat in your right hand. Tell Pepe to "Sit," but this time, don't give him the treat as soon as his butt touches the floor. Instead, move your left hand sideways stopping just in front of his nose (palm facing him) and say "Stay" at the same time. That's the traditional Stay signal. Now let a long second pass before giving Pepe a treat. Gradually — very gradually — work up to a ten-second Stay before presenting the reward. Decide how many seconds each Stay will be before you start, and vary the time. Otherwise, your Chi soon outguesses you.

What should you do if Pepe moves before time's up? Absolutely nothing. Don't reward, don't pet, and don't punish. Just try again and praise your dog when he does it right. Once Pepe learns how to Stay in place in Sit position, use the same procedure to teach him what Down-Stay means.

A soft treat, such as a nibble of cheese, makes a good training treat. It's healthy, and Pepe can eat it fast so you can continue training.

Making "No!" effective

Your petite pup may amaze your friends by walking on leash like an obedience champ and performing Sits and Downs on command. But if he's a brat when show-off time is over, he isn't the pure pleasure he can be.

All dogs need to respond to two words: "No!" and "Enough!" "No!" means, "Stop that right now and don't ever do it again." Bark out the word "No!" in a sharp tone and your attitude won't be lost on your Chihuahua. Just don't use it too often, or Pepe gets used to it. Reserve the word "No!" for really bad behavior like teething on a table leg, or nipping at feet or clothing. If your voice isn't emphatic enough, clap your hands (once) right after you say "No!"

What if Pepe ignores you and continues chewing the chair leg? Go to him, grab the scruff of his neck and shake him slightly with a delicate downward pressure (about as hard as another Chihuahua would chasten him — never harder, or it could be dangerous) while repeating your sharp "No!" Pepe understands that type of chastisement because it's similar to what a mama dog does to teach her puppies the limits of her tolerance. Just keep your cool, and never touch your dog in anger. If you have a temper (you know who you are), stick with a verbal "No."

Enough already

"Enough" means: "What you are doing was just fine for awhile, but you've been doing it too long, so stop now." Use "Enough" when you don't want to

Techichis believed to be true soulmates

During the 12th century in Mexico, the Aztec Indians wiped out the Toltec nation but spared their dogs, the Techichis, because the dogs had such an impressive job description. Believed to be holy, their task was to guide their dead owner's soul to safety. This concept appealed to the Aztecs because they needed all the help they could get. After all, they believed the dead had to cross nine perilous lands and a treacherous underworld river before their souls reached safety. So when the Aztecs burned a dead warrior, they burned his dog with him. They thought the little holy dog would race on ahead, fight off evil spirits, and wait on the far bank of the raging river until it saw its master, and then swim back across, guiding him safely to the other side.

Sacrificing a dog with red skin by burning it along with a human corpse was also popular with the Aztecs. They believed the sins of the deceased were transferred to the dog and not taken out on the person. No doubt that's why archeologists discovered a number of graves in Mexico containing both human and Techichi remains.

pet Pepe anymore, but he keeps pawing your hand. Say "Enough" if he gets too wound up during play, or continues barking long after the meter reader leaves. Said firmly, but without anger, "Enough" works on puppies, adult dogs, and the kids that play with them.

How often do you and your Chihuahua need to practice simple commands such as Sit, Down and Come? Every day. But don't set aside a special time for it. Instead, use the commands during daily life: Sit, for the dinner dish. Come, for a treat. Down, for petting. You get the picture.

Preventing Common Problems

Besides housetraining issues, common puppy problems include destructive chewing, persistent barking, jumping, nipping, and possessiveness. Okay, that was the bad news. The good news is that if Pepe is still young, you can prevent most of the typical pitfalls of puppyhood. And that's a whole lot easier than correcting problems once they become bad habits. Yes, that's possible too (see Chapter 12), but why do it the hard way when prevention is so much easier?

All dogs need toys but don't overdo it. A dog with too many toys may begin to believe that everything is a toy. Then he won't learn to discriminate between his toys and all the taboo items in the house.

"Shopping spree" teaches what's okay to chew

Your puppy needs to chew, but teaching him what to chew isn't always easy. Here's a nifty training aid compliments of my friend Amy Ammen. She serves as host of the television series *Amiable Dog Training* on Channel 14/47 in Milwaukee, Wisconsin, and is the author of several training books.

After your puppy knows how to walk on lead, teach him to discriminate between his toys and taboo items by taking him on a shopping spree right in your living room. First choose a word that means *get that out of your mouth,* (most people opt for Out or "Drop It"). Then place some personal objects — such as a wallet, slippers, or purse — and some paper products — like napkins, or a roll of toilet tissue — on the floor along with two of your puppy's toys.

With the props in place, put a leash on your puppy and let him explore the clutter. When he picks up a taboo item, say your "Drop It" command along with a tiny jerk on the leash (just enough so he feels it — if it moves his body, it's too hard). Then walk toward an appropriate toy and encourage your puppy to play with it. Take your puppy shopping a couple times a day, and he soon takes pride in leading you to one of the correct objects. When he does, be sure to praise him and let him keep his toy. And now that Pepe knows the command for releasing an object, use that command, and only that command, whether he's holding a slipper, a finger, or a dead mouse.

Controlling barking

Chihuahuas make good watch dogs because they have excellent hearing and a loud bark, considering their size. Some barking is a good thing. Most of us are glad our dogs tell us when a stranger is approaching the house. But it's best to be glad quietly, taking Pepe's protective tendencies for granted rather than praising them. For example, the first time Pepe goes into a prolonged barking fit at a door-to-door salesman, don't act like it's adorable unless you want him to bark long and hard at visitors all his life. Instead, keep incessant barking from becoming a habit by letting him know right from the start when he's barked long "Enough." It isn't barking but rather *excessive barking* that drives us mad. What's behind all that noise and what you can do about it?

Even though you take Pepe's warning barks for granted and don't bother to praise him for giving you advance notice when a visitor arrives, he usually feels rewarded anyway. That's because every time the meter reader or the encyclopedia salesperson leaves (after being barked at, of course), Pepe thinks he chased them away. And that makes him feel real macho.

Prevent problem barking by never praising Pepe for barking.

Trying to thwart Pepe's natural tendency to protect his family only frustrates him. Worse yet, he may learn to keep quiet no matter what, rather than acting as your early warning system. Countless Chihuahuas have alerted their families about fires and scared off burglars with their shrill bark. The trick is being able to turn off your live alarm on command. So use the "Enough" word (see previous "Enough already" section) to let him know when he's done his duty and it's time to quiet down. If that doesn't work — and only as a last resort — buy an inexpensive water pistol (small and wimpy, not high-powered) or a spray bottle. Keep it in your pocket and give him one surprise squirt, right in the face, to enforce the "Enough" word. Avoid the tendency to threaten him with the water treatment. It's best if Pepe thinks his barking, not you, flooded his face.

Don't punish Pepe after the fact. Not even if he has a *guilty look.* The truth is, dogs don't feel guilt. That's a people thing. Nor do they remember what they did five minutes ago. Sure there's poop on the rug and Pepe looks worried, but what you're seeing in his eyes is confusion. He senses that you're angry with him but he doesn't know why, and that makes him apprehensive. Hence, the guilty look.

Is jumping okay?

Is it? Only you can answer that. After all, Chis weigh hardly anything, so the danger of being knocked over is nonexistent.

Some people like having their dog joyfully jump on them. If you're one of those people, nothing is wrong with that as long as you enjoy having Pepe jump on you no matter what you're wearing. Your Chi isn't clothes-conscious enough to understand that jumping on you when you're wearing jeans is okay, but it isn't okay when you're dressed to impress. The point is, don't let Pepe do something one day that you don't want him to do another day. So decide if jumping is okay or not, and if it isn't, read on.

You'll have to change Pepe's method of greeting people when you teach him not to jump up. Teach him to Sit on command (see previous "Sitting Pretty" section), then tell him to sit (in a happy but firm voice) as soon as you open the door. When he does (even if you have to put him in sit position), kneel down to his level and give him plenty of praise. Pepe jumps on you for instant attention, but if you withhold your attention until after he's sitting, he soon learns to Sit for your approval.

Nipping nipping

Puppies use their mouths to investigate things, much the same way humans use their hands. They also use their mouths in play, and sometimes, to vent their high spirits. But needle-sharp teeth hurt, so puppies must be taught that nipping isn't nice.

Resist the urge to jerk your hand away from your puppy when he clamps down on it. That's the canine version of an invitation to play, so pulling away just makes him come back for another nip.

It's fine to pet your puppy as he licks and mouths you, but if he clamps down with his teeth, tell him it hurts. How? Say ouch! And say it like you mean it. Screech it out in a high pitched voice that lets Pepe know he hurt you. Most pups lick you in apology. If a week or two of yelping "Ouch!" doesn't make a difference, choose a command that means, "Don't Bite." Then say it every time Pepe touches you with his teeth, while putting your finger on his button nose and pressing gently. The last resort (use only on confirmed nippers) is dabbing Bitter Apple on the part of you your puppy nips. It works especially well on shoelace and sock chasers.

Preventing possessiveness

Most possessiveness starts over the food dish. That's because puppies compete with their littermates (brothers and sisters) for food, and sometimes have to be deprogrammed when they enter a human family. Nothing to it. Just mix up these three choices — using one during one meal and a different one at the next meal, and so on. After a couple weeks, Pepe should stop being possessive of his bowl.

- ✔ Give Pepe only one-fourth of his dinner. Then, just as he finishes the tiny portion, put the rest of his meal in the bowl.

- ✔ Pet Pepe for a few seconds as he begins his dinner, then walk away and let him eat the rest of his meal alone.

- ✔ When Pepe is nearly finished eating, walk up to him and place a tiny, but very special treat, in his dish. A slice of hot dog, a sliver of cheese, or a bit of burger makes him happy that you put your hand in his bowl.

Chapter 11

Going Beyond Basics: Fun and Games

Many Chihuahuas make the most of their intelligence and dexterity by participating in dog sports like AKC Obedience and Agility, earning Canine Good Citizen Certificates and serving as therapy dogs. In this chapter, I tell you about some activities you and Manchita can participate in as partners.

Beginning Obedience Training

I like to call Obedience *companion dog training,* because it teaches the dog to be a happy and responsive partner, while showing the owner how to train, understand, and enjoy the dog. During classes, Manchita discovers how to work with you despite distractions like strangers and other dogs. The happy result is enhanced companionship. Some simply call it teamwork. Whatever you call it, obedience training also provides a great background for any other activity you may want to do with your dog.

If an instructor suggests a training method or correction that doesn't feel right to you, don't do it. It's your dog and you have the final say in her training.

Years ago, common knowledge said that dogs don't attend obedience school until they are at least 6 months old. Back then, obedience exercises (such as the Long Sit, see Figure 11-1) were just something people practiced on the training field once a week and for a few minutes a day at home. Today, obedience schools have modernized. Contemporary classes concentrate on the practical, as up-to-date instructors tell their students how to incorporate the training into everyday life. Modern instructors also emphasize positive reinforcement rather than punishment, so younger dogs learn without becoming stressed. Four months is an ideal age to enter a novice class (although dogs profit from the training at any age).

In a novice obedience class, Manchita finds out how to Heel (walk in the traditional position by your left side) on and off lead, Sit when you stop, Down on command, Stand quietly while a friendly stranger pets her, Come when called, and remain in both the Sit and Down positions amid distractions from other dogs. Best of all, provided the training is positive and upbeat (don't stick around if it isn't), she gains considerable confidence from it.

While the ultimate goal of obedience trainers is a happy partnership with their dogs, obedience is also one of the more popular dog sports. If your Chihuahua enjoys it, you can turn obedience into a hobby and enter trials. When Manchita qualifies for her novice title, she officially becomes Manchita, CD (the title becomes part of her registered name). The CD stands for — you guessed it — Companion Dog.

The fun doesn't have to end after Manchita earns her CD. Plenty of challenging exercises can be accomplished in advanced competition. Among them are retrieving a small dumbbell; jumping various hurdles; discriminating between your scent and a stranger's; and responding to hand signals instead of verbal commands. Are you worried about Manchita making it over the jumps? If she has a sound body, it won't be a problem. Your Chihuahua is measured before she enters the ring and the jumps are set at the right height for her size.

In addition to the CD, American Kennel Club (AKC) Obedience titles include the CDX (Companion Dog Excellent), the UD (Utility Dog), the UDX (Utility Dog Excellent), and the OTCH (Obedience Trial Champion). The United Kennel Club (UKC) also offers a series of titles.

Choosing an Obedience Instructor

Dog clubs and private instructors offer obedience classes. They are advertised in the yellow pages or the newspaper. Your veterinarian and local pet supply store may also have info about nearby classes. Shopping around is a good idea — not for a bargain but for the best school for you and your Chihuahua. Manchita needs an instructor who has experience with dogs of all sizes, especially tiny ones.

Believe it or not, you'll recognize a first-rate teacher even though you don't know much about dog training. How? By observation. Watch a session or two of each beginner class offered in your area before signing up for one. Any instructor can bark out commands, but top-notch teachers have several attributes in common. Look for the following traits:

- **Good instructors are safety conscious.** They demand that all dogs be vaccinated. They don't crowd too many students into too small a space, and they provide a training area with sufficient traction and no hidden obstructions.

- **Good instructors are master of positive motivation.** They show their students how to use praise, petting, and toys to encourage correct responses.

- **Good instructors are flexible.** They adapt their methods to fit their student's needs.

- **Good instructors are approachable, friendly, and helpful.** They have upbeat attitudes.

- **Good instructors are creative.** They vary the drill by initiating group games, so handlers and dogs have a good time while performing the necessary repetition.

- **Good instructors are attentive to all their students.** They work well with handlers and dogs of all sizes, shapes, and ages, and aren't prejudiced against any breed or mix.

- **Good instructors have lesson plans.** They discuss training goals and explain how to work each new command into everyday life. Their classes are never chaotic.

- **Good instructors keep the class moving.** They don't allow one student to monopolize the lesson.

- **Good instructors respect their students and have empathy.** They are aware that everyone in the class has feelings, including the dogs.

Sporting events for dogs may occur indoors, or outside in all kinds of weather, and Manchita won't be allowed to wear a sweater during competition. Your Chihuahua won't do her best when she's chilled, so plan to attend dog events during the warm months unless the trial takes place indoors.

Figure 11-1: Maxie and Ginny demonstrate an obedience exercise called the long sit. They are litter sisters but have different expressions, because Maxie has typical Chihuahua ears while Ginny's ears never stood up.

Getting Active in Agility

How much fun can you handle? If you're thinking "a whole lot," then agility may be the sport for you. Thousands of dog owners swear that it's the most fun you can have with a dog.

At agility trials, dogs are timed as they navigate a course that resembles a colorful playground. They soar over hurdles, weave through poles, stride across balance beams, sprint up A-frames, play seesaw, and crawl through tunnels. Meanwhile their handlers point out the next obstacle (obstacles must be taken in the correct order), and direct them through the course. Audiences at agility trials are traditionally encouraging, but when the crowd sees a Chihuahua, the applause always amplifies.

One of the really cool things you discover in obedience and agility school is that dogs, because they are closer to the ground, see things differently than we do. When a student's dog seems leery about something, good instructors tell the student to get down and look at it from their pet's perspective. Try it sometime.

Many owners do agility training with their dogs just for fun, but plenty of titles await you if competition is your thing. Not only that, four major (and some smaller) organizations offer agility. Your Chi could add so many titles to her name that it sometimes takes two breaths just to say it.

Few people want to landscape their yard with agility equipment (at least not at first), so most agility enthusiasts attend a private instructor's classes or join an agility club. Besides the attributes that I told you that an obedience instructor needs (see "Choosing an Obedience Instructor" above), a good agility teacher also:

✔ Provides sturdy obstacles with neither rough edges nor a hint of a wobble.

✔ Goes slow and keeps the obstacles low, making sure every dog and handler in the class has a firm foundation.

✔ Provides new challenges by building on that foundation.

Smart handlers know the rules of the game before they play. Rulebooks for obedience and agility are available through the organizations that sanction these events. Their addresses are in Appendix B.

Qualifying as a Therapy Dog

More than a decade ago, the scientific community realized that interacting with friendly animals is therapeutic for people. Since then, polite pets are welcomed at nursing homes and other institutions.

Well-socialized Chihuahuas make top-notch therapy dogs because they are world class lap-sitters. Lap-sitting, after all, is one of the more important tasks of a tiny therapy dog. But becoming qualified to perform pet therapy isn't easy. This special service calls for a pet that keeps her cool in an institutional setting.

Therapy dogs must have dependable dispositions and impeccable manners. Although Manchita's main assignment is lap-sitting, she still needs plenty of confidence to remain relaxed in an institution. After all, she'll be sitting on strange laps amid the distractions of hospital equipment (like wheelchairs and walkers), institutional odors, crowds, and noise.

Many Chihuahuas help the hearing impaired through hearing dog programs. After a training regimen where they learn to alert their handlers to the doorbell, telephone, alarm clock, smoke alarm, oven timer, or baby crying, each dog is paired with a deaf person. The two practice obedience commands together, and the owner is taught how to care for the dog. Then they go home together, and the dog serves as that person's ears. Because they are so small that they fit anywhere, and so smart that they easily take to the training, Chihuahuas are popular hearing dogs.

Hundreds of clubs across the United States are dedicated to pet-assisted therapy. These groups prepare their members through classes and tests. At least two national organizations, the Delta Society and Therapy Dogs International (see Appendix B), have local clubs or certified instructors in many cities who are eager to help owners prepare their pets for therapy work. Your local dog club also may have a volunteer program.

The test used most frequently to certify dogs for therapy work is the AKC's Canine Good Citizen Test (see next section, "Passing the Good Citizen and Temperament Tests"). Some organizations modify it to include institutional equipment. A health certificate from your veterinarian may also be mandatory.

Requirements vary among organizations and institutions, but the rewards remain the same. Bored eyes light up and tired faces break into smiles at the sight of your Chihuahua. And the warm feeling remains with you and those you help for hours. But don't take my word for it. Give it a try.

If Manchita is a Chihuahua mix, or a purebred without *papers,* she can still participate in every event in this chapter. The AKC will grant an Indefinite Listing Privilege to spayed and neutered unregistered purebred dogs to allow them to compete in Obedience and Agility. The UKC welcomes spayed and neutered unregistered purebreds and mixed breeds. And three out of four organizations that sponsor Agility events welcome mixed breeds, too. Addresses are in Appendix B. Therapy dogs, Canine Good Citizens, and Temperament Tested dogs may be any breed or mix.

Passing the Good Citizen and Temperament Tests

"A Canine Good Citizen is a dog that makes its owner happy without making someone else unhappy," according to the AKC's CGC program booklet. That means Canine Good Citizens behave at home, are good neighbors, and are polite in public.

The CGC test is pass-fail and noncompetitive. It evaluates practical training, not formal obedience. Manchita is tested on how she behaves during everyday situations like being touched by a friendly stranger, walking on a crowded street, meeting another dog while out for a stroll, and coming when called. She's also graded on her reaction to distractions and her attitude when you are out of sight (separation anxiety). In addition, she must obey simple commands such as "Sit" and "Down," but not with the precision of a competitive obedience dog. All tests are performed on lead. If Manchita passes the ten-part test, she earns a certificate proclaiming her a Canine Good Citizen.

While preparing for the CGC test, owners find out how to train their dogs, and their dogs become better companions. Many dog clubs and private obedience schools offer short courses in CGC training, and some of them give the test as their graduation exercise. In addition, the AKC offers free info to help people train for the test. Contact AKC (see Appendix B) for Canine Good Citizen training material and information about how to find a test site near you.

The Temperament Test

The American Temperament Test Society (ATTS), Inc., also offers a ten-part test and rewards those that pass with a Temperamental Tested, or TT Certificate. The test takes no special training but requires a well-socialized dog with self-confidence and a reliable disposition. During a walk simulating several situations, Manchita encounters friendly, neutral, and threatening scenarios, and is evaluated on her reactions. ATTS provides free information about the test (see Appendix B).

Although they don't become an official part of a dog's registered name, owners of dogs that earn CGC and TT certificates, or belong to a therapy dog club, traditionally use the letters after their dog's names, as in Manchita, CGC, TT, TDI.

Chapter 12

Retaining Your Place as Head of Household

• •

In This Chapter

▶ Dealing with crying and barking

▶ Housetraining — one more time

▶ Dealing with humping and possessiveness

▶ Understanding separation anxiety

• •

*U*h oh! Chief Chihuahua rules at your house. He growls when someone tries to sit in *his* chair, barks as loud and as long as he pleases, refuses to drop forbidden objects, and sometimes even snaps to keep his spot on the bed. Obviously, a coup is long overdue. It's time to overthrow your tiny tyrant and put policymaking back in the hands of the people. With dogs, a benevolent dictatorship works best. First, elect yourself president for life. Then read this chapter. It helps you turn your tiny tyrant into a true friend.

Curing the Cry Baby

Most puppies whine and bark the first several times they're confined to a room or a crate. Whatever you do, don't take Pepe out of his place of confinement to stop the racket. That's exactly what he wants and doing so makes him feel rewarded for barking nonstop. Instead, wait until he's silent for a least a minute before going to him and letting him out.

You can squelch Pepe's complaints in several ways. Try them in the following order, moving on to the next one only if you need to:

✔ The first few times you confine Pepe and leave him alone, try to put up with the noise for ten minutes without doing anything. Some dogs simply quit sounding off when they realize they're dramatizing to an empty theater.

✔ Play a radio softly near Pepe. It relaxes some dogs. Just be sure to keep both the radio and the cord out of his reach.

✔ If Pepe is still mouthing off, make a sudden loud noise from another room such as stamping your foot or slapping the wall. But be sure not to say anything. It's better if Pepe thinks that his own racket, not you, caused the noise. As soon as he whines again, make the noise again. Repeat as often as necessary.

✔ From the room next to the one Pepe is confined in, bang two metal pots together (once only) every time he barks or whines.

✔ Here's your last resort: Fill a spray bottle or a wimpy water pistol (not a high-powered one) and every time Pepe makes a racket, walk in silently and squirt him one time, directly in the face. Then walk out again. When Pepe is quiet for a minute or two, go to him without the water pistol and pet and praise him. Repeat as necessary. It won't be necessary long.

Pepe should always have a chew toy and something to snuggle under when he's confined.

Quieting a Barker

Of course, you want to scream when your barking dog drives you to distraction, but resist the urge. If you yell when Pepe barks, he thinks you're joining in. Then the excitement of leading his best friend in a bark-a-long eggs him on all the more.

Mouthing off at the door

Pepe needs to learn the word Enough (see Chapter 10), so you can appreciate his warning bark when a stranger comes to the door, but turn it off on command (see Figure 12-1). You can also use the Enough word to stop him from barking for attention. If Pepe wasn't taught to respond to Enough as a pup, try the wimpy water pistol method I discuss above. It usually does the trick. In rare cases where a wet face doesn't work, you want to try the following.

Hang a leash near the door so you can clip it on Pepe when he pitches a fit at the sound of the doorbell. On your way to the door, tell him "Enough" firmly but without raising your voice. Snap on the lead, and if Pepe is still mouthing off, give the lead a slight sideways jerk — just enough so he feels it. If it moves his body, you've jerked too hard. Release the pressure immediately and repeat "Enough."

While talking to the person at the door, jerk the leash slightly and repeat "Enough" as often as you need to, but don't lose your temper. Screaming makes things worse, and a hard jerk is dangerous to a Chihuahua. Besides, if you want a calm pet, it's up to you to set an example. Don't get exasperated and pick up Pepe either. All that does is make him feel even braver. Why? Because in your arms he's taller, and protected by you.

One of the best ways to cure a Chihuahua who barks like crazy at the door is to set up situations where friends bearing treats ring the bell. At the sound, put a leash on your dog, open the door, and invite the person in. Then give the Sit command, and as soon as your dog shuts his mouth and sits, have the visitor give him a treat. This system may take several tries, but eventually your dog finds out that the doorbell doesn't signal the boogydog.

Yapping for attention

If Pepe barks incessantly for attention, don't give in and cuddle him or he discovers how to manipulate a petting session whenever he wants one. Instead, either ignore him or use the Enough word — reinforcing it, if necessary, with your wimpy water pistol (one squirt only, right between the eyes). Don't let him see the shower coming. Pepe should think he triggered it by barking after he heard the word Enough.

Figure 12-1:
Cricket guards the entrance to *her* motor home, but quiets down on command.

Housetraining (After All This Time)

Because so much of housetraining is up to the owner, let me ask you a few questions. Does the cliche, "when all else fails, read the instructions," fit you? Did you set up a routine, as suggested in Chapter 10, and follow it without fail? Did you clean up every mistake right away (without using ammonia or yelling at your dog)? Did you praise Pepe every time he relieved himself in the right place? Did you give him an opportunity to go potty as soon as you got up in the morning, and every time you arrived home, as well as after every meal, nap, and play session (that's up to ten times a day)? Be honest with yourself. If your routine is haphazard, or you're not taking Pepe out often enough, it's you who are sabotaging housetraining. Get a crate, read Chapter 10, and start over.

Maybe it isn't your fault at all. If you did everything right and Pepe still leaves doggy-do on the carpet, keep the routine going, but add the following:

- ✔ When you come home, don't greet Pepe or give him any positive attention until after he eliminates in the proper place. Then praise the devil out of him.

- ✔ Learn to read your dog's bathroom language. Most Chihuahuas (and other dogs) circle several times before squatting. If your dog starts circling, pick him up and head for the potty place. Then praise him for going there.

- ✔ Control his intake of water (Careful! Dehydration is dangerous!). Give him free access to water during the day, especially with and after his meals and following activity, but take away his water dish about three hours before you go to bed. If it's hot in your house or if Pepe plays hard later in the evening, let him lap some ice cubes. That way he gets the liquid he needs without bloating himself.

- ✔ Crate Pepe when you go out without him — even for just a few minutes.

- ✔ When you are home, keep Pepe with you on lead until he's reliably housebroken. That way he can't sneak a whiz behind the sofa. It also gives you a chance to catch him in the act. If you do, keep calm, tell him "No!" emphatically (but don't yell), pick him up, and take him outside. Then tell him how wonderful he is for finishing the job in the right place.

Marking — it's a macho thing

Male dogs have an instinct to mark their territory and they use (you guessed it) urine to say, "This land is mine." It's a macho thing. While dogs think their scent warns male dogs to stay away and attracts the ladies, owners feel like bawling when their dog lifts its leg on table legs and bookcases. Neutering provides the quickest cure. Otherwise, just keep the housetraining routine going, crate Pepe when you're away and be patient. It *is* possible to house-break an intact (unneutered) male Chihuahua. But it takes longer.

Sometimes, just as you relax and congratulate yourself on your housetraining accomplishment, your dog reaches puberty, learns to lift his leg, and must be reminded of his manners. A few weeks of keeping Pepe on lead in the house, and confining him when you are away, is often all it takes to put him back on schedule.

Submissive urination

When you come home, does your dog greet you happily, but with a hint of shyness, while squatting and dribbling several drops of urine? That's submissive urination. Though often mistaken for a housetraining problem, it's really an anxiety problem, and has nothing to do with housetraining at all. The tendency may be inherited, or it may be caused by harsh or too-frequent corrections, or even by abuse your Chihuahua suffered before you got him.

Between wolves in the wild, *submissive urination* means, "Hi boss. Sure hope I didn't do anything to upset you, but if I did, I'm sorry." Though it happens most often during a greeting, that dastardly dribble may also occur when you bend over Pepe to pick him up, or when you chastise him. It's a conditioned reflex to *dominant treatment,* and your puppy isn't doing it on purpose. In fact, he doesn't know he's doing it at all.

Never chastise your Chi for submissive urination because that makes it worse. Instead, correct the problem by making homecomings low key. Toss a treat for Pepe the instant you arrive home, instead of bending over to pick him up. After he eats the treat, ignore him until he comes to you for attention. Then tickle under his chin or rub his chest (with your palm up), instead of reaching over his head or bending over him.

Teach Pepe a few easy commands so he learns how to please you and earn praise. Then use a simple command, such as Sit, when you greet each other. Now Pepe has a positive way to express his devotion and earn your praise. It's compliments from you that eventually break the submissive urination cycle. Being praised for a correct response builds confidence, and confidence is what Pepe needs to conquer submissive urination.

The easiest way to prevent a host of problems, including submissive urination, whining when confined, separation anxiety, and jumping, is to come and go without making a fuss. Long apologies before leaving and boisterous homecomings overstimulate many dogs. And excited dogs behave erratically.

Disregarding the Drop It Command

Pepe's a portable vacuum cleaner with the mouth muscles of Jaws Jr. How can you get him to release forbidden objects without prying his tiny trap open? First try taking him on a "shopping spree" (see Chapter 10). If he still refuses to drop taboo booty, put a drop of Bitter Apple on your finger, and slide your finger along his gum line as you give the Drop It or Out command (choose a command and use the same one every time). He soon discovers it's smart to let go. The "Trading for Treats" section later in this chapter offers yet another technique.

Humping (How Humiliating!)

Oh no! Pepe humped Aunt Amelia's leg during the family reunion. Why does he do these nasty things?

Rampaging males' hormones are more often to blame when Pepe embarrasses you by humping someone's leg or puts on a sex show with a throw pillow. Dogs don't have sexual inhibitions like people do, so when the scent of a female in season wafts by and stimulates their libidos, they try to satisfy their frustrations with whatever is available. Since legs are close enough to the right height and width, many dogs mount them.

Neutering cures many males of mounting and relieves their frustrations, making them better pets in other ways as well. But if humping is habitual, you may not notice a difference for a month or more after surgery.

While neutering (see Chapter 13) is the cure of choice, some of you may not want to neuter your Chihuahua, because you plan to use him for showing and breeding. Because dogs that mount legs are also displaying dominance (the urge to be boss), dealing with that may break the habit. The following methods have worked on many males, and they also cure females who are so dominant that they have a mounting habit.

Don't get angry with your dog to teach him who's boss. All that does is teach him aggression. Instead, start by withholding petting and praise until Pepe earns it. Make him work for attention by obeying a command (Sit) or performing a trick (see Chapter 16), and give him more exercise.

You'll soon recognize the signs when your dog's libido is becoming overactive. If Pepe heads for a leg with that telltale vacant look in his eye, distract him by using a command such as Sit to stop him in his tracks. Keeping a shaker can handy also helps. (That's an empty soda can with a few pennies in it and a piece of tape over the opening). If Pepe tries to attach himself to his favorite throw pillow or your spouse's ankle, break his focus by tossing the can so it hits the floor near him.

Adjusting a Possessive Pup

If Pepe has a tendency to be possessive, it may extend beyond the food dish (see Chapter 10). Some Chihuahuas (and other breeds) demand sole ownership of their favorite chair, their end of the sofa, or even their snuggle spot on the bed. And when anyone tries to sit in *their* spot, the resentful dog snarls a warning, and in some cases, even snaps. Granted, Chihuahuas tend to be sassy — but surly is unacceptable.

Preventing possessiveness

The same techniques both prevent and cure possessiveness (but prevention is always the best policy). At the first hint of possessiveness, make sitting on the furniture a privilege, not a right. Invite Pepe to sit beside you by saying, "Come On Up" and patting the sofa when you say it. Then lift him up beside you if necessary. At the same time, teach him to Get Down by giving that command while pointing at the floor. He learns the signal if you place him on the floor every time you say it. Eventually he jumps up and gets down on command under his own steam.

Changing your attitude

Is possessiveness already becoming a problem? Then change your own attitude first. Instead of taking the path of least resistance, like backing away when Pepe growls (which teaches him that growling gets him what he wants), resolve to take command of the situation. Read the "Dealing with Dominance" section earlier in this chapter and make Pepe work for every bit of attention. Use commands often, and give your dog affection and praise only for complying. If Pepe growls when he's on the bed, don't allow him on the bed. The same applies with the sofa, chair, or wherever he displays dominance (see Figure 12-2). After several days of making him earn attention, you can let him share your chair again. But only on your terms — by invitation only — from now on.

Figure 12-2:
Possessive dogs defend *their* chairs, but Tiko hopes her owner will join her.

Hard cases

If your dog has been boss for a long time, and is serious about biting when you try to reform him, don't try to deal with him yourself. A Chihuahua may be small, but he can still do damage, especially if he snaps at your face. Instead, ask your veterinarian to recommend a professional trainer or behaviorist. It's worth it. A good pro puts your relationship back on the right track and teaches you how to maintain it.

Young puppies can't jump up on the sofa themselves and shouldn't be allowed to jump down even if they want to, because they can damage their legs or shoulders. Using the cue words Come on up, and Get down, before your puppy matures is a good idea, but place him on the furniture and always lift him down.

Trading for treats

Some Chihuahuas become possessive over treasured objects (that's anything they have that you want to take from them; a pencil that fell off your desk, for example). Prevent possessiveness over objects by teaching Pepe what Out means.

Get a small plastic container with a lid, break up a few of your dog's favorite biscuits, and place them inside. Now shake the container, open it, and give Pepe one treat. Do that two or three times a day until the mere sound of the shake excites him. Then graduate to shaking the container while Pepe gnaws on his toy. Say "Out," give him a treat when he drops the toy, and walk away without touching the toy. After several days of this, pick up the toy when you give him the treat, hold it for a second or two, and put it down again. Soon you'll be able to get Pepe to open his mouth and trade you any object for a treat. When the object is a taboo item, keep it after making the trade. Then show Pepe his own chew toy. For an alternative method, see "Disregarding the Drop It Command," earlier in this chapter.

Reducing Separation Anxiety

Most mature dogs catch a nap when their owners leave the house, but some pitch a fit when they're home alone. They may chew on the carpet, shred the toilet paper, urinate, bark nonstop, or any combination of other destructive behaviors. You're probably thinking, poor owners. But believe it or not, the destructive dogs are miserable too. They have a problem called *separation anxiety*.

To understand separation anxiety in dogs (see Figure 12-3), consider phobias people have. Some people are afraid of heights, others are afraid of tight places, and still others are afraid of the water, or snakes or spiders. Well, dogs are social creatures, and some of them are afraid of being alone. They panic, pure and simple, then make noise or destroy stuff to release pent-up nervous energy.

Figure 12-3: Dogs hate to be left alone but most eventually get used to it within reason. Cricket looks out the motor home window, hoping to see her people coming back from fishing.

Exits and entrances

Some dogs seem to be born with tendencies toward separation anxiety. Others develop it after a major change . . . like their owner's divorce, or being given up for adoption. But a surprising number of dogs catch the problem from their owner. It sounds something like this:

"Oh, poor poor Pepe. I'm leaving now. Are you gonna miss me? Are you? I'm gonna miss you. Poor sweetums. You'll be all alone. (kiss, kiss) Now you'll be a good boy won't you? Give mama a kiss. That's my boy. Poor baby. I'll be back soon. I promise (kiss, kiss)."

And then the owner leaves.

Now what does Pepe make out of all of this? He just got a lot of attention and sympathy, and then his human left. Maybe she's not coming back. Maybe he'll never see her again. Maybe he'll never see anyone ever again. No wonder he feels anxious.

The best way to prevent separation anxiety is to make comings and goings low key. Ignore Pepe for ten minutes before you leave, and take him for granted when you return. That's easy. But what can you do for a dog that already suffers from the problem?

Alleviating anxiety

Let's start with what you shouldn't do. If Pepe becomes a demolition demon when home alone, the worst — yes, the absolute worst — thing you can do is punish him when you get back. All that does is give him additional anxiety. Instead of being scared only when you leave, he also is terrified of your return. That means double trouble.

Okay. You know you have a problem, so don't set up your dog for another dreadful day of demolition. Instead, crate him comfortably when you leave the house (Chapters 5 and 10). In addition to keeping him out of trouble, being in his own den may calm Pepe. Yes, I know, that's a just a quick fix and doesn't actually cure the problem. But it's a start. We have to start somewhere, and keeping Pepe out of trouble so he doesn't sense your aggravation is the best possible place.

Don't make the mistake of thinking your dog has human emotions. He doesn't tear up the house out of spite because you left him alone. And he certainly doesn't have fun doing it. Instead, he's miserable. Separation anxiety can be compared to a person with claustrophobia getting stuck in an elevator. Pepe needs help, not punishment.

Now that we have the destruction under control, let's work on alleviating Pepe's anxiety problem when he has the run of the house (or even a whole room). To do this, you must leave the house frequently for short periods of time. Eventually that teaches Pepe that comings and goings are unimportant because you always return. Here's how to set up your scenarios:

✔ Take Pepe outside to eliminate about 10 minutes before you leave.

✔ Turn on the radio and make sure two of his favorite toys are available.

✔ Leave Pepe's crate in its normal place with the door open, so he can go inside if he wants to.

✔ Don't say good-bye or reassure Pepe in any way. In fact, don't give him any attention at all for several minutes before you leave.

✔ Leave, close the door behind you, and count to ten. Open the door, go inside, and ignore Pepe for a minute or two. Then tell him to "Sit" and praise him for obeying.

✔ Gradually increase the amount of time before you come home. Make progress slowly at first. Take two weeks to go from 10 seconds to 10 minutes.

✔ If you find a puddle, or the beginning of any destruction, don't call it to Pepe's attention, but make a mental note of how long you were gone. Next time, decrease the amount of time you stay away. Then gradually work your way back up.

✔ With a lot of practice (and patience, too) you may be able to work your way up to spending a few hours away from home without Pepe having an anxiety attack. Unfortunately, it doesn't work with every dog. If your dog doesn't learn to accept separations, he may need professional help. Ask your veterinarian for referral to a behaviorist (if you're lucky, there may even be a Board-certified veterinary behaviorist in your area). The solution will include desensitization work, and may include a temporary prescription of a drug to help keep him calm as he completes his desensitization program.

If your dog used to suffer from separation anxiety but overcame it, put him in a reputable boarding kennel when you go on vacation instead of hiring a dog-walker or housesitter. Otherwise, your leaving home and not returning for a week or more could make him regress.

Part IV
Keeping Your Chihuahua Healthy

The 5th Wave   By Rich Tennant

Dr. Doug and his Chihuahua shared a unique companionship

C'mon Misty-scissors, scissors! That's a scalpel. You know that!

In this part . . .

Selecting a skilled and caring veterinarian is the most important step in keeping your Chihuahua healthy. This part shows you how to find that special person, how to make the most of your visits to the vet, and how to preserve good canine health at home.

Chapter 13

Visiting the Vet

....

In This Chapter

▶ Choosing your Chihuahua's veterinarian

▶ Covering all the essentials during a check-up

▶ Preventing problems

▶ Spaying and neutering

▶ Implanting permanent I.D.

....

Next to you, no one is more important to Pepe's health than his veterinarian. That's why choosing his vet is one of the more important decisions you ever make for him. This chapter helps you find a veterinarian you can to trust with your Chihuahua's life.

But it takes two to save a sick dog — one to diagnose the illness and prescribe treatment, and the other to follow up at home. Because the other is you, I help you become the kind of client every caring veterinarian wants — one who prevents problems whenever possible, sees the signs of sickness before they become severe, keeps calm (uh oh), remembers instructions, and carries them out exactly as prescribed.

Choosing Your Chihuahua's Veterinarian

By now you know that all dogs are not the same, and toys like Chihuahuas have special needs and sometimes specific problems. So you need a veterinarian who likes and understands Toy dogs. Depending upon where you live, you may have several excellent choices right in town, or you may have to drive 50 miles to visit the vet most of the Toy owners in your community trust. Near or far, picking Pepe's vet is a major decision. Someday his life may depend on the dog doctor's diagnostic ability.

Some of the better ways to find a good veterinarian are:

- ✔ Ask Pepe's breeder. If the breeder lives within a reasonable distance, try his or her vet first. Even if the breeder lives far away, he or she may have sold pups to other people in your area and can tell you how to contact them. Then you can find out which vet they use.

- ✔ When you see people walking Toy dogs in your neighborhood, ask them who they use and if they are satisfied with the quality of care.

- ✔ Call the nearest major veterinary referral hospital or the local or state veterinary association (find them in the phone book) for recommendations.

Let your mouth, not your fingers, do the walking when looking for a good veterinarian. Asking Toy dog breeders and members of the local kennel club beats looking in the Yellow Pages.

Evaluating your veterinarian

After you choose a vet with an awesome reputation and make the first appointment for Pepe, you must decide whether you're satisfied with your choice.

The right veterinarian will:

- ✔ Handle your Chihuahua with professional proficiency. Whether Pepe is everybody's pal or shy with strangers, your veterinarian handles him gently but firmly. The complete physical examination needs to be performed carefully but with practiced ease (see Figure 13-1). Steer clear of any vet who seems rushed or rough, or says or does anything that leads you to believe he or she may not like Chihuahuas.

- ✔ Weigh Pepe and take his temperature and a complete history, including where you got him, how long you have had him, his age, diet, vaccinations, wormings, activity level, appetite, and previous illnesses.

- ✔ Explain the examination and discuss the results with you — possibly giving you tips on how to improve Pepe's condition or keep him healthy over the long term.

- ✔ Answer your questions thoroughly in language you understand. Any vet who purposely talks over your head, or has an arrogant attitude, doesn't need you (or me) for a client. Good vets answer their client's questions in everyday language without talking down to them.

- ✔ Make provisions for emergency care during weekends, holidays, and the middle of the night. Some veterinarians handle emergencies themselves, while others refer their clients to a service that specializes in emergencies. If your vet opts for the service, make sure a vet knowledgeable in toys is always available.

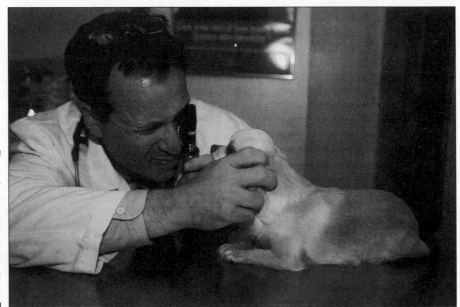

Figure 13-1:
Your
Chihuahua
needs a
veterinarian
who
likes and
understands
small dogs.

✔ Have a pleasant receptionist and staff, and a clean waiting room. (The exception is the small-town vet who cheerfully operates a tidy, one-person office.)

✔ Have an organized and well-equipped facility.

✔ Discuss fees. While most clinics expect you to pay for regular office visits right away, you may want to ask about their policy for unexpected, expensive emergencies.

✔ Be caring. If you sense coldness or indifference, Pepe's in the wrong place.

Being the best kind of client

If Pepe becomes seriously ill, it takes more than an excellent vet to cure him. It also takes you — a conscientious and composed client. A dog does best if his veterinarian and his owner work together to pull him through a crisis. Here's how you can be the type of client a veterinarian is glad to have on his or her team:

✔ Calling and making appointments for routine visits, such as annual exams and booster shots.

✔ Arriving on time.

✔ Not asking your veterinarian to diagnose Pepe over the telephone. Why? Because it can't be done. A variety of canine illnesses display similar signs. It takes a hands-on examination, and possibly some tests, to find out what's causing the problem and decide on the best method of treatment.

✔ Having an understanding attitude when the vet runs late because he or she had to drop everything to take care of an emergency.

✔ Knowing Pepe's normal behavior and calling the clinic immediately if something doesn't seem right.

✔ Bringing along a written list of recent behavior changes, if any exist (for example: excessive thirst, loss of appetite, change in activity level, unexplained fear or aggression).

✔ Bringing along the health and vaccination records the breeder gave you (on your first visit).

✔ Keeping Pepe on leash on your lap or in his crate in the waiting room. Don't let him play on the floor or sniff strange dogs. It's easy for pups to pick up germs.

✔ Being honest. When your veterinarian asks if your Chihuahua has been on any medication, don't be ashamed to admit you tried an over-the-counter medication from the pet shop. Admitting it may make you feel like a fool, but your vet has to know exactly what your dog ingested to make a correct diagnosis. Not only that, but mixing medications can be fatal.

Also, if Pepe seemed slightly sick for several days and you kept hoping he'd get better on his own, admit that too. Don't try to make yourself look better at your dog's expense by saying that you just noticed something wrong that morning.

✔ Making a list of your dog care questions and bringing it along. Vets are glad to answer appropriate questions about feeding, grooming, toenail trimming and anything else related to your Chihuahua's health; but they don't have time to listen to you ramble on about how Grandma Mildred thinks Pepe should be a TV star.

✔ Taking notes when the veterinarian gives instructions.

✔ Following instructions exactly. Medications must be given at the right time and in the correct dosage or they won't work. If you don't understand how to administer a medication, ask. Your veterinarian can explain or demonstrate.

✔ Staying as composed as possible, even during an emergency. The more serious the injury or illness, the more your veterinarian needs you as a clear-thinking partner in your Chihuahua's treatment.

No matter how frightening the emergency and how fast you want to get your dog to the vet, securing his crate so it doesn't roll or slide while you drive is of the utmost importance. The last thing a sick Chihuahua needs is a terrifying tumble.

> ✔ Not being argumentative or belligerent. Most vets care about their clients and understand how deeply people love their dogs. But they aren't magicians and can't guarantee that a badly injured or gravely ill dog will recover, no matter how skillfully they treat it. If you lose confidence in Pepe's vet, the best thing to do is change clinics.
>
> ✔ Paying your bills according to clinic policy.

Never increase the dosage of a medication (not even a little) hoping to make your Chihuahua feel better faster. Medication doesn't work that way. In fact, what cures at the proper dosage can kill when overdosed.

The When and Why of the First Exam

The best time for Pepe and his veterinarian to meet is within 48 hours after you acquire him. Although most puppies purchased from reliable breeders are healthy, the first examination is especially important for three reasons. First, your veterinarian either confirms that Pepe is healthy, or gives you the bad news if he isn't (we're talking major problems here, not a minor infestation of worms or a loose baby tooth that needs attention). If something is seriously wrong, finding it out while you can still return your Chihuahua is better than after you're hopelessly in love with a puppy so sick that it can never live a normal life.

The second reason why Pepe needs an immediate examination is so the clinic establishes a permanent record of what's normal for him (assuming he's fine). Then, if he ever shows signs of sickness, tests quickly disclose deviations. Besides, why not get to know your vet when Pepe is healthy, rather than entrusting your Chihuahua to a total stranger during an emergency?

The third reason for a prompt visit to the vet is that Pepe probably needs vaccinations, a checkup for internal and external parasites, and medicine to prevent heartworm. I tell you more about preventative medicine later in the section titled "Those vital vaccinations" and in Chapter 14.

Unfortunately, we don't always get to decide when to visit the veterinarian. In case of emergency, take Pepe to the vet ASAP. Speedy treatment is often the difference between death and complete recovery. Call the clinic first and explain what happened, so the staff can prepare.

Write down your dog's normal vital signs and keep them handy. Yes, your vet keeps a record, but Pepe may get sick while you're traveling together, and knowing what's normal for him helps the emergency vet make a better diagnosis.

Let's get organized

A checklist of what to do before your dog's first visit to the veterinarian includes:

- ✔ Feeding your Chihuahua a couple dog biscuits an hour or more before driving him to the veterinarian. That may keep him from getting car sick.
- ✔ Putting a roll of paper towels and a container of the wet wipes in your vehicle in case a quick cleanup is necessary.
- ✔ Taking along a copy of your dog's health record.
- ✔ Collecting a recent stool sample. (Some vets want you to bring one along the first time in a resealable plastic bag. Be sure to ask about that when making Pepe's appointment.)
- ✔ Transporting your dog in a crate
- ✔ Tying down the crate to make sure it doesn't take a tumble if you have to swerve or make a quick stop.
- ✔ Bringing cash or your checkbook. Veterinarians are paid at the time of treatment, and some of them don't take credit cards.

No coddling allowed

Even if the thought of Pepe getting a shot makes you cringe, don't let him know that. Be friendly with the veterinarian, not nervous, or your dog feels your tension and gets scared. Your ideal attitude is patient but matter-of-fact. Hold Pepe in place gently but firmly for the examination and talk to him in a happy tone, without letting sympathy creep into your voice. Consoling and coddling your Chihuahua only makes him sure something terrible is going to happen. Pepe takes his cues from you, so if he senses that you're relaxed and like the vet, he likes the vet, too.

Making the most of your first visit to the vet

Surely you have questions about dog care. The initial visit is the time to ask. Write your questions down at home as you think of them, so you don't forget anything. To get you started, here are a few questions new Chihuahua owners often ask:

✔ When is it safe to start taking my dog to public places?

✔ What do normal bowel movements look like?

✔ How often should my dog have a bowel movement?

✔ What is a good balanced diet for my Chihuahua?

✔ How often can Pepe have treats, and what makes a good treat?

✔ Does my dog need a vitamin and mineral supplement?

Those Vital Vaccinations

Modern dog owners are lucky. We don't have worry about losing our pets to the host of deadly diseases that wiped out dogs by the thousands just a few canine generations ago. Today, the main focus of dog care is preventative medicine. The vaccinations your veterinarian schedules are the best safeguards to keep Pepe from contracting a variety of potentially fatal diseases.

An allergic reaction to an injection is called anaphylaxis or anaphylatic shock. The sooner treatment to counteract the reaction begins, the better the chances of survival.

Extra precautions for Toy puppies

Don't be surprised if Pepe's vaccination schedule is different from the plan your friend follows for her Doberman Pinscher puppy. Chihuahuas and other Toy dogs are more likely than large dogs to have allergic reactions to some of the common combination vaccines. In fact, sometimes they come through their first vaccination just fine but then get sick from the second or third. That's why many vets separate the shots and give tiny dogs their parvo shot alone rather than in combination with other vaccines. The leptospirosis vaccination is also an issue with toys, so discuss it with your veterinarian. Depending on your lifestyle, it may not be included. If you plan to travel a great deal with Pepe, tell your vet, because exposure to strange dogs and new places may demand extra precautions.

Don't take Pepe on any outings until you're sure his puppy series of inoculations is complete. Following his puppy series, he needs a booster shot every year of his adult life.

If your dog is allergic to a vaccine, a reaction (swelling around the muzzle, difficulty breathing, or even collapse) usually occurs between 20 and 30 minutes after the shot. If you live far from the clinic, don't drive home immediately after your dog is vaccinated. Instead, stick around for an hour (read a book or listen to music in your vehicle with your dog on your lap). That way, immediate help is just seconds away.

What do those letters mean?

Although your Chihuahua may not get the whole combination in one shot, the most common vaccine given to dogs is the *DHLPP.* Here's what the letters mean.

D is for distemper

Distemper is the number-one killer of unvaccinated dogs and is highly contagious. Its victims are usually puppies, although older dogs may come down with it too. Because distemper manifests itself in various forms, it can be difficult even for experienced veterinarians to diagnose. Symptoms include some, but not all of the following: diarrhea, vomiting, reduced appetite, cough, nasal discharge, inflamed eyes, fever, convulsions, exhaustion, and lack of interest in toys, games, or attention. While dogs with distemper occasionally recover, they may suffer permanent damage to the brain or nervous system. Dogs that receive treatment immediately have the best chance of survival.

H is or hepatitis

Infectious hepatitis in dogs affects the liver just as it does in humans, but humans don't catch the canine form. In dogs, it spreads through contact with an infected dog's stool, saliva or urine. Intense thirst is one specific symptom, but all the other symptoms are similar to those of distemper. Hepatitis progresses rapidly and often is fatal, so prompt veterinary treatment is critical.

L is for leptospirosis

Leptospirosis (lepto) is caused by a *spirochete* — a microorganism that often is carried by rats. It can infect a dog that has contact with a rat, or eats something contaminated by rats. Symptoms include bloody diarrhea or urine, fever, exhaustion, red and congested eyes and mouth membranes, painful mouth ulcers, vomiting, increased thirst, loss of appetite, pain when moving, and the whites of the eyes may become red or jaundiced. Lepto can permanently damage the liver and kidneys, so prompt veterinary treatment is essential. Since humans can catch Lepto, it's important to keep from infecting yourself when caring for a sick dog. You vet will explain the proper precautions.

Although they are often referred to as permanent shots, don't believe it. No canine vaccine gives permanent immunity. That's why dogs get booster shots throughout their adult lives. Your vet recommends the proper schedule for Pepe.

P is for parvovirus

Parvovirus (parvo) attacks the stomach lining, bone marrow and lymph nodes, and in young puppies, even the heart. It is highly contagious and spreads through contaminated stools; easily encountered via dog paws or shoes. Beginning with depression or exhaustion and a loss of appetite, symptoms soon progress to vomiting, diarrhea (sometimes bloody) and fever. Puppies with infected hearts *(myocardial parvovirus)* often die suddenly or within a day or two of contacting the disease. Those few that recover may suffer chronic heart problems. How severely adult dogs are affected depends on the individual. Some dogs become extremely ill, while others just lose their appetite and lower their activity level for a day or two.

P is also for parainfluenza

Parainfluenza, also know as *infectious canine tracheobronchitis,* spreads rapidly from dog to dog. It is caused by several different viruses, as well as a bacteria. Symptoms are a frequent dry, hacking cough, and sometimes a nasal discharge. Other than that, the dog usually appears to feel fine, and many dogs infected with parainfluenza don't even miss a meal.

Dogs vaccinated against parainfluenza sometimes get it anyway, but usually have milder symptoms than unvaccinated. dogs. Although the disease usually runs its course, it is more dangerous to puppies than it is to mature dogs. They should be kept in a warm, humid room while recovering. No matter how old Pepe is, your veterinarian will probably prescribe antibiotics to prevent complications, and medication to control the cough. Whether Pepe is 9 weeks or 9 years old, see your vet right away if he starts coughing. It could be a sign of something serious.

You puppy's vaccinations must never be closer than two weeks apart. Three to four weeks apart is ideal.

Rabies

Rabies always is fatal. And a dog with rabies is a danger to humans and other animals. The disease is a virus that can infect dogs that come in contact with squirrels, cats, raccoons, skunks, foxes, bats, or other warm-blooded animals that already have the virus. It affects the nervous system, and is generally passed from animal to animal, or animal to human through infected saliva — usually from a bite. Rabies can also infect a victim through cuts or scratches that come in contact with saliva from a *rabid* animal.

One of the first signs of rabies is a difference in disposition. A gentle dog may act aggressive, or an independent dog may suddenly crave affection. Soon the dog's pupils may become dilated and light may seem to cause him pain. Eventually the dog won't want any attention and may develop stomach trouble and a fever. As the disease progresses its symptoms can include bared teeth, random biting, lack of coordination, twitching facial muscles, and loss of control of the facial muscles, resulting in an open mouth with the tongue hanging out. The dog's voice may change, and it may drool, paw at its mouth, and cough. Finally, it slips into a coma and dies. All warm-blooded animals are susceptible to the disease, so anyone bitten by a dog (or any other animal) needs to see a doctor right away.

Rabies vaccine prevents this dreaded disease. Your veterinarian gives the rabies shot separately, not in combination with other vaccines. Some rabies vaccinations are good for longer than a year, so ask your vet when Pepe's shot should be renewed.

Just say "No!" to deadly diseases

Sorry about all the gloom and doom, but for Pepe's sake, you must know the worst. The good news is that preventative medicine keeps your beloved Chihuahua safe from all those dastardly diseases. Just follow the vaccination schedule your vet recommends.

Besides the diseases you read about in the previous sections, your vet may also recommend vaccinations against *Lyme disease* and a viral diarrhea called *coronavirus*. Lyme disease (spread by the deer tick), is more of a danger in some parts of the country than in others. In addition, your Chihuahua needs to be on a regular program that prevents heartworm. I'll tell you more about it in Chapter 14.

Spaying and Neutering for Happier, Healthier Dogs

If showing in conformation (see Chapter 17) is not your game, the nicest thing you can do for yourself and your Chihuahua is have your dog spayed or neutered. Females spayed before their first season (usually around 6 months of age) are at much less risk of developing breast cancer than unspayed females. Because spaying removes the female's reproductive organs, spayed females never suffer cancers or infections of the ovaries or uterus. In addition, they don't have unwanted pregnancies, and won't drip blood all over your carpet and furniture for several days twice a year.

Spayed females also are nicer to live with. Their sexy scent won't entice males to serenade in chorus on your front lawn, and they won't suddenly develop a desire to roam. Spaying helps to keep a female's disposition consistent, and lets her participate in competitive events such as obedience and agility without taking three weeks off every six months (females in season are banned from performance events). In short, spaying Manchita when she is young gives her a healthier life, gives you fewer hassles, lessens the risk of a big dog mounting her, and doesn't add to the pet overpopulation problem.

Please don't breed your female Chihuahua so you can *get back your investment* or so your children can witness the miracle of birth. A beloved female may need an emergency Caesarean section, or even die giving birth, leaving you with traumatized children and orphan puppies. And as far as your investment goes, any emergency results in big vet bills, and raising even healthy puppies is an expensive endeavor.

Neutering your male dog before he's a year old can save him the pain of prostate problems, including cancer, when he ages, and it makes him easier to live with. Here's why:

Male hormones make dogs desire every female in season whose scent wafts by on the wind, and some of them perform Houdiniesque feats to escape and find the female. Male hormones also make dogs more aggressive toward other dogs and are often implicated in housetraining problems, such as scent marking (when the male lifts his leg and urinates on objects inside the home to stake out his territory). Frustration (also caused by male hormones) is what may make Pepe embarrass you by making love to Aunt Amelia's leg during Thanksgiving dinner. While neutering won't immediately cure a frustrated, dog-aggressive, escape artist with a housetraining problem, it eliminates the production of male hormones and almost always starts him on the road to improvement.

Don't believe it!

Several myths and old wives tales started long ago about spaying and neutering, and every one of them is wrong. Here's the real story:

✔ Spaying or neutering does *not* make a dog fat and lazy. Overfeeding and lack of exercise do that. The truth is, spayed and neutered pets are often the top performers in competitive events. Neutered males can keep their minds on their work, and spayed females can compete throughout the year without losing several weeks because of being in season. In fact, almost all service dogs (hearing dogs, guide dogs for the blind, and dogs that help the physically handicapped) are spayed or neutered.

✔ Spaying or neutering does *not* prevent a dog from being an alert watchdog. Neutered males concentrate on their home better than males that have the scent of sex on their mind. And spayed females alert to strange sights and sounds every bit as quickly as unspayed females.

✔ Comedians and cartoonists often get laughs by implying that males dogs are sad or resentful about being *castrated*. But in reality, dogs don't have human feelings about romantic love and sex. Males never miss the hormones that made them feel frustrated and constantly steered them toward trouble, and females don't feel unfulfilled because they didn't have a litter. In fact, spayed and neutered dogs usually become closer to their human families. And that's where dogs really want to be.

An I.D. for Your Dog

The traditional form of doggie identification is a tag inscribed with the owner's name and telephone number that is attached to the dog's collar. With luck, this is enough so that the nice family down the block sees to whom Pepe belongs if he ever wanders out the door unseen. But collars can come off, and tags can get lost, so here are two newer and better methods to discuss with your veterinarian. They ensure you that Pepe carries his I.D. all the time.

Sporting a tattoo

No, we're not going to decorate Pepe's handsome bod with hearts or eagles. *Tattooing* is a relatively painless procedure that permanently places a number on the inside thigh or groin area of a dog's back leg — out of sight unless someone looks for it. Animal shelter personnel and other humane workers know where to look to find a dog's tattoo. The most convenient number you can have tattooed on Pepe is his American Kennel Club registration number. Then, if Pepe is found, his number can be traced to you instantly through the AKC's records. If your Chihuahua isn't AKC registered, there's another excellent option. Have your social security number tattooed on your dog. Enroll Pepe in the AKC's Companion Animal Recovery program and/or the National Dog Registry (see Appendix B). Both organizations are amazingly apt at reuniting lost dogs with their owners. Ask for enrollment information when you have Pepe tattooed or *microchipped*.

If you want to have your dog tattooed and your veterinarian doesn't offer the service, contact your local kennel club. Sometimes dog clubs conduct tattooing clinics where a veterinarian or a trained club member tattoos pets for a reasonable fee. Even if your local dog club doesn't offer the service, the members can tell you where they have it done.

Computer-age I.D.

The modern method of permanently identifying dogs is the microchip. This tiny device (about the size of an uncooked kernel of rice) is encoded with identification information and implanted under your dog's skin (usually at the juncture of the neck and the withers) by your veterinarian. The procedure is similar to receiving a vaccination.

If Pepe becomes lost and ends up in a shelter, a device called a scanner reads the microchip and identifies him. Although more and more humane facilities are acquiring them, the problem remains that not all of them own a scanner yet. To be on the safe side, have Pepe microchipped, but use another form of identification as a backup.

Home again and more confused than ever

You and Pepe visited your vet for the first time and now you're home again, filled with new information — some of it different from what you read in this book. What should you do? Who should you believe?

Trust your veterinarian. This book is a general reference, meaning that it contains good, solid information about Chihuahua's in general. But your dog is an individual who just had a thorough examination, and now you have personalized instructions. Follow them. They were meant especially for Pepe.

Chapter 14

Debugging de Dog

*A*host of creepy-crawlies are looking for a free lunch and a cozy condo, compliments of your Chihuahua. Some prefer camping under a tent of hair, while others set up housekeeping indoors and homestead in the intestines, bowels, and even (horrors!) the heart. In this chapter, I unmask these intruders and tell you how to protect your dog from parasitic invasions.

The dictionary defines a *parasite* as an organism that relies on another living thing for its survival but contributes nothing to the host organism. That's true as far as it goes, but many parasites do contribute something in a negative sense — they hand their hosts an array of afflictions.

Turning Worms Away

Don't be embarrassed if Manchita gets intestinal worms. No matter how carefully you care for her, she can still become infested with them. Heartworms, however, are a different story. Those deadly dependents are preventable, so if Manchita is unlucky enough to be diagnosed with them, someone screwed up. Here's the poop on the low-down critters that may try to munch on Manchita.

Heartworms

Heartworms are transmitted from dog to dog by mosquito bites. As the worms mature inside the dog (a process that takes about eight months), they migrate to the heart and lungs. There they interfere with heart action, eventually killing their canine host. Symptoms include a chronic cough, weight loss, exhaustion, and eventually death. Whatever you do, don't wait for symptoms. Prevention is the only defense, and it must start as soon as you get Manchita and must continue all her life.

If you acquire Manchita as a puppy, ask your veterinarian to put her on a heartworm prevention program. You may be offered a choice between giving the medication daily or monthly. Either schedule is effective provided that you stick to it without fail. Depending on where you live (the length of your mosquito season), you must keep Manchita on medication anywhere from seven months at a time to year-round.

Even after she's on preventative medication, your Chi still needs an annual blood test for heartworms. Why? Because prevention is the best thing going, but it isn't 100 percent perfect (and neither are we, the people who have to remember to give our dogs pills). The annual test is critical, because if a dog already has heartworms and takes preventative medication, the combination can be fatal. In fact, if you acquire Manchita as an adult dog, your veterinarian must give her a blood test before prescribing preventative medicine.

A single heartworm can grow up to 14 inches long.

What if you acquired Manchita as an adult and she tests positive? Now that's a real bummer. On the plus side, you caught it while she's still breathing — and where there's life, there's hope. Treatment needs to start immediately. Unfortunately, the procedures to rid a dog of heartworms are dangerous, although less dangerous than the deadly worms. Many (but not all) dogs survive the treatment. Good luck. Once your dog is heartworm-free, rely on preventative medication to keep her that way.

Roundworms, hookworms, whipworms, and tapeworms — Yuck!

Many puppies are born with *roundworms,* and some get hookworms from their mothers' milk. In fact, your Chi can pick up one of several species of worms, including *hookworms* and *whipworms,* when simply out for a walk. She might even ingest a *tapeworm* while nipping at the flea that suddenly sprang from the grass and landed on her well-groomed back Fleas play host to tapeworms. So what can a dog owner do?

Prevention through clean quarters and quick removal of internal parasites is the best policy, and works best if started as soon as you get your puppy. In addition to vaccinating Manchita (see Chapter 13), and putting her on a heartworm prevention program, your veterinarian also needs to examine her stool to find out if she has intestinal parasites.

The symptoms of roundworms, whipworms, tapeworms, and hookworms are similar, and include dull eyes; a rough, dry coat; weakness; weight loss despite an enormous appetite; coughing; vomiting; diarrhea (sometimes bloody); and a big belly (all the time, not just right after eating). Most dogs have only two or three symptoms, while others totally lose their appetites when harboring worms. Occasionally a dog may have no symptoms at all but then suddenly becomes severely anemic from a heavy infestation. Hookworms, for example, are bloodsuckers, and can kill a dog as tiny as a Chihuahua puppy within weeks.

Don't try to diagnose and worm your Chihuahua using over-the-counter medications. Many symptoms of worms also are signs of other serious illnesses. Not only that, but different worms demand different treatments. Likewise, the amount of medicine is determined by your dog's weight, and the medication is downright dangerous if misused.

On the brighter side, getting rid of intestinal worms is a routine veterinary procedure. If your veterinarian discovers that any of these worms are living inside Manchita, he or she may give her a shot or prescribe medication. A follow-up treatment also will be scheduled. Don't overlook or reschedule the follow-up visit, because timing is important.

After Manchita checks out negative for worms, take a stool sample to your veterinarian at least twice a year (three times the first year). That way, if it comes up positive, you'll get rid of the new worms before they become overwhelming and endanger her health.

Giardia

Giardia are found in lakes, ponds, and other outdoor water sources. Chihuahuas seldom contact Giardia because the *protozoans* (one-celled microscopic organisms, not worms) are most often ingested by thirsty hunting dogs, and dogs accompanying backpackers — not comfort-loving critters like Chis. After a dog ingests them, Giardia chew on the inner lining of the small intestine. Naturally this creates irritation, which is accompanied by inflammation, stools coated with mucous, weight loss, diarrhea, and bloating. If you travel with Manchita, Giardia are one more reason to carry water from home. But dogs can also pick up the protozoa from licking an affected dog's stool (yes, sometimes dogs do yucky stuff like that). If Manchita gets diarrhea after eliminating at highway rest stops, let your vet know that Giardia is one possibility. Prompt treatment is important.

Coccidia

Coccidia, another protozoan, lay their eggs in animal's stools. And (yes, I have to repeat it), dogs sometimes get up close and personal with poop. Once inside Manchita, coccidia line her intestinal tract causing watery stools, bloating, straining during elimination, vomiting, weight loss, and sometimes a streak of blood on the stool. Is there any good news? Yes. Coccidia are easily diagnosed by your vet, and quickly eliminated when treated early.

Parasites that live inside their hosts are called *internal parasites*. Those that stay on the skin are called *external parasites*. For example, worms are internal parasites, while fleas are external parasites.

Controlling the Externals: Fleas, Ticks, Mites

Fleas, ticks, and a mixture of mites are the more common external parasites that annoy and endanger dogs. In the following sections, I explain what you need to know to keep Manchita safe from a variety of bloodthirsty bugs.

Defeating the terrible tick

I'm going to give you the good news first. If you walk Manchita in the sunshine during the warm months, and keep her away from tall grass and profuse plants, chances are she won't pick up any ticks. Why? Because like Dracula, these bloodsuckers, prefer darker areas, especially the woods. But occasionally ticks appear in unexpected places, and because they are so dangerous, your best bet is to check Manchita's body daily from late spring through the end of summer. It takes several hours for a tick to do its dirty work, so if you remove ticks quickly, your dog probably won't come down with any of the dire diseases ticks can cause.

When checking for ticks, pay special attention to Manchita's head, face and neck, and the inside of her ears. Those are the tick's favorite lunch counters. Another choice spot is between the toes. But a tick can cling to any part of Manchita's body, so run your fingertips everywhere — up and down her legs, under her pits, and down her back, sides, belly, and tail. It sounds like a big job, but you can easily complete the whole exam in a minute. Now aren't you glad you chose a Chihuahua?

If you find an attached tick, don't try to pull it off by hand. The safest way to remove ticks is with a preparation recommended by your veterinarian. If you are far from a veterinary clinic and don't have a preparation on hand, remove the tick with a tweezers. Some pet shops sell special tweezers just or that purpose, but unless you live near the woods and have to remove ticks often, the tweezers in your medicine chest will do just fine.

First separate Manchita's hair so you can see where the tick embedded itself in the skin. The embedded part is the tick's head. If you have rubbing alcohol handy, put a drop of it right on the tick. That makes some ticks release their hold. Then use your tweezers to clamp down as close to the head as possible and pull it out. Sometimes part of the head remains under the dog's skin after you use the tweezers. If that happens, apply an antiseptic.

If you're sure you removed the tick within an hour or so of when it attached itself, Manchita's probably home free. But it's a good idea to keep the tick in an escape proof container so your vet can identify it in case Manchita shows signs of sickness. Watch her closely for the next couple of weeks and take her to the vet if something seems wrong. You'll know the signs after you read the next few paragraphs. They tell you all about the many miseries ticks carry.

Dogs seldom get all, or even half, of the symptoms that a particular disease can cause. If you found a tick on your dog within the last two weeks, just one or two symptoms of a tick-related illness warrant an immediate trip to the veterinarian.

Tick Bite Paralysis

The American *dog tick* (sometimes called *Eastern Wood Tick*) and the *Western Mountain or Rocky Mountain Wood Tick* all inject toxins into their hosts through their saliva. Early signs of sickness are weaknesses, fever, a change in the dog's voice, vomiting, dilated pupils, and lack of coordination. These symptoms are followed by paralysis, difficulty breathing, and death.

Rocky Mountain Spotted Fever

This deadly disease is brought to your dog by the same ticks that can cause paralysis, *Rocky Mountain Spotted Fever* occurs when a tick injects a particular protozoan under the skin. Signs of this disease are a high fever, a tender abdomen, water retention (look for swollen legs and feet), blood in the urine or stools, nosebleeds, difficulty breathing, and general weakness. Symptoms may not show up until two weeks after the tick bite.

Lyme Disease

Transmitted in the Northeast by the deer tick, in the West and Midwest by the California black-eyed tick, and in the South by the black-legged tick, Lyme disease occurs when a carrier tick transmits a particular bacterium into a dog (or person) through its saliva. An estimated 50 percent of deer ticks are carriers. These ticks are also more difficult to find on your dog because they are small. The good news is that they must be attached for nearly two days before infection can occur.

A dog with Lyme disease may become lame, depressed, weak, and feverish, suffer painful joints, and be reluctant to move. If you live in a rural area known for having a large population of deer ticks, your veterinarian may suggest vaccinating Manchita against Lyme disease.

Lyme disease has currently been diagnosed in 47 states. It also attacks people, so check yourself and your dog after a walk in the woods. A preventative vaccine for humans is available, and is probably a good idea if you live near a wooded area. Ask your doctor about it.

Fleas are no circus

I wish I could offer you a quick and easy method for getting rid of fleas, but unfortunately, eliminating fleas never is easy . . . not even with all the new formulas that are marketed every year. The truth is fleas quickly become resistant or actually adapt to insecticides. That's why new flea dips, powders, and sprays appear on the pet shop shelves annually.

With flea prevention, earlier is better. Those bad little buggers are capable of producing another generation every 21 days, and one female can produce thousands of eggs in her lifetime. Not only that, but they itch something awful, often cause an allergic reaction that turns into an oozing *hot spot,* and can carry tapeworms.

Dogs react to fleas in a variety of ways. A dog with a fleabite allergy is miserable with just one or two fleas on her, while another dog may have a severe infestation without even bothering to scratch. Chances are, Manchita will let you know when she has fleas. Most Chihuahuas scratch themselves silly when a flea bites them.

The only way to control fleas is to eliminate them not only from your dog, but also from inside and outside your home . . . and from your car and RV if Manchita travels with you. This is best done by interrupting their life cycle through an insect growth regulator (commonly called a *flea tablet),* that your dog eats once a month.

Once your dog has fleas, your house does too, so you'll also have to treat your home and yard. That's because fleas don't live on dogs all the time — they just feed on them and ride around for awhile. Then they hop off and camp in the carpet, dog bed, or grass until they get hungry and hitch a canine ride again. Meanwhile their eggs hatch, go through four larval stages, and hop back on Manchita when they mature.

Flea tablets are prescription medicine, and insecticides for the home and yard must be used with great care . . . especially when you own the smallest of all breeds. Don't try to come up with a flea management program on your own. The use of more than one product often is necessary, and your veterinarian knows which ones can be safely used at the same time and which products become toxic when combined. If you're like me and prefer natural products instead of parasiticides, tell your veterinarian.

An easy test for fleas in the house

Finding out if your home has fleas is easy. Fill a large, shallow pan with water and add some liquid dish soap. Before retiring for the night, put the pan on the floor and place a desk lamp right next to it with the light cocked over the water. After you go to bed, and the lamp is the only light on in the house, fleas will jump at it, fall in the water, and sink immediately, because dish soap makes the water soft. If you find drowned fleas in the pan the next morning, you know your home has been invaded. Some people set this flea trap every night during the summer and say it's a big help in controlling fleas.

Your vacuum cleaner is your best friend when fighting fleas. Besides inhaling the adults, it also sucks the eggs and larva right out of the carpet and upholstery. Vacuum every room often when fighting fleas. Just be sure to throw away the bag away when you finish. A mature flea is a match for Houdini.

Managing mites

A myriad of microscopic bugs, including one commonly called *walking dandruff,* feed on the skin, blood, and even hair of the dog. Manchita may never be bothered by any of them, but it's smart to be familiar with the symptoms. Chances are your dog doc will do a skin scraping (it's painless), to find out what kind of mite is making Manchita miserable. Don't try to diagnose and treat skin problems yourself. Some of them have such similar symptoms that even your vet won't be sure without a test, and each mite demands different medication.

Saracoptic mange

Saracoptic mange, sometimes called the *scabies,* is caused by crab-shaped mites that literally get under your dog's skin. After burrowing in, they sip Manchita's blood, mate, and lay eggs. These mange mites make Manchita itch. Symptoms are relentless scratching, tiny red bumps, and patchy crusted areas. Visit your veterinarian before Manchita suffers hair loss or a bacterial infection. Scabies responds to medication.

Follicular or demodectic mange

Commonly called *red mange,* follicular or *demodectic mange* is caused by a different type of mite. Because itching is a symptom in some dogs but not in others, look for small, circular, moth-eaten-looking patches. They are usually found on the head, or along the back, sides, and neck.

In young dogs, red mange is often stress related. Anything that produces anxiety — such as going through the hormonal changes of adolescence, or staying in a boarding kennel for the first time — can trigger a minor outbreak. So, do mites crawl around with miniature blood pressure cuffs so they can tell when a dog is stressed out and launch an attack? Not exactly. The truth is, most dogs have some of these mites on them all the time and never have a problem. But when they are under stress, their defenses break down and the result is a small patch of demodectic mange (sometimes called *juvenile mange*). It is easily treated by your veterinarian.

Generalized outbreaks of red mange are another story. If Manchita or Pepe ever gets a case of mange that covers much of their body, have them spayed or neutered (if they aren't already). Never breed a dog with a generalized case of mange — the disease and its misery can be passed on to the puppies. Severe cases of *demodex* are treatable, but the treatments are much more intense, may include antibiotics, and should be performed at the veterinarian's office.

Few house pets get lice because the bugs are spread through crowded conditions. But a dog from a shelter or pet shop could come with lice. These bugs live on the hair shaft and symptoms include itching and patches of thinning hair. Getting rid of them is quick and easy. Your vet can tell you how.

Ear mites

Does Manchita continuously scratch her ears or shake her head? She may have ear mites. These critters move into the ear canal and proceed to eat the outer layer from the walls of their cottage (yup, that's your dog's skin). Wipe gently inside the ear with a cotton ball. If it comes out with rusty-brown or blackish goop on it, Manchita has mites. They are easily treatable when caught early, so see your veterinarian.

Walking dandruff

Yes, this mite has a real name. If you want to remember or pronounce *Cheyetiella,* may the Force be with you. But to return to earth, does Manchita try to turn her body into a circle so she can nip and nibble along her spine? Does she lie on the rug upside down and wiggle around in an effort to scratch her back? Have you noticed an abnormal amount of flaking when you groom her? Those signs all point to walking dandruff, a mite that devours the skin along a dog's spine (and sometimes other places too). Your veterinarian can get rid of these itchy critters, but it may take several treatments. You'll have to clean all your dog's bedding and favorite rugs too.

Chapter 15

Recognizing Signs of Sickness

- -

In This Chapter

▶ Watching carefully when Pepe is off stride

▶ Handling emergencies

▶ Popping pills

▶ Understanding ailments specific to Chihuahuas

▶ Keeping an old dog comfortable

▶ Facing the facts of life and death

- -

*A*lthough prevention is the best plan when it comes to health care, being perceptive and prepared run a close second. That's because the sooner you seek help for a sick dog, the better his chance of recovery. This chapter helps you sense the earliest signs of sickness. It also describes some hereditary ailments that occasionally inflict Toy dogs, and shows you enough first aid, so that you can act in an emergency until professional help is available. With luck, this chapter has more info than you'll ever need. I hope you never have to use it, but it's here for you just in case.

One section of this chapter I do hope you have to use. It's about taking care of a golden oldster. We all hate seeing the signs of aging in ourselves or our pets. Yet, as the cliche goes, getting old is a whole lot better than the alternative. So don't let a little gray on your dog's muzzle depress you. Your sassy senior can enjoy a high quality of life for many years, and this chapter helps you keep him in super shape.

Finally, I'll discuss the most painful fact of life — death. Losing a precious pet is heartbreaking enough without having to make sudden decisions, so I'll discuss options such as euthanasia, and different methods of caring for the body. I've also included some info on the stages of grief and healing. Finally, I end on a happier note — bringing another dog into your life.

TIP

The average dog's temperature is between 100°F and 102.5°F. He has a pulse rate of between 80 and 120 beats per minute, and takes 20 breaths per minute.

Reading the Signs of Sickness

Many signs of sickness in Chis, although subtle at first, are symptoms that you may sense rather than actually see — the way you instinctively know when something is troubling your spouse or your child. So if something seems wrong, but you can't figure out what it is, don't chalk it up to an overactive imagination. It's probably an early warning, which is the best kind because quick treatment, before your Chihuahua weakens, has the greatest chance of success.

Years ago, when I showed American Staffordshire Terriers, I had a female named Frankie who bounded over obedience jumps with several inches to spare. One day, at a Chicago show, she seemed a little less spirited than usual during breed judging but still started the morning on a high note by winning Best of Breed. Later on, she also earned a qualifying score in open obedience competition; however, I noticed that she just cleared the jumps with no room to spare. I wanted to attribute her sedate attitude to a muggy Midwest afternoon, but it nagged at me on the long drive home.

The next morning, I called the vet for an appointment, telling him only that something about Frankie didn't seem quite right. It turned out that she had a uterine infection. Caught early, it was easily cured, but if I had waited for more evidence of illness, her problem might have become serious. What's the moral of the story? No one knows your dog better than you do. If something doesn't seem right, even though that *something* doesn't appear in this chapter, trust your intuition and take Pepe to the vet for a checkup.

Wait and see (but not very long)

Some problems often go away on their own, but Pepe needs medical attention if they continue longer than 24 hours: If your Chihuahua has any of the following symptoms, watch him carefully:

- Refusing to eat anything at all but having no other signs of sickness.

- Limping, or refusing to put weight on one of his legs, yet eating normally and showing no obvious signs of a fracture or other pain or sickness.

- Changing personality or activity level but exhibiting no other signs of pain or sickness.

- Mild diarrhea. The stool is loose but not liquid, and doesn't have any blood in it. No signs of straining or stomach pain.

- Vomiting two or three times but showing no other signs of sickness (lots of perfectly healthy dogs vomit after eating grass).

✔ Scratching or nipping an itchy spot or two but not hard enough to break the skin.

✔ Drinking and urinating more than usual but showing no other signs of sickness.

 To take Pepe's temperature, use a rectal thermometer with a rounded end. Shake it down below 100 degrees Fahrenheit, smear it with petroleum jelly, and insert it carefully, between one and one-and-a-half inches. Talk soothingly while holding Pepe firmly, in a standing position, for two minutes (don't let him sit). Remove the thermometer and check the reading. Normal temperature is between 100 degrees and 102.5 degrees Fahrenheit. Disinfect the thermometer before putting it away.

Call your vet now

If Pepe has any of the following problems, call your vet and explain the symptoms in detail. You'll probably need a same-day appointment.

✔ Refusing to eat and seeming depressed or lethargic. May also be suffering from stomach pain.

✔ Suffering an eye problem. This includes excessive tearing; eye swollen shut or partially shut; or an eye that looks cloudy or off-color.

✔ Breathing that is labored, or fast and shallow. May or may not be in combination with a cough.

✔ Vomiting frequently combined with depression or exhaustion.

✔ Incessant diarrhea. A liquid stool, combined with a terrible odor and possibly pain and straining.

✔ Swallowed an object but isn't choking. A swallowed object can turn into a life-threatening problem if Pepe can't pass it. The sooner your vet assesses the situation, the better.

✔ Swelling on any part of the body. It may feel hard and hot to the touch, or be infected and oozing.

✔ Suffering injuries like a deep puncture that can become infected, a cut that needs to be stitched, or severe lameness with no indication of a fracture.

✔ Scratching and/or biting at the skin until it is inflamed, with possible hair loss brought on by intense itching.

Emergency!

A real emergency is a situation so scary that Pepe needs the attention of a vet immediately — no matter if it's Sunday, New Year's Eve, or three o'clock in the morning.

Emergencies resulting from accidents include:

- Broken bones
- Heavy bleeding
- Severe trauma (possibility of internal bleeding and/or shock)
- Burns from fire, scalding, or chemicals
- Poisoning

Emergency illnesses include:

- Seizures
- Staggering and/or falling down
- Uncontrollable diarrhea (sometimes bloody)
- Frequent vomiting
- Breathing problems
- Allergic reactions
- Obstruction in the throat (choking)
- Obstruction in the intestine or urinary tract (straining to eliminate)
- Paralysis
- Heatstroke
- Bloat (extremely rare in Chihuahuas)

Emergency situations demand the service of a veterinarian ASAP. In the meantime, handling Pepe properly until he's in the hands of a pro is important. Keeping calm is the hardest part. If a wave of panic doesn't rush over you when you first see your sick or injured pet, you're stronger than I am. But panic won't help Pepe, so take a deep breath and resolve to stay calm and think straight. Then get to work.

First Aid and Transportation

If Pepe ever has an emergency, call your veterinary clinic (or its emergency number) immediately and tell the receptionist (or whoever answers the phone) what happened. That way, the clinic can prepare for Pepe's arrival. Then give him first aid and transport him to the clinic. Unless the clinic gives you other instructions for transporting your Chihuahua, put him in his crate with a lot of clean, soft bedding, secure the crate in your vehicle so it won't slide or roll, and drive to the clinic.

Be careful when handling a dog that's in pain or panicking. He will bite.

Heavy bleeding

Use a pressure bandage (not a tourniquet) to control heavy bleeding or blood spurting from any part of your dog's body. It's best if you have a helper, so one person can keep the pressure bandage on Pepe while the other one drives to the clinic.

With clean hands, apply direct pressure to the wound by holding a gauze pad firmly against it for 30 seconds. If bleeding continues, apply a second gauze pad on top of the first and continue applying pressure. With Pepe wrapped in a clean towel and one person carrying him and holding the gauze pad(s) in place, go to the veterinary clinic.

If you don't have a helper, wrap a wide adhesive bandage around the wound and the gauze pad, put Pepe in his crate with a towel or blanket around him, secure the crate in your vehicle so it won't slide or roll, and head for the clinic. If the clinic is many miles away and the adhesive bandage is around one of Pepe's legs, stop and check the foot below the bandage after half an hour. If it is swollen or cold, loosen the bandage but leave the gauze pad in place.

Resist the urge to clean or wipe a wound while it's still bleeding. Stopping the bleeding is the first priority and cleaning the wound often makes it bleed even harder.

Choking

If Pepe paws at his mouth, drools, seems unable to close his mouth, coughs, tries to vomit, strains for breath by stretching his head and neck, or appears frantic he may be choking.

If Pepe is getting enough air to sustain himself, put him in his crate and take him to the clinic immediately. If he appears on the verge of passing out, or if his tongue is turning blue, first wedge something (the handle of a small screwdriver works well) between the top and bottom molars on one side of his mouth to keep it open. Use a flashlight, or put him under good lighting, and look into his mouth and down his throat. Pull his tongue straight (careful, he may try to bite) to see if the offending object is on top of it. If you find the problem, remove it with your fingers or long-nosed pliers. If all else fails (you can see the wedged object but Pepe can't catch his breath), hold him upside down by his hind legs and shake him. With luck, that will dislodge the object so he can breath again. Visit the vet anyway. Pepe just suffered a major trauma.

If you suspect that your Chi has been poisoned either by ingesting or inhaling poison, absorbing a toxic substance through the skin, or by injection (snake, scorpion, or spider bite), get professional help immediately. If you are far from a vet, call the National Animal Poison Control Center hot line at (900) 680-0000. The fee is charged to your phone.

Can't catch breath

If Pepe is gasping for air, or his tongue is turning blue, or his breathing is loud and labored, or he's not breathing at all, you don't have a second to spare. If he is getting enough air to sustain himself, transport him to the vet immediately in his crate. But if he isn't breathing, start mouth-to-nose resuscitation right away. Here's how:

1. First try the methods recommended under "choking" above.

2. If Pepe still isn't breathing, lay him on his right side on a table. Close his mouth and tilt his head back.

3. Keeping Pepe's mouth closed, place your open mouth over his nose (you can do it through a handkerchief if you prefer) and breathe five or six shallow (short) breaths into it. Of course you're terrified, but try to control your breathing. Your dog is so small he doesn't have much lung capacity. If Pepe starts breathing, you've saved his life. Now take him to the vet for observation.

4. If Pepe still isn't breathing, keep giving him mouth-to-nose. Try to give him approximately 20 shallow breaths per minute. When he starts breathing by himself, go to the clinic. Keep trying for a full ten minutes. If breathing doesn't resume by then he's probably dead, but at least you'll know you did everything possible to help him.

Broken leg

When transporting a dog with a broken leg (or any broken bone), your job is to get him to the clinic without making the injury any worse by moving it. Steady the limb (without pulling on it) by wrapping absorbent cotton around the entire leg. Then use gauze bandage, held in place with adhesive, to keep it from moving during transport.

Dogs don't sweat. The only way they can regulate their body temperature is by panting.

Heatstroke

Symptoms of heatstroke include rapid or heavy breathing, a bright red mouth and tongue, thick saliva, unsteadiness and possibly falling, diarrhea, vomiting, a hot and dry nose with legs and ears hot to the touch, and complete collapse, often combined with glassy eyes and gray lips.

To save your dog, you must start cooling him immediately — even before you call the clinic. First take him to a shady or air-conditioned place. Then soak a towel in cool (not ice) water, wring it out, and apply cold compresses to his belly and groin. Next, lay the cool towel on Pepe's back and gently wet his head with it. Let him drink a small amount of cool water at intervals, not all he wants at one time. If he's too weak to drink, wipe the inside of his mouth with the water. Now call the clinic, put the cold, wet towel in the bottom of his crate, and take Pepe to the vet.

While most emergencies are the result of bad luck rather than bad management, heatstroke is absolutely preventable. Please don't overexercise Pepe on a muggy day or leave him alone inside your vehicle. The temperature inside a car or truck, even one parked in the shade, is usually 25 degrees hotter than outside the vehicle. Every year hundreds of pets die from being left alone in parked vehicles for just a few minutes.

Popping Pills

It usually takes two people to give a Chihuahua a pill. With your helper holding Pepe firmly, open his mouth and place the pill as far back on the center of his tongue as you can. Then hold his mouth shut while tilting his head upward (careful, don't cover his nostrils). Stroking his throat gently may induce him to swallow. After Pepe swallows, look inside his mouth to make sure the pill went down.

Liquid medication is easier on both of you, so opt for it if your veterinarian gives you a choice. Use an eyedropper to give Pepe liquid medication. Lift his lips slightly and place the eyedropper in the back corner of his mouth, where the upper and lower lips form a pocket. Now hold his head up and his lips shut and squeeze the eyedropper. Keep holding Pepe's muzzle, tilting it slightly upward until you are sure that he swallowed. Gently stroking his throat may help.

Chihuahua Considerations

While Chihuahuas have fewer genetic defects than many breeds (maybe because so many breeders try hard to eliminate problems), no breed is perfect. In the following sections, I tell you about some idiosyncrasies — a few serious but most not — that are sometimes seen in Chihuahuas and other Toy breeds.

Subluxation of the patella

In dog lingo, this defect is called *slipped stifles* or loose kneecaps. When it occurs, the kneecap (we're talking about the rear legs) slips out of it's groove — sometimes often and sometimes rarely — depending on the severity of the problem. If your dog is one of the unlucky few whose kneecaps slip often, surgery may be the solution. A dog with a mild case can live a normal life, kind of like a person with a *trick knee. Subluxation of the patella* is a relatively common problem in small breeds and some large ones as well.

Hypoglycemia

Hypoglycemia means low blood sugar and is a common problem in young Toy breed puppies, although most of them grow out of it before they are old enough to leave the breeder. But for a few, it's a danger throughout their lives.

Symptoms of low blood sugar are a staggering gait, glassy eyes, and sometimes either limpness or rigidity. If the dog doesn't receive immediate help, he can suffer seizures, unconsciousness, and finally, death. Treatment involves putting some sugar in your dog's mouth, calling your veterinarian, and heading for the clinic. Once you know your dog has a tendency toward hypoglycemia, you can prevent further attacks by changing his feeding schedule to small amounts several times a day and avoiding sugary treats (check the ingredients before buying dog treats). Too much sugar in his food can put Pepe on a roller coaster ride of sugar highs and lows rather than keeping his blood sugar nice and level.

If you get your Chi used to taking delicious liquid from an eyedropper, administering liquid medication becomes a cinch. Occasionally melt a teaspoon of vanilla ice cream, put it in an eyedropper and give it to her just as if it was medicine.

Collapsing trachea

Collapsing trachea is a problem for Toy dogs of many breeds. The symptoms include coughing, shortness of breath, and exhaustion. Although it appears more often in dogs older than 5 years, an occasional puppy has it from birth. To understand the condition, think of the trachea as a straw made of cartilage that carries air from the neck to the chest. When the cartilage collapses, breathing becomes difficult, kind of like sipping soda through a flattened straw.

Your vet can treat the condition with medication, but if you smoke, your Chi's prognosis may be poor. Secondhand smoke is a proven contributing factor to the problem . . . and smoke tends to settle low, where a little dog's nose is.

Heart murmur

Heart murmurs are relatively uncommon in Chihuahuas and even those that have one usually have the functional type. As in people, that means they can be as active and athletic as they want and live long, normal lives.

Molera

The Chihuahua's molera (a.k.a. fontanel) is considered a breed characteristic and not a defect. Most Chihuahuas (80 percent to 90 percent) have a *molera* — a soft spot on the top of their head similar to a human baby's soft spot. But unlike babies, most Chihuahuas don't outgrow it. Although it usually shrinks as the dog matures and ends up between nickel- and dime-sized, Pepe's molera won't be a problem as long as you're gentle when petting or handling his head.

In rare cases, the molera remains quite large and can be a sign of a serious problem called hydrocephalus (see the next section). But don't borrow trouble. Hydrocephalus has several other signs besides a larger-than-usual molera.

Hydrocephalus

A dog with *hydrocephalus* (a.k.a. water on the brain) may have an unusually large head for his size caused by swelling. Other signs of this fatal condition are frequent falling, seizures, a lot of white showing in the eyes, an unsteady gait and east-west eyes (the opposite of crossed eyes). A dog with hydrocephalus is in pain and won't live long, so euthanasia is the humane solution.

Euthanasia is the medical term for a humane, vet-assisted death.

Going under anesthesia

The possibility that your dog may someday need anesthesia is one main reason why you need to choose a veterinarian who is accomplished in treating Toy dogs. Although deaths from anesthesia are rare, and usually the result of an allergic reaction, its use is potentially dangerous. Your vet uses anesthesia only when necessary (before surgery, for example).

Be sure to read about how to clean Pepe's teeth (see Chapter 7) so that cleaning them under anesthesia isn't necessary. And when your dog has to go under anesthesia (during spaying or neutering, for example), ask your veterinarian if any necessary dental work (such as pulling impacted baby teeth) can be done at the same time.

Be sure your vet uses one of the modern gas anesthetics. They are much safer than the old fashioned intravenous products.

Watch those eyes

It's certainly not a *condition,* but because Chihuahuas have big eyes and live close to the floor, they are more prone to eye injuries than a lot of other breeds. Put several drops of saline solution in your dog's eye if the injury seems minor. That's often all it takes to flush out a foreign object that was accidentally kicked up by someone's shoe. If that doesn't relieve the problem, or if the injury appears more serious, take Pepe to the vet.

Keeping Your Senior Sassy

Oh no! Pepe's getting gray hairs. Even though he's healthy and still in his prime, seeing the first signs of aging is scary. But it doesn't have to be. Keeping your oldster healthy and happy isn't hard at all. If you are lucky enough to share your life with a golden oldie, you can help him feel feisty by keeping his infirmities in mind.

Aid for your aging dog

Dogs age much like we do. Even though Pepe led a worry-free life, one of the first signs that he is becoming a senior is sprouting gray (white) hairs (see Figure 15-1). They appear first on his face, encircling his eyes and giving his muzzle a grizzled look. Don't let them spook you. Chances are your Chihuahua will have gray hairs for several years before feeling the first creaky joint of old age.

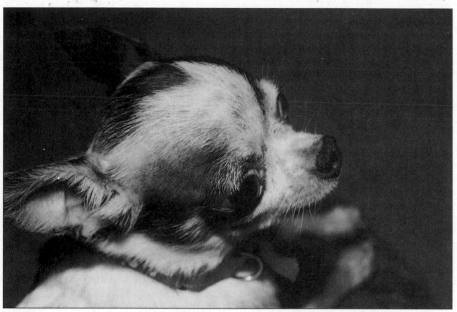

Figure 15-1: Manchita is 11 years old in this photo. Notice her gray and thinning hair and compare it to her 2-year-old picture in Chapter 1. But nothing else has changed, and she still plays like a pup.

Other signs of aging are dental problems, including the loss of teeth. Eventually Pepe may no longer be able to crunch his kibble (dry food). One solution is to soften it by soaking it in warm water for several minutes and mixing it with canned meat. If Pepe develops kidney trouble (or other organic or allergic problems) your veterinarian can prescribe an easily chewed food made especially to ease such difficulties.

While recovering from an accident or illness, or when suffering the dental problems that could come with old age, your Chihuahua may welcome baby food. You'll find boxes of rice cereal and jars of strained meats in the baby food section of the supermarket. A combination of rice cereal and strained meat (warmed slightly) may entice your dog to eat when nothing else works.

Older dogs often are even less tolerant of cold than puppies, so be sure Pepe has a warm sweater for outings, keep him away from drafts, and put an extra baby blanket in his bed. And speaking of his bed, he may start spending more time in it, preferring an afternoon nap to a brisk walk. We've all heard the saying "use it or lose it," and that advice applies to dogs as well as people. Pepe still needs his exercise, although don't expect him to take part in strenuous activities. Make your walks together leisurely instead of lively, and when playing indoor exercise games (see Chapter 11), don't be surprised if he shuffles rather than speeds through the house. No matter what speed Pepe chooses, playing helps him stay mentally sharp and keeps his muscles oiled too. Not only that, but exercise helps him avoid obesity.

Aching joints and other signs of aging

Arthritis often attacks older dogs and although nothing cures it, your veterinarian may be able to provide relief. Other ancient Chihuahuas may not have severe enough cases to require medicine but may need a little help at home. If Pepe can't jump on and off the sofa anymore, lift him up and down. Same with the stairs. And if he can't reach his traditional easy chair when he's home alone, make sure he has a place to nap and stay warm while you're away. Either build a ramp so he can reach his favorite spot, or place a doggie bed by it.

If Pepe were an older person, he might need bifocals and a hearing aid. The problem is, they don't make them for dogs. So if your Chi always came when you called him, and then suddenly starts to ignore you, chances are he has a hearing (not a behavior) problem. And if he was on the same elimination schedule for a dozen years, and then starts waking you up at 4:00 a.m. to take him outside, he's not just looking for attention.

Pepe may become a crotchety old codger too, detesting even minor changes and become unwilling to make new friends (perhaps because of failing senses or twinges of arthritis). Report sudden changes in routine and disposition to your vet. Many problems can be relieved. Others can't, and some of them probably bother you more than they bother Pepe. After all, dogs don't agonize over the signs of aging like people do. As long as Pepe still enjoys life (and isn't suffering severe pain), he'll be happy as long as you love him.

Problems peculiar to aging are treated by the branch of medicine called geriatrics, and gerontology is the study of aging in people or their pets.

Coping with the Death of a Pet

We often know in advance when death is threatening our pet, but sometimes dogs die without warning, leaving us not only saddened, but shocked. Complicating the process are the decisions we may have to make concerning euthanasia and a final resting place. Understanding these options in advance may make things a little easier.

Is euthanasia ever the best ending?

Euthanasia is the best ending if Pepe is in severe and constant pain with no hope of recovery. It consists of a lethal dose of a strong anesthetic humanely administered by your vet. The injection puts your dog to sleep instantly and stops his heart. Only you can decide when the time is right, but it won't be as hard as you think. Trust your instincts. They tell you when ending your dog's misery is the most merciful thing you can do for him.

After you make that painful decision, the receptionist asks if you want to leave your dog or stay with him during the procedure. Staying may be harder on you in the short run but is best for most of us in the long run. Take care of all the paperwork first, so you won't have to handle it through your tears. Then hold Pepe in your loving arms while the vet administers the injection. That way you'll know for sure that your dog didn't suffer, and he will die peacefully, nestled against your chest.

Do you get over it? Well — no. You'll probably always miss Pepe. But some day you'll be able to talk about his antics without a tear in your eye or a catch in your throat. Instead, you'll smile as you relate some of your favorite Pepe stories. And you'll know that the good times you had together will never be gone. They'll always remain in your mental bank of happy memories.

Handling your dog's body

Many people choose to leave their departed pet's body at the veterinary clinic. Usually the clinic notifies a service, which picks up the body and cremates it. Several dogs are usually cremated at the same time, and the *cremains* (ashes) are buried in the earth. Don't be shy about asking your vet how he or she will dispose of the body. Some clinics have their own facilities for cremation, and others have different procedures.

Let him die while he's living

One of the saddest sights I ever saw was an ancient Chihuahua lying on her side in a puddle of urine, her hind legs and tail soiled by feces. Sadie's owner loved her too much to have her put down. When the owner had to spend a couple days in the hospital, she asked my friend to care for Sadie, warning her that the poor puppy (Sadie was 16), couldn't stand up anymore and would have to be cleaned up and force fed. My friend asked me to come along on her first visit, and although we expected it to be bad, it was worse than we expected. We bathed and dried Sadie, cuddled her, pushed prescription pills down her throat, got some strained chicken down her the same way, gave her water from an eyedropper, and covered her with clean blankets. Through it all, Sadie's expression remained blank. Her spirit was gone, leaving her miserable shell of a body behind. Please don't love your dog so possessively that it makes you selfish. To paraphrase a Jimmy Buffett song, let him die while he's living, not live when he's dead.

Private cremation is another option. It may be handled at either a pet cemetery, a private pet crematorium or your veterinary clinic. Then you can keep the ashes in an urn; bury them; or scatter them in a place your pet loved.

Some people prefer to bury their dogs in their own yards. You can mark the spot with a beautiful perennial plant. That's an excellent option, provided that it's legal in your area. If not, pet cemeteries offer regular burials, and these can be as simple or as elegant as you choose (and can afford). Because not all pet cemeteries are created equal, look for one that is neat, clean, and has been around for a long time.

Finding Ways to Heal

Shock and disbelief, anger and alienation, denial, guilt, and depression are all stages of grief, and most of us go through every one of them, although not always in that order. To help yourself through these painful stages, you need to:

- ✓ Understand that mourning the loss of a beloved dog is natural. Pepe wasn't "just a dog." He was your dog. You had a strong bond with him, and broken bonds cause broken hearts.

- ✓ Take time to mourn. Don't tell yourself to "get over it," and then bury your grief so deep that it eats you up from the inside. No guidelines exist for working through the stages of grief. Some of us need more time to mourn than others.

- ✓ Make a few changes in your habits and decor. Put Pepe's bed, bowls, crate, and toys out of sight. Take his treats out of the cookie jar and his leash off the hat rack. Since walking him was probably one of the first things you did each morning, create a new morning routine.

- ✓ Talk about your feelings. First find an understanding ear — someone who also adored Pepe or who loves their own dog deeply — and discuss your feelings of loss. Many cities have support groups that help people through the pain of losing a pet. Ask your vet for a recommendation.

- ✓ Read a book about pet loss (see Appendix A for some suggestions).

- ✓ If Pepe's death was preventable, forgive yourself but learn from it. Maybe you didn't feel up to walking him one morning so you turned him loose "just that one time" and he ran in front of a car. Or maybe you lost track of when his booster vaccination was due and he caught a deadly disease. If you caused Pepe's death you're probably beating yourself up with guilt. But that won't bring him back. Instead, face what you did, learn from it, and go on. Give Pepe's death meaning by resolving never to make that mistake again. After all, none of us are perfect pet owners. We're just people who love our dogs but are occasionally prone to poor judgment.

Don't use Pepe's death to make a point to your children. Even if you had to nag Julie when it was her turn to walk Pepe, resist forever any urge to say something like, "If you hadn't made Pepe wait so long to go potty, he might not have had kidney failure." Grieving kids need compassion, not guilt.

- ✔ If you have other pets, give them extra attention.

- ✔ Consider getting another dog. No, not a replacement. It's impossible to replace Pepe because he was an individual and no other dog will be just like him. But you can love other dogs, as long as you don't expect them to act like Pepe. If you think you'll have a problem with that, buy a different color Chihuahua or a different breed entirely. That helps you learn to love your new dog's unique personality.

Resolution

Helping your spouse and your children cope with the loss of their pet can be soothing to you at the same time. One of the ways families come to terms with the finality of the situation (and then go on) is by combining their efforts and creating a memorial ceremony for their dead dog. You can do this regardless of whether you have remains to scatter or a body to bury, and it can be performed indoors if you don't have a yard.

Explain the ceremony to your family as a celebration of Pepe's life and all the joy he brought to your family. Then ask each one to think of why they loved Pepe, or something funny that he did, and tell it during the ceremony. (Youngsters who have a problem expressing themselves may want to begin their contribution with "Thanks, Pepe, for . . . .") Before the ceremony, the family may want to go out together and choose a plant (indoor or outdoor, depending on the situation) in Pepe's memory.

Sometimes sadness may sweep over you at work, and your co-workers may notice. If they ask you what's wrong and you don't want to talk about it, or you aren't sure how they feel about pets, just tell them you recently lost a good friend. After all, it's the absolute truth.

In the days that follow Pepe's death, don't be afraid to say that you miss him in front of your family. Encourage your kids to talk about their feelings, too. Look at pictures of Pepe together, and recount his hilarious escapades. Tell the kids (more than once) that Pepe will always be part of them, because the good memories they have of him are theirs forever.

If you're going to get another dog, never refer to it as a *replacement*. Tell your children that Pepe can't be replaced, but learning to love another dog is okay too. In fact, some say the greatest honor you can give your dog is to love another of his kind.

Part V
Taking Your Chihuahua on Stage

The 5th Wave   By Rich Tennant

"Oh, we've got to nip this little trick in the bud right away."

In this part . . .

So, your Chihuahua is (as we all know) the cleverest canine this side of Broadway! It's time to teach that dog some tricks and take your show on the road. Chapters 16 and 17 give you the basics. All that you, Manchita, and Pepe have to provide is pizzazz. Curtain up!

Chapter 16

Teaching Your Dog a Trick or Two

C lose your eyes and visualize Manchita greeting people with a paw shake, waving hi and good-bye, asking for a cookie (or better make that a taco?), even dancing on her hind legs while you whistle the Mexican Hat Dance. Does that image make you smile? Good. Manchita loves showing off and it surprises you how fast she learns. So what are you waiting for? Put some treats in your pocket and call your Chi. In this chapter, I show Manchita enough tricks to tickle your family and friends.

Motivating Manchita

Chihuahuas like learning tricks. After all, during training they have what they want most — your full attention, plus praise and treats. Manchita thinks trick training was created just to make her feel special, but you reap rewards too. Besides having fun and impressing your friends, teaching Manchita to perform tricks enhances her vocabulary, encourages closer bonding, and leads to better behavior.

Another advantage to trick training is that it makes your Chihuahua an impressive ambassador for her breed. Many people believe tiny dogs are brainless and lack character, but a Chi that waves and barks "Hi" changes their thinking in a hurry.

Besides all those benefits, once a shy Chi learns how to pull off a trick or two, she has something other than fear to focus on in social situations. And making people laugh improves her confidence.

Pushing Your Dog's Performance Buttons

Let's talk motivation. The happier Manchita is about learning a new *move* the faster she perfects it. So if you're a good motivator, she can be a terrific trickster in no time.

Praising Manchita works only when your tone is sincere and maybe a little silly — okay, mighty silly with some dogs. Praising your pet in a drab monotone won't turn her on. In fact, colorless compliments stimulate her about as much as elevator music excites you.

How can you make the praise so powerful that Manchita wants more? Give it with gusto. Give your Chi a big smile when you say, "Good girl." If she's a little lethargic, accentuate your praise with a little applause. Use joyful words that come naturally to you and say them in an excited voice every time Manchita willingly gives her trick a try. Don't become boring by using the same praise words and treats every time. Sometimes, surprise Manchita with new words, "Way to go, girl!" "All Right!" "Yes, Yes!" Scratch her back. Give her a taste of cheese, a sliver of hot dog, a bite of burger, or. toss a toy. Manchita never knows exactly what her reward will be when she does something right, but she sure wants to find out.

Read your Chihuahua's reactions to rewards. Your praise should make her eager to continue the lesson. Don't make it so shrill that it scares her, or so invigorating that it distracts her.

Soon you discover which phrases inspire Manchita to try harder, which treats she finds most tempting, and whether she'd rather chase a squeaky toy or have a back rub. Those are Manchita's buttons. Pushing them makes her happy, and when she's happy she's willing to try the trick again — do it with more pizzazz — learn to perform it on cue. And as a result, that makes you happy too.

Putting Manchita in the mood

Because treats are an important part of trick training, try to train when Manchita is hungry — before, not after, her meals. Before beginning a training session, take her outdoors and give her an opportunity to relieve herself.

When you get back inside, let Manchita watch you prepare and pocket some treats. Now that you've got her undivided attention, start with something she knows. Have her Sit for a tidbit. That sets the tone and puts her in a cooperative mood to learn her first trick. Don't try trick training until Manchita sits on command (see Chapter 10). That's a prerequisite to most tricks.

Using praise and treats

When teaching tricks, use praise and treats or toys to motivate Manchita, and don't bark out, "No!" when she makes a wrong move. When she does something right, reward her. When she does something wrong, or does nothing at all, don't reward her. It's as simple as that. Neither force nor punishment is ever involved.

Reward every correct move, no matter how tiny or tentative, when your dog is learning something new.

Shaking Hands or Gimme Five

As soon as the Sit command is second nature to Manchita, you can teach her to Shake Hands or Gimme Five (see Figure 16-1). Be creative. It doesn't matter what verbal cue you use as long as you use the same words every time.

Kneel down to Manchita's level after she sits and say the cue words. Then pick up one of her forelegs, lift it from underneath, and gently release it. Praise Manchita as soon as you drop her leg, and give her a tiny treat. Repeat the process five times, then try it again later, or tomorrow. After Manchita is comfortable with you picking up her leg, gently move it up and down before releasing it. The big breakthrough comes one day when Manchita lifts her leg as soon as you say the cue word. Let her know how happy you are.

Gradually wean Manchita away from expecting a treat every time she gives you five, but always tell her what a good girl she is. And even after she performs reliably for praise, surprise her with a treat occasionally. After she has this trick down pat, have family and friends practice it with her (but not more than five tries at a time).

Figure 16-1:
Glad to
meet you,
Manchita.

Waving Hi and Bye

After Manchita shakes hands as easily as a state senator, you can start teaching her how to wave. Use your cue words and ask her to shake hands. Then, just as she lifts her paw, pull your hand away while repeating your cue words ("Yes," for the handshake) in a happy voice. Most dogs wave their paw in the air in an effort to make contact with your hand. The instant Manchita waves even a little, say "Wave," and give her a treat. Keep at it, making her wave just a microsecond longer each time before she gets her reward. When she waves well, eliminate asking for the handshake by going directly from "Sit" to "Wave." Finally, wean Manchita off the treat by giving it once every few times. But continue praising her for every wave.

It's also fun holding your Chihuahua at chest level in both hands and asking her to wave at someone. You can teach it the same way, except that you'll need a helper. Hold Manchita while your helper walks up, asks her to shake hands, and then pulls their hand away to elicit a wave. Some Chis wave with both front legs when in their owner's arms (see Figure 16-2).

Use the command Wave instead of the obvious Hi or Good-bye because it's more versatile. Besides cuing your Chihuahua to Wave Hi and Wave Good-bye, you can personalize the trick by telling her to "Wave to Aunt Amelia."

Figure 16-2:
Chiquita
waves with
both paws.

Speak and Shhhhh

You'll have to get silly to teach your Chi how to Speak. Start by showing Manchita her favorite treat. Wiggle it right in front of her but don't let her take it. Instead, get her all wound up by teasing her with it. As she prances around, say "Speak" excitedly, over and over. The object is to get Manchita to make a sound (any sound). When she does (even if it's a wimpy squeak instead of a full-fledged bark), give her the treat and plenty of praise. After she eats the treat, try again. Stop after five tries no matter how much fun she's having.

It won't be long before Manchita makes the connection and barks as loud as she can when you say "Speak" and show her the treat. That's a good start. Continue using the treat until you have to say "Speak" only once. Gradually wean Manchita off the treat, just as you did when teaching her to shake hands. The real fun begins when you get creative. "Speak to Me." "If you want a cookie, Speak." "Speak to Aunt Amelia." "Speak Spanish."

Some Chihuahuas anticipate this trick and begin barking before you say the cue word. Every time Manchita tries that, tell her "Shhh," and don't give her the cue (or the treat) until she quiets down and stays quiet for several seconds. After a while, she'll learn that "Shhh" means hush — an extra bonus that may come in handy.

Dancing the Tango

Chihuahuas make marvelous dancers with moves that are the envy of larger breeds. To teach Manchita the tango (or the waltz, jitterbug, two-step, or mambo), turn on your favorite tune or hum a few notes. Hold a treat several inches above her head and say, "Let's dance." The object is to get her to walk a few steps on her hind legs, so move the treat forward slightly after she rears up.

When Manchita realizes what you want, it may take several weeks until her leg and back muscles are developed enough to let her dance on her hind legs for several seconds. As soon as she balances on her hind legs rather well, start moving the treat in a circle above her head to teach her to turn. Soon she pirouettes in either direction.

What do you do with a dancing dog? Join in, of course. As your Chihuahua swings and sways on her hind legs, start moving to the music along with her so you're dancing together. Having a partner encourages her to make up steps of her own. She may soon add hops, skips, and jumps to her repertoire.

Chapter 17

Showing Your Chihuahua

. . . .

In this Chapter

▶ Making sense of judging

▶ Keeping score at the show

▶ Deciding whether this game is for you

▶ Beginning to show

▶ Talking like a dog show expert

. . . .

*I*f you want to see more than a hundred breeds of gorgeous dogs gathered together in one place, treat yourself to a dog show. Besides seeing beautifully groomed and trained representatives of all your favorite breeds, you'll also become acquainted with rare breeds that few people ever get to see.

Dog shows are fun regardless of whether you understand the judging procedure, but a little knowledge makes your first experience more rewarding. In this chapter, I tell you about the basics of dog judging, so you understand what the exhibitors and judges are doing. Then I give you the upside and the downside of the *dog game* and help you get started if you want to be a player.

Unentered dogs are not allowed at dog shows, so leave your Chi at home when you go to a show. Instead of a dog, put a notebook on your lap and jot down your impressions of why certain dogs won. Later, when and if you get into the dog game, dig out that notebook and read what you wrote. Your first impressions may help your handling.

Understanding How Dogs are Judged

Dogs don their finest fur when competing at a dog show, and with so many gorgeous creatures to choose from, your first reaction may be to pity the poor judge. But the judge has help in the form of guidelines called the *breed standard* (see the Chihuahua standard in Chapter 2). The standard describes an *ideal specimen* of the breed, and the judge's job is to select as the winner, the dog that most closely conforms to this written description of physical perfection. In other words, no matter how many dogs compete in the show ring, the winner should be the one that most closely resembles the ideal dog described in its breed standard, second place goes to the next closest dog, and so on.

When watching a show, you see dogs of the same breed judged together early in the day. But later, you see the winning dogs of each breed competing against each other. That's when novices really get confused. After all, how can a judge choose between an animated Chihuahua and an elegant Pekingese? Bet you know the answer already. The judge isn't really comparing the Chihuahua to the Pekingese. Instead, the judge is comparing how close the Chihuahua matches its breed standard with how close the Peke matches its own standard.

When exhibitors compete at dog shows, they say they are showing their dog in *breed* or *conformation*.

An elimination contest

Shows where dogs are judged on their conformation are actually elimination contests. To begin with, all the dogs of a single breed (or variety of a breed) compete with others of their sex in one of the regular classes — Puppy, 12-to-18-Month, Novice, Bred-by-Exhibitor, American-bred, or Open. Next, first-place winners of the same sex from each of the above classes compete against each other for Winners Dog and Winners Bitch. These two *winners* are awarded points toward their championship (see "Becoming a Champion," later in this chapter) and return to the ring for *Best of Breed* (or Variety) competition. Dogs that are already champions are called *Specials* and they also compete for Best of Breed or Variety.

Three awards are presented in the final elimination contest at the breed level. The top specimen is awarded Best of Breed or Variety. The best dog of the opposite sex than the Best of Breed is presented the Best of Opposite Sex (BOS) ribbon. And, the best of the two class winners is named Best of Winners (BOW). Sometimes a class dog (a dog that isn't a champion yet) goes to the top and takes Best of Breed or Variety as well as Best of Winners.

When Chihuahua judging is complete, all but the Best of Variety winners are finished for the day. The Best of Variety Chihuahuas are eligible to compete in the Toy group. That's where all the Toys that won Best of Breed or Variety compete for group placements.

Following group competition, only seven dogs — the first place winners from each group — are left in the show. During the climax, they compete for Best in Show (BIS). When the show is over, only one undefeated dog remains — but a couple hundred dogs may have earned points toward their championship, and many others thrilled their owners by placing high in their classes.

Group Classifications

For purposes of showing, the American Kennel Club (AKC) divides dogs into seven groups as follows:

Group 1	Sporting Dogs
Group 2	Hounds
Group 3	Working Dogs
Group 4	Terriers
Group 5	Toys
Group 6	Non-Sporting Dogs
Group 7	Herding Dogs

Only two Toy breeds, the Chihuahua and the English Toy Spaniel, are represented by two varieties in the Toy group. The two Chihuahua varieties are long coat and smooth coat. Two other Toy breeds, the Manchester Terrier and the Poodle, also come in varieties, but only the Toy Manchester Terrier and the Toy Poodle compete in the Toy group. Their larger counterparts compete in other groups.

Becoming a champion

To become an AKC champion, Pepe must win 15 points, including points from at least two major wins (majors are shows where three or more points are awarded). The two majors must be awarded by different judges and at least one of the remaining points must be won under a third judge.

The number of points Pepe may be awarded for going Winners Dog at a show varies. It depends upon how many Chihuahuas competed, the schedule of points established by the AKC, and whether he goes on to win Best of Winners, Best of Variety, the Group, or even Best in Show. The most points ever available at a show is five, and the fewest is one, so Pepe must win points at a minimum of three shows to earn a championship. But five-point majors are few and far between, and competition is keen, so most Chihuahuas are shown several times before becoming champions.

When a dog *finishes its championship,* it is permanently recorded as a champion of record and is entitled to the word *Champion* before its name. The AKC abbreviation is *Ch* as in Ch Pepe.

Winning or Losing — It's the Judge's Call

Your first experience with subjective judging may make you feel a little confused while you watch the competition. Most of the better-known sports are judged objectively. During games of baseball, basketball, football, golf, or tennis, you always know the score. But it's different at dog shows, where winning or losing depends on the judge's opinion. This can be confusing at first, especially when you see a dog go Best of Winners one day and not even place in its class the next day.

The more you learn about canine conformation and the Chihuahua standard (what it means and why those attributes are important), the better you'll understand how each judge picks his or her winners. One judge may be a stickler for movement. Another may be swayed by a superior head. Because judges interpret the standard in their own unique (and individual) ways, different dogs may win under different judges. And that's a good thing, because it lets many excellent dogs have their days.

Dogs are also judged *on the day,* or to be more precise, in a moment of time — something like the way we judge ourselves when we confront our image in the mirror each morning. On Saturday, you may smile and congratulate yourself on looking years younger than you really are, but then on Sunday you may appear drawn and weary. Well, dogs have good days and bad days too, and the judge can only go by what dogs look like during the few moments they're exhibited. So if the owners of yesterday's Best of Breed Chihuahua kept superdog up too late while they celebrated, he may look like sleepydog during the next day's competition.

Many people hire professional handlers (agents) to show their dogs. If you decide to hire a handler, choose one who has an excellent reputation for taking care of and winning with Toy dogs.

Deciding to Show

All hobbies have their good points and bad points. Some of the things, both positive (upside) and negative (downside), you may want to consider before deciding if you want to show dogs are listed below.

Charmed — utterly charmed

Americans traveling through Mexico during the mid-1800s, occasionally visited the ruins of a castle that was believed to have belonged to Montezuma, the last Aztec emperor. It was located near Casas Grandes in northern Mexico. A few American tourists were so charmed by the tiny dogs owned by some of the locals that they bought puppies as souvenirs. The dogs had large ears, long nails and a soft spot (molera) in the middle of their heads, all typical of today's Chihuahua.

When the little lap dogs first became popular in the United States, they were often referred to as *Texas dogs* or *Arizona dogs,* because Americans who lived in the states bordering Mexico usually owned them. But soon more Americans wanted a wee wonderdog, and some of them traveled to Mexico to select their pets. Because the Mexican state of Chihuahua is the largest northern state in Mexico, most Americans shopped for their puppies there and dubbed their dogs Mexican Chihuahuas. Eventually, the word Mexican was dropped and the dogs became known in the U.S. simply as Chihuahuas. Their Mexican name is *Chihuahueno.*

In 1888, James Watson, a noted dog authority, bought a Chihuahua for $3 during a visit to Mexico and brought it back to the U.S. Although his dog was extremely tiny and lived less than a year, he was captivated by the breed and went back to Mexico for more dogs. Watson also traveled along the border studying and writing about the dogs. He reported that Chihuahuas varied in size, shape, and coat, but all had one thing in common — the soft spot or molera. In fact, he decided that a Chihuahua without a molera was not purebred. Watson's magazine articles on the breed portrayed the dogs as smart and affectionate, contributing to their early popularity. But even more important, his descriptions match today's dogs, proving that the Chihuahuas of the mid-1800s were *not* that different from modern specimens.

Although its history is as much fantasy as fact, most historians agree that the Chihuahua is a true *American Toy dog* — not bred down from anything else — and the only true domestic dog indigenous to our hemisphere.

The upside of showing dogs:

- ✔ Competing with your dog is fun and exciting.
- ✔ Making new friends with people who have similar interests and being invited to join dog clubs.
- ✔ Depending on your goals, it can be a casual or an absorbing avocation.
- ✔ Showing dogs is educational. If you have an open mind, you find out something new every time you attend a show.
- ✔ Meeting the top Chihuahua breeders.
- ✔ Becoming seriously involved means you may become a breeder (at least occasionally).
- ✔ Training your Chihuahua for the show ring strengthens the bond between you and your dog.

✔ Showing involves traveling.

✔ Learning from your losses makes you a better competitor.

✔ Winning feels wonderful.

The downside of showing dogs:

✔ Winning at dog shows means you'll need a dog with superior conformation.

✔ Showing dogs is expensive and requires some special equipment.

✔ Training your Chihuahua for the show ring is time consuming.

✔ Showing can be stressful to dogs and their owners.

✔ Showing involves traveling.

✔ Once you become involved, breeding dogs (at least occasionally) becomes a probability.

✔ The sport can take over your life. Between conformation classes, club meetings, dogs shows, and breeding, showing dogs can become all-encompassing.

✔ Losing feels lousy (until you learn to turn losses into learning experiences).

Getting Started in Showing

I hate to be the bearer of bad news, but no matter how handsome you and your friends think he is, if you didn't buy Pepe as a potential show dog, chances are he won't win at dog shows. Some dogs are rare exceptions, of course, but your Pepe is probably tops at exactly what you bought him for in the first place — companionship. Eventually, you'll need another Chi if you want take up showing, but in the meantime, make Pepe your compadre for learning the ropes. Take him to conformation class (see info coming right up) and discover how to train and handle him in the ring. He loves the attention, and you make your novice mistakes on him, becoming a better handler for your next pup — the one you buy with showing in mind.

Take your time purchasing a show-potential Chihuahua. Study the standard and attend a couple shows. Watching the judging helps you develop an eye for a show-quality dog. Soon you find out which attributes are more important to you, and which breeders' dogs are strong in those traits. Then talk to the breeders whose dogs you most admire, and check out their available show potential pups. But don't expect to get one right away. You may have to put your name on a waiting list and fork over a deposit.

When you arrive at the show, buy a show catalog right away. Then you can match each dog's catalog number with its handler's armband number, thus finding out who's who.

What show dogs do

Assuming Pepe is show quality, what's next?

Besides possessing physical beauty and a steady temperament, Pepe must take travel, crowds, noise, and strange dogs all in stride. He also must stand still for grooming; pose while the judge examines him; circle the ring at a smooth trot in a line with his competitors; gait solo in the designated pattern; and keep his cool from the first burst of applause through the hush that settles over the arena just before the judge points to the winner.

Yikes! You'll know what to expect after watching a show or two, but how will Pepe get used to all that? And how will you ever be able to handle him in the show ring? Easy. You take lessons together. Dog clubs and private instructors offer conformation classes where you become familiar with the finer points of handling. At the same time, your dog gets used to stacking (posing) and trotting (gaiting) around other dogs and people. Check your yellow pages or ask your vet where show training is available.

When you attend conformation classes, you find out when matches take place in your area. Matches are practice dog shows — much like the real thing except they're informal and no championship points are awarded. They're great for honing your handling skills and getting your dog used to the show atmosphere.

Where's the show?

Your conformation instructor knows where shows are scheduled in your area, but you need some written material when you're ready to enter. The "Events Calendar," a supplement to the *AKC Gazette,* and a few other dog magazines (sold in pet shops and at bookstores and newsstands) list upcoming AKC shows. They also include the names and addresses of the show superintendents you need to contact if you want to receive show information. The superintendents make your mailbox bulge with premium lists about shows in your area, complete with entry forms, fee information, and closing dates for entries. If Pepe is ready to show, enter well ahead of the closing date so you aren't disappointed. Late entries are not accepted.

Speaking Dog Show Lingo

Every sport has its own terminology and dog showing is no exception. When studying the breed standard (see Chapter 2), or evaluating dogs with other fanciers, certain words always come up. Knowing and understanding these terms early in the game is a good idea.

Type

Type is what sets one breed of dog apart from every other breed. The concept of breed type is easiest to understand if you remember that each breed has only one correct type. It's type that makes you instantly recognize the features that combine to make up a Chihuahua. Type enables people to differentiate your dog from a Papillon, Miniature Pinscher, or any other breed. And in the show ring, the *most typey* dog is the one that comes closest to matching the characteristics described in its breed standard.

When fanciers advertise their wins, they usually abbreviate the awards. You'll see *BIS* for Best in Show, *Gr. 1* for first place in the group, *BOB* for Best of Breed, *BOW* for Best of Winners, *BOS* for Best of Opposite Sex, and *WD* or *WB* for Winners Dog or Winners Bitch.

Soundness

Soundness is the ability to function well, and it includes a correct skeleton, proper musculature, and a stable temperament, along with no handicaps, temporary or permanent, that inhibit the dog from using these attributes. A dog that is deaf, blind, lame, overly aggressive, missing a testicle, or painfully shy, is *unsound.* If a sound dog steps on a smoldering cigarette and limps because the burned pad hurts, he is *temporarily unsound* and can't be shown. But as soon as he heals enough to move normally, he becomes sound again.

Not all faults in a dog are considered unsound. For example, Pepe's ears may be on the small side (the standard specifies large), yet function just fine. Since having smallish ears doesn't interfere with his ability to hear, they do not make him unsound. However, small ears are uncharacteristic of the breed, so he lacks type.

Manchita's story

Show breeders sell their top quality puppies as *show potential.* That means the pup appears to have all the attributes necessary to become a champion. But it's still only potential. As the dog matures, things may change. That's what happened to real-life Manchita, a show potential puppy that I got when she was going on 4 months old. At 6 months, she still looked mighty fine, so we entered a show. She won the Puppy class and then beat the other class winners for Winners Bitch. That day Manchita was awarded her first (and last) championship points. During the next few weeks, her bite changed big time, and she matured with a wry mouth and the habit of letting the tip of her tongue dangle. So much for showing.

Note: Manchita's breeders guaranteed her for show potential, as many top breeders do. When her mouth went wry, they were prepared to trade for a different pup and place Manchita in a pet home. But we wanted to keep her (and the timing wasn't right for raising a second pup), so we never asked them to honor the guarantee.

Balance

Balance means that all parts of the dog fit each other without exaggeration of any single part. The size of the head corresponds with the size of the body; and height, width, and weight are proportionate. If people look at Pepe and say, "My, what long legs he has," or "Doesn't he have a big head for his size?" chances are he lacks balance.

Don't fret over balance too soon. Puppies often go through stages where they're temporarily out of *proportion,* another word for balance. When Pepe is young, his head may look too big for his body. He may have a well-developed front and a wimpy rear, or he may seem to be walking downhill because his back legs grew faster than his front legs. However, by the time he matures into a good show dog, all his parts must be balanced.

Condition

When it comes to *condition,* the ball is in your court. You can't control whether Pepe matures typey or balanced, but his condition depends on you. Pepe's in condition when he carries the right amount of weight for his size and has an immaculate coat with a healthy sheen, good muscle tone, clean ears, and clear eyes.

Style and showmanship

Style and *showmanship* are similar terms with reference to the show ring, but they're not quite identical. *Stylish* is the dog-show term used to describe a dog that carries itself elegantly and with pride, while a *good showman* indicates a dog with a pleasantly bold attitude that performs well during the judging. If Pepe has showmanship and style, he shows off his breed characteristics, making the most of his typiness. Judges recognize a dog like that easily. He steps out with pride — neck arched, head up, aspect bold, happy, and eager — yet remains under control. A good showman that lacks style may still be appealing because of his saucy, outgoing manner but never fools a knowledgeable judge.

At a dog show, style often separates the superior from the good and the winners from the losers when all other points are nearly equal. Style or elegance is a quality you can't give Pepe. He was either born with it or he wasn't. Pepe may be typey, sound, well balanced, and in fine condition, yet still lack style. That doesn't mean he won't win, because a correct dog, especially one with showmanship, wins his share. What it does mean is that when competing against an equally correct dog that also is stylish, Pepe's going to come in second.

Unlike style, which you can't instill into a dog through training, you can help your puppy grow into the best showman he can be. Give Pepe socialization to bolster his confidence. Lead-break him with praise and patience. Keep training periods upbeat and brief so he doesn't become bored, and you'll elicit his best attitude.

Part VI
The Part of Tens

The 5th Wave   By Rich Tennant

"We're very careful about grooming. First I'll check his teeth and nails, then trim any excess hair from his ears, nose, and around the eyes. After checking for fleas and parasites I'll let Roger go off to work so I can begin grooming the dog."

In this part . . .

Part VI contains lots of little topics that I think are important enough to have their own special space, including a list of 10 questions to ask when you're buying or adopting a dog, and sources of much more information on the Internet. And finally (no, I haven't forgotten!) a spotlight on Gidget, the Taco Bell Chihuahua, and other celebrity dogs.

Chapter 18

Ten Questions to Ask When Buying or Adopting a Chihuahua

. . . .

In This Chapter
▶ Committing to a permanent relationship
▶ Selecting a breeder
▶ Picking a pup
▶ Getting everything in writing

. . . .

Did canine cupid sting you with an arrow? Even if you've memorized the singular sensation of a precious puppy's warm body snuggling in your arms, make sure your head rules your heart and take your time before committing to a permanent relationship. With good management and good luck, you and your Chi can expect to be best buddies for well over a decade — so before making that momentous decision, be sure that you know the answers to these important questions.

Ask Yourself:

1. Do I (and my family) really want a doggie dependent?

Pepe needs you from puppyhood through old age. Not only must he be fed, watered, groomed, trained, and exercised, but Chis also need frequent affection to feel happy and secure. Most dog owners enjoy spending time with their pets and consider daily dog care a pleasant routine. But alas, some people grow tired of taking care of a dog and begin neglecting their pets after the newness wears off. The result? An owner with guilt pangs and a lonely little dog. Neither of you deserves that, so think hard and consider your finances, lifestyle, and future plans before making a decision. Only you know if the time is right for you and your family to take on the joys and responsibilities of dog ownership.

2. Is a petite pet the right choice for me?

Portable pups are delightful. They travel well, love attention, are amazingly bright, and can get enough exercise in a small apartment. Many of them are also alert watchdogs. But dogs as small as Chihuahuas aren't for everyone. For example, Pepe is a housedog. He can't tolerate a damp basement or being outdoors in the rain. And he's too small to endure any rough stuff. For more on the pros and cons of Toy dogs in general, and Chihuahuas in particular, see Chapter 1.

3. Is there some sizzle between this Chi and me?

Good chemistry is an important part of successful relationships, so pay special attention to the first pup that catches your eye. But don't make any instant decisions. Make sure your first choice is healthy, socialized, and has a pleasing personality. On the other hand, don't pick a puppy that doesn't particularly appeal to you just because he is available or inexpensive. Although you may learn to love him, your best bet is to keep looking until you and a pup pick each other.

Ask the Seller:

4. Did you breed this puppy (or dog)? If not, where did it come from?

The best place to buy a healthy Chihuahua is from its breeder. Beware of puppies that are being sold by middle-people. For example, no matter how clean the pet shop, that appealing pup in the window may have been born in a puppy mill. The combination of poor breeding practices and lack of human attention during the formative weeks can cause lifelong complications. Buyer beware.

When dealing with a rescue organization, chances are no one knows where the dog originated, but the person fostering the dog can tell you the circumstances of the rescue and everything that is known about the dog's health and temperament.

5. How many litters a year do you breed and what other breeds do you sell?

Okay, you found a Chihuahua breeder. But how do you recognize a good one? The best breeders specialize in only one or two breeds and never have more puppies than they have time to care for. And that means individual attention. Good breeders adore their pups, give prospective owners the third degree, and may exhibit their stock at dog shows. Their facilities are clean, their puppy play areas contain toys, and their dogs enjoy being handled.

6. You know this puppy (or dog) better than anyone. Please tell me all about him.

Some people are more talkative than others, so if the seller needs some help getting started, ask about the pup's position in the litter, or how the pup was socialized. Good breeders know all about each and every one of their pups, and most of them are be happy to fill you in on a particular puppy's life story. Beware if the breeder hesitates when asked whether the pup is dominant or submissive with its littermates, or hems and haws about how he was socialized. Caring breeders can tell plenty of stories about puppies no more than a few weeks old. That's because they're observant when the puppies play together and make time to give each one individual attention.

7. May I see the pup's family?

Now that you've found a breeder you trust and a puppy or adult dog that twangs your heartstrings, it's time to meet your prospective pet's family. Expect to see at least the dam (that's mom in dog lingo) and the pup's littermates (siblings). With luck, you may also see an aunt or uncle, and maybe even a grand-dam or an adult brother or sister from an earlier litter. Don't be disappointed if you don't see the sire (papa). He may live far away, but his picture and pedigree will probably be available.

8. May I test this puppy's temperament?

If the breeder is sure that you know how to hold and handle a tiny dog, he or she is more likely to be willing to let you test the puppy's temperament. This involves taking the puppy away from its dam and littermates and out of sight of the breeder — for example, into another room or around the side of the house. Take this book with you. Easy instructions for temperament testing are in Chapter 4.

9. May I have a copy of the puppy's feeding schedule and health record? What kind of health (and possibly show) guarantee comes with him?

Many breeders give new owners a copy of the puppy's feeding schedule and health record. If the breeder just tells it to you verbally, write it down. Making sudden changes in a dog's diet can be dangerous. Also, your veterinarian needs to know what vaccines your dog already had and when they were given to be able to set up a vaccination and worming schedule.

Most sellers offer some type of health guarantee, giving you a certain amount of time (usually 24 to 48 hours) to take the dog to your own vet for a complete physical. When buying a show-potential puppy (one you plan to exhibit in dog shows), find out if a replacement pup will be offered if the dog is not show quality at adulthood.

10. Is this puppy eligible for AKC registration and will I receive the application for registration at the time of purchase?

In addition to this important question, you'll also want to ask if you can have a copy of the pup's pedigree. A registration application that has been filled out and signed by the seller should accompany every AKC registrable dog. The form has a section for you to complete. Do it ASAP, enclose the required fee, and send it to the American Kennel Club (the address is on the form). A registration certificate soon arrives in the mail. Then, and only then, do you own a registered dog.

If you want an AKC-registered dog and the seller doesn't have a registration application ready to go with your puppy, proceed with caution. Yes, it's possible that the paperwork is still at the AKC offices and will arrive soon. If you trust the seller enough to take the puppy with papers pending, request a bill of sale signed by the seller that includes your dog's breed, date of birth, sex, and color. It must also contain the registered names and AKC numbers of the dog's sire and dam and the full name and address of the breeder. Now if the important paperwork doesn't show up in a week or so and you want to contact the AKC, you'll be able to identify your dog.

Most breeders automatically offer a copy of the puppy's pedigree. The pedigree is Pepe's family tree and it gives more information than just names. If any of his ancestors were illustrious in the show, obedience, or agility ring, abbreviations of their titles may be included too. For details, see Chapter 4. Or ask the proud breeder to decipher the mysterious letters.

Chapter 19

Ten Web Sites Where Chihuahuas Gather

In This Chapter

▶ Finding a breeder

▶ Info on Chi care, temperament, and training

▶ Adopting a homeless Chi

▶ Just-for-fun stuff for people and their dogs

*T*he Internet is often called the *Information Superhighway* and there's no denying that you can find information about everything and anything while cruising along its wide lanes. But, like the gorgeous Alaska Highway, it can suddenly disintegrate into dirt and deep ruts, so navigate with care and avoid some sites altogether. The problem is, people can say anything they please on the Net, and they don't have editors to make sure the info is useful, or even correct. When I typed the word *Chihuahuas* into a search engine, I came up with 45,830 matches. Naturally, that changes daily. A few of my favorites start you on your way. I'm sure you'll find many more worthy sites as you cruise along, so keep on clicking.

Something for Everyone Who is Charmed by Chihuahuas

For a wealth of practical information ranging from basic Chihuahua care, to introducing your new Chihuahua to your cat, try *My Chihuahuas,* www. geocities.com/Petsburgh/1014/. Whether you're thinking about acquiring your first Chihuahua or you are already an accomplished breeder, this site has something for you. One of its neatest topics covers variations in the Chihuahua breed. It illustrates how Chis are perceived in commercials, cartoons, and movies, and invites you to view top show dogs. Chihuahua rescue also is covered. Rescue organizations are listed by state and you can find out what to expect from a rescue organization and a rescue dog.

Toys for Toys

Is finding the right-sized toys for your tiny Chihuahua a challenge? Then take a look at www.Dogtoys.com. This on-line store sells play and dental health toys sized especially for each breed. They even feature a *breed pack,* touted to contain everything for your Chihuahua's playing needs. Included are ball toys, snack toys, floss toys, plush squeaky toys, and rubber toys — all neatly packaged in a bone-shaped toy box.

Settling Down and Staying Awhile

Once you click on the American Kennel Club's (AKC) site, www.akc.org, you'll probably want to visit for awhile. Sure you can type in **Chihuahuas** and go directly to the breed standard for additional info on temperament, history, and care, but don't stop there. Click the link chihua.mov and see the ideal Chi gait. Then click Breeder Search and find respected kennel clubs and their breeder referral contacts. These are people who help you find a responsible Chihuahua breeder in your area.

The AKC site also contains a wealth of general info. Learn all about purebred dogs, including training, nutrition, and health care, and share the kids' corner with your youngsters. If you want to find out about AKC registration, or learn more about dog shows, obedience, and agility trials, that info is handy too. The AKC also has an online store featuring books, videos, magazine subscriptions, a purebred dog poster, and order forms for copies of your dog's pedigree or show records. And if you've seen the whole site and still have a question, ask dogdom's advice expert, Mr. Murf.

Truth is, once you click on the AKC site, you can spend several entertaining hours perusing purebred dogs and their activities. Just for starters, the AKC recognizes 147 breeds of dogs and every one of them is individually illustrated and described by its official breed standard. Have you ever seen a Spinone Italiano? No, it isn't on the menu at the Olive Garden. Look it up at the AKC site. It's a fun place to learn about dogs.

Good Deeds for Chis in Need

Chihuahua Rescue and Transport (CRT) is a network of volunteers dedicated to the welfare and rescue of Chihuahuas in the United States. The CRT site, www.chihuahua-rescue.com, tells you about the Chihuahuas currently available for adoption and includes photos. Besides an online newsletter, the site is a super place to visit on the Web if you want to buy something unique to show off your favorite breed. Featured merchandise includes a Chi Gang Beach Party T-shirt, a Chi Pride T-shirt, a Chi Rescue tote bag, and a charming cookbook of recipes sure to please people and their dogs. Profits go to help homeless Chis. If you want to be part of this caring group, info about becoming a volunteer is available. And if your heartstrings need tugging, read CRT's Chi rescue stories. But be sure to crack open a box of tissues. You'll need them.

Comforting Canada's Homeless Chis

Canadian Chihuahua Rescue and Transport (a sister organization to CRT above), rescues, fosters and provides veterinary care for homeless, abandoned, and abused Chihuahuas in Canada. Its site, www.ccrt.net, provides detailed profiles of dogs available for rescue, matches homeless Chis with carefully screened adoptive homes, and provides follow-up support for new owners. Educating the public about the breed is a priority. For a good read, try their heartwarming stories of successful rescues. If you want to help, info is available about becoming a volunteer and there is a link to CRT in the United States.

Chihuahuas, a Good Short Course

For solid general information on the breed, including temperament, health, grooming, exercise, and living conditions, try http://www.dogbreeding.com/chihuahua.htm. You'll also find splendid pictures of smooth and long coated Chis, and even Chihuahua jokes. Includes links to North American and some foreign kennel clubs that recognize the breed.

Gaga Over Gidget?

If you didn't see enough of Taco Bell's Gidget on TV commercials, click your way to the Taco Bell site, www.tacobell.com. Besides nutritional info, corporate opportunities, and the location of the Taco Bell nearest you, you'll find Chihuahua images directly from the Taco Bell TV spots. Before you leave, send someone a Cyberlunch. Why not? It's free.

Gidget Galore

Gidget fans can view old Taco Bell commercials to their hearts' content at www.everwonder.com/david/tacobelldog.html. This fun site features audio and video clips of all your favorite ads. It also offers answers to frequently asked questions (FAQ's) about Chihuahuas, and includes info on history, temperament, and care. Merchandise, such as talking Chis, head-bobbing Chis, and Chi key chains are available through the online store, and the site also includes a chat room.

Fetching a Breeder

Looking for a Chihuahua breeder? Go to www.breeders.net, click "Find nearby breeders," then click "Chihuahua" from the breed list. Now enter your zip code and click "Fetch!" and you'll get a list of the Chi breeders nearest you. If you are shopping for your first dog, read "How to Find a Dog." The authors of this site explain the difference between good and bad breeding practices, give you tips on selecting a dog, and remind you that being listed on this site is no guarantee of quality. In other words, it's up to you to check out the breeder for yourself. But that's okay. You can find out how to do that in Chapter 4.

Seeing the Mini Marvels of the Agility Ring

Discover all about the exciting sport of agility, its history, a description of the obstacles, and the terrific Toy dogs who have scored big at www.agilityability.com. Also enjoy photos of Chihuahuas training for agility and the few fearless Chis who've earned agility titles.

Chapter 20

Gidget and Nine Other Celebrity Dogs

Thanks to Taco Bell's commercials, today almost everyone is a Chihuahua fan. Yet, artists and entertainers adored this bright breed long before television was invented. In this chapter, I tell you about diminutive dog stars and celebrity Chi owners. But choosing only ten of them is just too hard, so I'm going to cheat a little and stuff several human stars and their Chis under one heading.

Taco Bell's Great Gidget

Gidget, Taco Bell's talking dog star, retired from the advertising business in 2000 after a long and successful career as chief spokes-dog for the fast-food chain. But it seems like only yesterday . . . .

She plays a cool-guy role and does her own stunt work, including riding on Godzilla's tail, running up a fire escape, riding a skateboard, and jumping on a taxi cab. She loves riding in limos, and has her own line of drinking cups, T-shirts, and talking toys. She even has two male stand-ins. But despite all her fame, this diva is easily pleased and willingly works for chicken and steak bits. Ay Chihuahua! That's gotta be Gidget, Taco Bell's TV star.

Gidget was born December 8, 1994, and is owned by animal trainer Sue Chipperton, who acquired her as a pup and trained her for stardom. Her expressive face appeared in a print campaign for The Limited, and she had a *carry on* role in "The Fan" with Robert De Niro, before becoming the hottest commercial canine since Spuds McKenzie. Although special effects enhance her brow and move her mouth, and comic Carlos Alazraqui provides her voice, Gidget dishes out a hip attitude that attracts fans of all ages. And she isn't even bitchy about it. Besides an occasional tidbit, her only demand is a blanket to keep her from getting chilled between takes. But don't expect to see this star gracing the covers of tabloids. Unlike some super-stars, she has only one vice — her Mrs. Hedgehog toy has to accompany her to every set.

At first, Gidget's only stand-in was a male named Dinky. When Taco Bell needed another Chihuahua, a search on the Internet led them to a homeless dog in an animal shelter in Orlando, Florida. The rescued Chi is called Taco, and is Gidget's second stand-in.

Early Animal Actors

How early were Chis recognized as talented animal entertainers? No one knows for sure, but they already had an avid audience in England during the latter part of the 19th century. That's when British performer Rosina V. Casselli popularized an animal act featuring a dozen or more Chihuahuas doing myriad tricks.

Madame Patti's Pet

When General Porfirio Diaz was president of Mexico (about a century ago), he presented world-famous opera singer Madame Adelina Patti with a bouquet of flowers containing a Chihuahua. She adored the dog, named him Bonito, and carried him with her wherever she went — including operatic tours all over the world. Eventually Madame Patti acquired several Chihuahuas and helped popularize the breed in England.

Remember the Alamo?

Victorious Mexican General Santa Ana had his Chihuahuas with him at the Alamo. Some say he never left home without them. In 1836, when Santa Ana was finally captured, several Chihuahuas were found in his camp. Unfortunately, no one knows what became of them.

The first Chihuahua registered with the American Kennel Club was a red-coated dog named Midget, owned by a Texan from El Paso. That was in 1904. The Chihuahua Club of America was founded in 1923 and has thrived ever since. Mexico took longer to acknowledge its own. It didn't register the breed until 1942.

And the Band Played On

Xavier Cugat, a popular Latin American band leader during the 1930s and '40s, took his Chihuahuas on stage with him. He often held a Chi in one hand while conducting his band with the other. According to a popular (possibly true) story, he once dressed a Chi like a baby, complete with a bonnet, so he could smuggle it into his hotel room.

Winsome Works of Art

Are Chihuahuas a fashion statement? At fashion shows during the late 1990s, it was chic to have one peeking out of a classy handbag.

In truth, Chis have been prized by the creative for centuries. For example, a pot-bellied pup with large ears and a roundish head similar to a Chihuahua's was a popular design on pre-Colombian pottery. And pictures carved on stones of dogs closely resembling modern Chihuahuas are displayed at the monastery of Huejotzingo, near Mexico City. The monastery was built by Franciscan Monks around 1530.

Is there a Chihuahua in the Sistine Chapel? A fresco depicting the story of Moses, believed to be the work of Sandro Botticelli, circa 1482, includes a short coated little dog with a round head and big eyes. That's a decade before Columbus reached the New World. If the dog is indeed a Chihuahua (other Toy breeds claim it, too), wouldn't that add a mysterious aura to Chihuahua origins?

Among artist Henri de Toulouse-Lautrec's many paintings is "Lady with a Dog," portraying a woman with a dog in her lap. The dog looks much like a smooth-coated Chihuahua. Check it out. The work hangs in the National Gallery in Washington, D.C.

Renowned animal artist, Sir Edwin Landseer, painted a smooth-coated dog that is probably a Chihuahua in his work, "Diogenes." Another Toy dog, a King Charles Spaniel, is in the same painting.

Today, collectors of ceramic and porcelain figurines can easily fill their shelves with Chihuahua images. New ones abound at gift shops, toy stores, and at vendor booths at dog shows. Vintage statuettes are fun finds at antique, consignment, and pawnshops, and of course, at yard sales. Is there a stamp collector in your family? Chihuahuas have been featured on several countries' stamps, including Mexico, Liberia, Paraguay, and Scotland.

Show Ring Roots

Owen Wister, author of *The Virginian,* owned Chihuahuas. One of his dogs was Caranza, the breed's first sire of renown. Two lines of top-winning Chihuahuas, Perrito and Meron, trace their roots to Caranza.

Palace Pets

Emperor Maximilian of Mexico and his wife Empress Carlotta, filled their palace with pet Chihuahuas.

Meet the Don

Do you like to read novels about the mob that are suspenseful and hilarious at the same time and best yet, have a Chihuahua as one of the characters? Then look for books by Laurence Shames. But don't expect the Chihuahua to be bright, or bold, or endearing. That isn't Shames's style.

Don Giovanni has traits undesirable in a Chihuahua. Fragile, frightened, and a veritable canine hypochondriac, he spends most of his waking seconds quivering in the arms of Bert the Shirt, his elderly ex-mafioso owner. But the Shirt has enough character for both of them, and his relationship with his ancient dog makes funny and heartwarming reading. Alive with zany characters, packed with action, and set in colorful Key West, Shames' novels are among my favorites. Two of them, *Florida Straits,* and *Sunburn,* feature Don Giovanni on the cover.

Super Stars Smitten by Chihuahuas

Madonna and Rosie O'Donnell have been seen sporting Chihuahuas.

Tennis great Martina Navratilova is a Chihuahua owner and so is former Yale football coach Herman Hickman. He had two exceptionally small Chis named Killer and Slugger.

Remember Christine Ebersole, '80s comedienne, actress and singer? She had a Chihuahua named Margarita. Other famous names linked with Chihuahuas include Jayne Mansfield, Lupe Velez, Billie Holiday, Vincent Price, Gertrude Stein, Mickey Rourke, and Charo.

Finally, try visualizing Arnold Schwarzenegger walking his Chihuahua. How about that for attractive opposites!

Appendix A
More Good Reading

●●●

Magazines

AKC Gazette (subscription or newsstand), 260 Madison Avenue (Fourth Floor), New York, NY 10016; phone 212-696-8351; www.akc.org/pubs/gazette.

Dog Fancy (subscription or newsstand), P.O. Box 6050, Mission Viejo, CA 92690; phone 800-361-4132; www.animalnetwork.com/dogs.

Dog World (subscription or newsstand), 500 North Dearborn, Suite 1100, Chicago 60610; phone 312-396-0600; www.dogworldmag.com.

Los Chihuahuas (subscription), 12860 Thonotosassa Road, Dover, FL 33527.

Books

Burch, Mary, Ph.D. 1998. *Volunteering with Your Pet.* New York: Howell Book House.

Cecil, Barbara, and Darnell, Gerianne. *Competitive Obedience Training for the Small Dog.* Council Bluffs, Iowa: T9E Publishing.

Nicholas, Anna Katherine. 1988. *The Chihuahua.* Neptune, New Jersey: T.F.H. Publications.

O'Neil, Jacqueline. 1998. *All About Agility.* New York: Howell Book House.

Sife, Wallace, Ph.D. 1998. *The Loss of a Pet.* New York: Howell Book House.

Simmons-Moake, Jane. 1991. *Agility Training, The Fun Sport for All Dogs.* New York: Howell Book House.

Terry, Ruth E. 1996. *The Chihuahua, An Owner's Guide to a Happy, Healthy Pet.* New York: Howell Book House.

Terry, Ruth E. 1990. *The New Chihuahua,* New York: Howell Book House.

Appendix B

Clubs and Connections

● ●

Organizations

American Kennel Club (AKC), 5580 Centerview Drive, Suite 200, Raleigh, NC 27606; phone 919-223-9780; e-mail info@akc.org. Provides information on breed, obedience, and agility clubs. Also offers dog shows and obedience, agility, and the Canine Good Citizen programs. Home of the AKC Companion Animal Recovery System (helping owners recover lost dogs). For information on purebred rescue organizations by breed, call the *AKC Gazette* at 212-696-8321.

American Mixed Breed Obedience Registry (AMBOR), 179 Niblick Road, 113, Paso Robles, CA 93446; phone 818-887-3300; e-mail Ambor@Amborusa.org. Provides information on shows, obedience, and agility for mixed-breed dogs.

Chihuahua Club of America, Inc., (CCA), Corresponding Secretary: Diana Garren, 16 Hillgirt Road, Hendersonville, NC 28792. This is the national or parent breed club for the Chihuahua. Write for breed info and to find the Chihuahua club closest to you.

Delta Society, 289 Perimeter Road East, Renton, WA 98056-1329; phone: 800-869-6898, fax: 206-808-7601; e-mail: info@deltasociety.org. Provides information about becoming a Pet Partner (performing therapy with your pet).

National Dog Registry (NDR); Phone: 800-637-3647; e-mail: info@ natldogregistry.com. Recovers lost dogs. Join as soon as your dog has permanent I.D.

North American Dog Agility Council (NADAC), HCR 2 Box 277, St. Maries, ID 83861; phone: 208-689-3803. Provides information on agility clubs and competition.

Small Dog Rescue League, P.O. Box 433, Mayville, MI 48744; fax: 517-761-7062; e-mail: smalldogs@centuryinter.net. Contact to adopt a dog or if you can't keep yours.

Therapy Dogs International (TDI), 6 Hilltop Road, Mendham, NJ 07945; or 88 Bartley Road, Flanders, NJ 07836; e-mail: tdi@gti.net, Web site: www.tdi-dog.org. Provides information on performing therapy with your pet.

United Kennel Club (UKC), 100 East Kilgore Road, Kalamazoo, MI 49001; phone: 616-343-9020, fax: 616-343-7037; e-mail: Tina@ukcdogs.com. Provides information on dog clubs, dog shows, obedience, and agility.

United States Dog Agility Association (USDAA), P.O. Box 850955, Richardson, TX 75085-0955; phone: (972) 231-9700, fax: (214) 503-0161; e-mail: info@usdaa.com, Web site: www.usdaa.com. Provides information on agility clubs and competition.

Index

• D •

• E •

• U •

Notes

Notes

Notes

Notes

Notes

Notes

Notes

Notes

Notes

Notes

Notes

Notes

Notes

FOR DUMMIES

A world of resources to help you grow

HOME, GARDEN & HOBBIES

0-7645-5295-3

Gardening
0-7645-5130-2

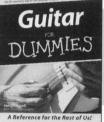
0-7645-5106-X

Also available:

Auto Repair For Dummies
(0-7645-5089-6)

Chess For Dummies
(0-7645-5003-9)

Home Maintenance For
Dummies
(0-7645-5215-5)

Organizing For Dummies
(0-7645-5300-3)

Piano For Dummies
(0-7645-5105-1)

Poker For Dummies
(0-7645-5232-5)

Quilting For Dummies
(0-7645-5118-3)

Rock Guitar For Dummies
(0-7645-5356-9)

Roses For Dummies
(0-7645-5202-3)

Sewing For Dummies
(0-7645-5137-X)

FOOD & WINE

0-7645-5250-3   **0-7645-5390-9**   **0-7645-5114-0**

Also available:

Bartending For Dummies
(0-7645-5051-9)

Chinese Cooking For
Dummies
(0-7645-5247-3)

Christmas Cooking For
Dummies
(0-7645-5407-7)

Diabetes Cookbook For
Dummies
(0-7645-5230-9)

Grilling For Dummies
(0-7645-5076-4)

Low-Fat Cooking For
Dummies
(0-7645-5035-7)

Slow Cookers For Dummies
(0-7645-5240-6)

TRAVEL

0-7645-5453-0

0-7645-5438-7

0-7645-5448-4

Also available:

America's National Parks For
Dummies
(0-7645-6204-5)

Caribbean For Dummies
(0-7645-5445-X)

Cruise Vacations For
Dummies 2003
(0-7645-5459-X)

Europe For Dummies
(0-7645-5456-5)

Ireland For Dummies
(0-7645-6199-5)

France For Dummies
(0-7645-6292-4)

London For Dummies
(0-7645-5416-6)

Mexico's Beach Resorts For
Dummies
(0-7645-6262-2)

Paris For Dummies
(0-7645-5494-8)

RV Vacations For Dummies
(0-7645-5443-3)

Walt Disney World & Orlando
For Dummies
(0-7645-5444-1)

FOR DUMMIES®

Plain-English solutions for everyday challenges

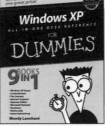

FOR DUMMIES®

Helping you expand your horizons and realize your potential

INTERNET

The Internet FOR DUMMIES

0-7645-0894-6

The Internet ALL-IN-ONE DESK REFERENCE FOR DUMMIES

0-7645-1659-0

eBay FOR DUMMIES

0-7645-1642-6

Also available:

America Online 7.0 For Dummies
(0-7645-1624-8)

Genealogy Online For Dummies
(0-7645-0807-5)

The Internet All-in-One Desk Reference For Dummies
(0-7645-1659-0)

Internet Explorer 6 For Dummies
(0-7645-1344-3)

The Internet For Dummies Quick Reference
(0-7645-1645-0)

Internet Privacy For Dummies
(0-7645-0846-6)

Researching Online For Dummies
(0-7645-0546-7)

Starting an Online Business For Dummies
(0-7645-1655-8)

DIGITAL MEDIA

Digital Photography FOR DUMMIES

0-7645-1664-7

Photoshop Elements 2 FOR DUMMIES

0-7645-1675-2

Digital Video FOR DUMMIES

0-7645-0806-7

Also available:

CD and DVD Recording For Dummies
(0-7645-1627-2)

Digital Photography All-in-One Desk Reference For Dummies
(0-7645-1800-3)

Digital Photography For Dummies Quick Reference
(0-7645-0750-8)

Home Recording for Musicians For Dummies
(0-7645-1634-5)

MP3 For Dummies
(0-7645-0858-X)

Paint Shop Pro "X" For Dummies
(0-7645-2440-2)

Photo Retouching & Restoration For Dummies
(0-7645-1662-0)

Scanners For Dummies
(0-7645-0783-4)

GRAPHICS

PowerPoint 2002 FOR DUMMIES

0-7645-0817-2

Photoshop 7 FOR DUMMIES

0-7645-1651-5

Macromedia Flash MX FOR DUMMIES

0-7645-0895-4

Also available:

Adobe Acrobat 5 PDF For Dummies
(0-7645-1652-3)

Fireworks 4 For Dummies
(0-7645-0804-0)

Illustrator 10 For Dummies
(0-7645-3636-2)

QuarkXPress 5 For Dummies
(0-7645-0643-9)

Visio 2000 For Dummies
(0-7645-0635-8)

Available wherever books are sold. Go to www.dummies.com or call 1-877-762-2974 to order direct.

FOR DUMMIES®

SELF-HELP, SPIRITUALITY & RELIGION

Sex For Dummies
0-7645-5302-X

Parenting For Dummies
0-7645-5418-2

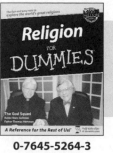

Religion For Dummies
0-7645-5264-3

Also available:

The Bible For Dummies
(0-7645-5296-1)

Buddhism For Dummies
(0-7645-5359-3)

Christian Prayer For Dummies
(0-7645-5500-6)

Dating For Dummies
(0-7645-5072-1)

Judaism For Dummies
(0-7645-5299-6)

Potty Training For Dummies
(0-7645-5417-4)

Pregnancy For Dummies
(0-7645-5074-8)

Rekindling Romance For Dummies
(0-7645-5303-8)

Spirituality For Dummies
(0-7645-5298-8)

Weddings For Dummies
(0-7645-5055-1)

PETS

Puppies For Dummies
0-7645-5255-4

Dog Training For Dummies
0-7645-5286-4

Cats For Dummies
0-7645-5275-9

Also available:

Labrador Retrievers For Dummies
(0-7645-5281-3)

Aquariums For Dummies
(0-7645-5156-6)

Birds For Dummies
(0-7645-5139-6)

Dogs For Dummies
(0-7645-5274-0)

Ferrets For Dummies
(0-7645-5259-7)

German Shepherds For Dummies
(0-7645-5280-5)

Golden Retrievers For Dummies
(0-7645-5267-8)

Horses For Dummies
(0-7645-5138-8)

Jack Russell Terriers For Dummies
(0-7645-5268-6)

Puppies Raising & Training Diary For Dummies
(0-7645-0876-8)

EDUCATION & TEST PREPARATION

Spanish For Dummies
0-7645-5194-9

Algebra For Dummies
0-7645-5325-9

The ACT For Dummies
0-7645-5210-4

Also available:

Chemistry For Dummies
(0-7645-5430-1)

English Grammar For Dummies
(0-7645-5322-4)

French For Dummies
(0-7645-5193-0)

The GMAT For Dummies
(0-7645-5251-1)

Inglés Para Dummies
(0-7645-5427-1)

Italian For Dummies
(0-7645-5196-5)

Research Papers For Dummies
(0-7645-5426-3)

The SAT I For Dummies
(0-7645-5472-7)

U.S. History For Dummies
(0-7645-5249-X)

World History For Dummies
(0-7645-5242-2)

FOR DUMMIES®

We take the mystery out of complicated subjects